HEALTHY AGING IN ACTION

HEALTHY AGING IN ACTION

Roles, Functions, and the Wisdom of Elders

JEFFREY A. KOTTLER

cognella®

SAN DIEGO

Bassim Hamadeh, CEO and Publisher
Amy Smith, Senior Project Editor
Rachel Kahn, Production Editor
Jess Estrella, Senior Graphic Designer
Kylie Bartolome, Licensing Coordinator
Natalie Piccotti, Director of Marketing
Kassie Graves, Senior Vice President, Editorial
Jamie Giganti, Director of Academic Publishing

cognella® | ACADEMIC PUBLISHING
3970 Sorrento Valley Blvd., Ste. 500, San Diego, CA 92121

Dedicated to Charles H. Kottler Muse, mentor, and model of the man—and grandfather—that I always aspired to become and to Aliya and Caia

Brief Contents

Detailed Contents

Preface

Niah had just celebrated her 64th birthday when her husband's cancer had metastasized to the point that recovery was no longer possible. A few months later she lost her life partner and felt crippled by her own incapacitating grief. Her appetite diminished, and she lost considerable weight, along with chronic sleep disruption. Her daughters became increasingly worried over the next few years as she continued to isolate herself.

When Niah's youngest daughter gave birth to a baby boy, it seemed like it was a gift from her Higher Power, a message from her late husband that it was time to let go of the past and think about her role in the future. Fortunately, she lived within driving distance of her infant grandson, allowing her to visit frequently, but more significantly, she now felt she had a purpose to her life, a compelling reason to get out of bed in the morning. She described this transition to becoming a grandmother as among the most satisfying and joyful periods of her life, one in which she wondered how she could ever imagine that her productive life was over. Now that she had an important reason to remain healthy and fit, she began working out with a personal trainer and even decided to resume her former career in real estate part-time. One significant change, however, is that she always scheduled work around her first priority: to assist her daughter's growing family. Niah couldn't recall a time when her life had ever felt more satisfying and her health more robust.

Kyle had also lost his partner a few years earlier, but he was never sure why his wife chose to abandon their 25-year marriage and relocate to another country with her new paramour. He tried to pick up the pieces of his life thereafter, struggling to maintain a semblance of reasonable functioning at his job and social world, yet it was the crushing burden of debt that seemed to pull him under. Even more concerning, his son was struggling with addictions that appeared to jeopardize the health and safety of Kyle's 3-year-old granddaughter. His daughter-in-law had decided she'd had enough, abandoning her troubled husband and daughter for some unknown location. She would never show up again.

With no other choice after his son entered rehab and eventually became homeless when repeated treatments failed to put a dent in his opioid addiction, Kyle was forced to become the custodial caregiver for his young granddaughter. There was no choice in the matter, made far worse by his relative cluelessness about how to take care of a little girl. Earlier in their marriage Kyle had been busy with work most of the time, delegating childrearing exclusively to his wife. He wondered now whether that accumulative resentment was the reason she decided to leave him. In any case, he now felt stuck, trapped even, into taking care of this abandoned child who was already displaying some disturbing behavioral patterns.

With the additional financial pressures and caregiving responsibilities, coupled with his own personal troubles that were spinning out of control, it was apparent that Kyle was singularly unprepared to assume this unwelcome role as the primary parental figure for a confused, angry little girl. Not surprisingly, the unrelenting stress and additional burdens played havoc on his health. Kyle became increasingly resentful and frustrated with the responsibilities of becoming a custodial grandparent, something he never wanted, never really chose for himself at this stage of life.

The profile of these two very different grandparent situations illustrates the interaction between what it means to age optimally, and the context under which someone transitions into the role of grandparent or elder either by choice or circumstances. For most older adults, caring for grandchildren (or others outside the family) is truly one of the highlights of their lives, the pinnacle of achievement, not only in the sense that their genetic line will continue, but also the feeling of pride and satisfaction that one's lifetime of experience and wisdom can be passed on to the next generations. For many people, this is the ultimate in what is experienced as a meaningful, productive life.

Yet for others who were pressured, recruited, or forced to take on major responsibilities of caregiving for grandchildren or others, this burden can have quite opposite effects on health, well-being, and life satisfaction. Depending on the person's financial resources, social support, living situation, personal characteristics, attitudes, capacity for resilience, health and fitness, and family dynamics, such additional responsibilities may feel like a crushing disaster. Many grandparents or elders serving in these custodial roles feel absolutely overwhelmed and miserable. It is therefore clear in these examples that healthy aging for older adults depends as much on the context and perceived choices of their lives as their actual physical health and functioning. Like almost everything else in life, attitude is everything.

Overview

Regardless of one's age and station in life, what does it mean to age in a healthy, optimal way? This process for a young adult, for example, might be related to mastering the key developmental tasks of that stage of life, preparing for a career, achieving a degree of independence and autonomy from parents, establishing a personal identity and value system, learning emotional regulation, maintaining intimate, supportive relationships with family and friends, remaining in good physical shape, eating healthfully, and so on. For those in the latter stages of life, the challenges and tasks are quite different, often related to continuing an active, engaged, and meaningful daily existence. While dealing with declining health and vigor are part of the journey, ongoing life satisfaction is usually related to feeling useful, productive in some capacity. While this can—and does—involve continuing one's career or employment, for close to 90% of the elderly in the United States and other countries, one significant role is as a grandparent or caregiver in the family.

The subject of grandparenting and later stage of life is particularly curious and interesting because it can occur at so many different ages—from age 50 to 100! It has been suggested that this stage of life may indeed qualify for its own unique classification, one that has been completely transformed by changes in life span, culture, technology, population trends, and family needs. This has also led to new and different images of what it means to be old, less about an inevitable stage to be dreaded and avoided and now more about a time that is anticipated and relished (Tropp, 2019).

This book is designed for a variety of courses in the social and behavioral sciences that explore the experiences and meaning of later life, especially as they relate to maintaining a sense of productivity and life satisfaction. After all, humans are among the only living creatures on earth that survive beyond their reproductive functions. This is all the more peculiar given that the stated purpose of all existence is to perpetuate our own genetic material. Most animals, insects, and other living things expire soon after they are done producing offspring so that they make room for newcomers and to avoid squandering valuable resources on organisms that are no longer viable for fertility.

This leads to a few essential questions that will be explored in this book. Why do older people even exist if they can no longer produce children who are necessary for the continuation of our species? What are grandparents and elders really for, and why didn't evolution kill them off just as it does with almost every other animal? Given their physical limitations, reduced life span, health risks, and possible burdens on the family and community, what is considered "successful" or "optimal" aging? And more specifically related to the main theme we will be discussing, what are the characteristics, features, behaviors, attitudes, and lifestyles of those elderly individuals who lead fully engaged and satisfying lives in which they are continuing to make a significant contribution to their families and communities?

Where Book Ideas Are Born

I'm often asked what sparks an idea for a new writing project, a logical question after completing more than 100 of such books. I always kind of shrug, partly because I'm a little uncomfortable with the query, and also because I'm not sure I've settled on a definitive explanation. Of course, each of us is confronted every day with curiosities we don't understand.

Related to this current volume, the idea first came to mind during a conversation with one of my granddaughters, Caia, age 3, while we were playing with her Barbie Dream House.

"Popi," she said to me while carefully rearranging a piece of furniture in one of the rooms of the playhouse, "do you have toots?"

"Um, Caia," I hesitated, "I don't know what you mean." Of course, I knew *exactly* what she meant, but I was stalling for time to figure out the most appropriate response that wouldn't get me in trouble.

"You know, toots." [Pointing to her bottom]

"Oh, like farts?"

[Nods head]

"Sure I do! Everyone has toots."

She stopped and looked at me curiously. "Well," she insisted, "Josie, my friend at school, doesn't have toots."

"What do you mean?" I challenged her. "Everyone farts, I mean, has toots."

Caia looked at me skeptically, "Well, Josie says she doesn't."

"Hmmm. Interesting," I replied, not sure where to go next with this; then I found inspiration: "I like the smell of my own farts. What about you?"

Caia started giggling. "Yeah, but I don't like to smell other people's when *they* have toots." Then we held up our hands to seal the deal with a high five.

So, what's the book idea, you wonder? It relates directly to the celebratory high five at the end of the discussion when we validated our shared experience, especially about something we don't talk about very often. This immediately brought to mind a host of other topics that remain mysterious and misunderstood. I was flooded with thoughts about all the things that we just take for granted but rarely talk about openly, even though almost everyone has these shared experiences like "tooting."

FIGURE 0.1   One of the most interesting mysteries related to aging healthfully in old age is how the role of caregiver or grandparent has led to such a dramatic increase in life expectancy for humans. There are few other species that survive after procreative functions are completed. Yet it has been suggested that one of the reasons that *Homo sapiens* have been so dominant on the planet is precisely because elders are available, not only to assist with childcare but also pass on the experience and wisdom that has been accumulated to the following generations. The author is pictured with his granddaughters.

I began to review all the things that we assume about healthful aging that are shaped by myths and misunderstanding. Supposedly as we age we become more lonely, more unhappy, and more frustrated and complain more about the state of one's life, as well as the world at large, not at all "like the good ole days." The elderly are often viewed as burdensome, frail, and brittle, both in physical condition and attitude, even though this is actually the time in life when people are *most* satisfied and content. People become obsessed with attempts to prolong their lives, believing that if they just take vitamins and placenta pills, drink celery juice, get coffee enemas, do hot yoga, that will guarantee a long, healthful, and joyful life. Although these might be reassuring and pleasurable illusions of self-care, none of them are likely to make much of a difference compared to one completely natural development that occurs in the transition to grandparenthood or some other form of active caring for others.

Tales of Wonder

Imagine the tales of wonder that elders and grandparents have observed and experienced in their lifetimes. Those of us of a certain age can remember the first time we saw color on a television (with only three stations!) and prewashed lettuce in a bag. When I was in graduate school the computer that processed my data, after meticulously typing the IBM punch cards, was the size of a whole building. The staff who operated the mysterious machine wore white lab coats and masks and were stationed behind glass walls. We had to wait 24 hours to get the results after submitting data entry cards.

And what about all the remarkable new inventions and discoveries of the previous generations during their formative years? Those who were alive during the end of the 19th century would have been dazzled by all the innovations displayed during the Chicago World Fair of 1893, witnessing the first electric lights, dishwashers, elevators, even a Ferris wheel. Then there were all the new foods that were introduced that single year—hamburgers, Cracker Jacks, Pabst Blue Ribbon beer, shredded wheat cereal, Juicy Fruit gum, pancake mix in a box.

Now consider all the advances in technology and lifestyle enhancements that the current crop of elders are experiencing with the redoubling of innovation almost every year. Mobile devices, autonomous vehicles, entertainment media, and even many jobs and professions have become increasingly obsolete. Then there are all the historical events that were survived by the current baby boomer cohort, only the most recent of which was the worldwide pandemic: The Cold War, Vietnam War, Middle East wars, fall of the Soviet Union, 9/11, space race, invention of the internet, civil rights movement, the assassinations, the conflicts, the new developments, all of which have shaped their worldview.

Although this book would be interesting and useful for almost anyone who loves to solve a mystery or understand a phenomenon about which we still don't fully understand, it is designed primarily as a supplementary text in a variety of courses in psychology, family studies, gerontology, human services, counseling, human development, health professions, and related fields. It is intended to augment the standard texts on aging that cover the classic theories, review standard concepts, and cover the comprehensive life cycle. Even within courses that focus specifically on older adults and aging processes there's increasing interest in not only covering the developmental tasks of this stage of life but also digging much deeper into the greatest sources of satisfaction, joy, and optimal function during later life.

Among all the different functions and roles that older people serve within contemporary life there is no other "job" that is more popular—and less understood—than grandparenting. Within the United States, close to 90% of all senior citizens will, at one time or another, eventually become at least a part-time caregiver for young people. Whether as the primary caregivers within "grandfamilies" that have "lost" one or both parents as a result of neglect, abandonment, abuse, sickness, or death, or else as occasional babysitters or more formal, traditional roles as respected elders, grandparents exist because they continue to provide critical responsibilities that better support families and the larger culture.

A Final Very Personal Confession

Perhaps one of the most significant findings as a result of this intensive investigation is the discovery of just how influential and powerful the relationships can become between grandparents and their grandchildren. Although we will examine these reciprocal effects in detail throughout the book, I was struck by one particular study that seemed to resonate most closely with my own life experiences—and, honestly, it is probably the real reason I wrote this book.

First are a few facts about our subject, or at least empirically supported trends. Throughout almost all of history, in every setting and context, and with the great majority of species, it is the maternal elders and parents that are most closely and intimately involved with young offspring. You will learn that it is somewhat rare, traditionally speaking, for the father's parents to become major players in the life of the nuclear family, at least in terms of supporting children. Secondly, during cases of divorce or separation, it is not uncommon that paternal grandparents are cut off completely, or at least blocked from easy access to the children. After all, grandparents have few, if any, legal rights.

I always found it surprising that my mother's parents were so disengaged from our family; maybe I'd see them a few times of the year, during holidays as an obligatory visit. Otherwise, they were distant figures, somewhat frightening to me. My father's parents, however, and especially my grandfather, functioned as surrogate parents in many ways, especially after my parents divorced. My father wasn't around very much, and my mother was a depressed alcoholic. It was my grandfather who was my main source of support. He was my hero. And it was his stories that beguiled me. He had endless versions of how he ended up bald—he was scalped while working as a scout for Kid Carson in the Old West. He slept too close to the headboard on his bed and it rubbed all the hair off. There were a dozen different explanations, and every single one made me giggle.

I had never fully appreciated how my grandfather actually "saved" me—until I saw this article describing how if children had a close relationship with a grandparent following the parents' divorce, they were likely to become more emotionally stable, have fewer personal problems, and be more involved in prosocial (helpful, altruistic) behavior (Buchanan & Rotkirch, 2018). *That*, in a nutshell, is the story of my own life.

As you review the material in this book, read the research and stories, study the theories that explain how and why aging unfolds the way it does, you can't help but internalize and personalize the content. Throughout this journey you will repeatedly apply some of the ideas to your own life. You will become "triggered" by memories and reminiscences within your own family experiences. Hopefully, you will also gain a much deeper understanding of what it means to age healthfully throughout the life span, but especially during the last stages of life when new identities, roles, functions, and responsibilities take precedent, not only for personal satisfaction, but ultimately programmed by evolution to bolster the family and community.

Jeffrey Kottler

Houston, Texas

CHAPTER 1

What Is Healthy Aging Anyway?

In most comprehensive textbooks about human development three quarters of the chapters focus only on the first few decades of life. It is as if once we achieve certain age-related markers we have essentially reached our peak; the rest of life is pretty much downhill. Although it is certainly true that there is a lot of spectacular action going on inside us during infancy, childhood, and adolescence, optimal development actually continues throughout every day of life thereafter, well into old age.

It has pretty much always been the policy to identify the most critical times during the life span when the most dramatic changes take place. Typical examples include when babies are first weaned, when puberty begins, or when children leave home. There have also always been evaluative judgments about the relative importance associated with various life stages and what it means to age successfully within each stage. When examining the words, labels, and terms to describe one's age, however, there is quite startling differences between what it means to be "young" versus "old" in many cultures, especially our own (Sokolovsky, 2008). Infants and children, for instance, are almost always portrayed as various forms of adorable or cute (peewee, tyke, bambino, cherub). But compare those labels to that of people who are viewed as "old" and the list of names is quite different: geezer, geriatric, old maid, dirty old man, old dog. Needless to say, this presents considerable challenges for the elderly in a culture where they are essentially viewed as being retired, over the hill, and barely able to keep up with everyone else.

Early thinkers like Aristotle conceived of the human mind as similar to a wax tablet. When you are born it is smoking hot and pliable, readily responsive to any slight impression. Yet with age memory supposedly begins to cool down, becoming so brittle that it can barely hold onto new impressions without them fading soon afterward. That's one reason why the elderly, especially grandparents, are so often portrayed in media, fairytales, shows, and films as feeble, tottering old fools who may, at times, be adorable, but also somewhat annoying as a meddlesome burden. As such, certain biases have not only been perpetuated within cultural scripts but also internalized by many older people in such a way that it affects their ability to function optimally, whether as a mentor, advisor, teacher, supervisor, sage, or grandparent.

Parts of this chapter are adapted from Jeffrey A. Kottler, "What Does It Mean to Age 'Successfully' in Later Life?," *Critical and Provocative Issues in Human Development*, pp. 322–327, 329. Copyright © 2021 by Cognella, Inc. Reprinted with permission.

It is also presumed that this latter stage of life is characterized by a dark, cascading collapse into chronic fragility, forgetfulness, suffering, emptiness, despair—and eventually oblivion.

Over the years it has been difficult to determine what it means to age successfully because it is a concept that encompasses so many different facets, not only how long one lives but especially the quality of those moments. Standard definitions often discuss an older person's expansion of functional years, relatively free of pain and disease, along with active social and relational engagement (Rowe & Kahn, 1987). It is also clear, however, that this refers not only to objective measurements of these variables but also someone's own subjective experience and personal assessment. More recently there has been a shift by researchers in gerontology to move away from an exclusively biomedical conception of aging well, meaning the person is healthy, mobile, and lucid, to a far more multidimensional conception that encompasses functional behavior in a variety of other contexts. These include but are not limited to meaningful work and family responsibilities such as sharing financial resources, childcare and grandparenting, satisfying social contacts, and active engagement with the world at large (Urtamo et al., 2019).

What Does It Really Mean to Age "Successfully" in Later Life?

The rate of developmental, behavioral, and personality changes are greatest during which stage(s) of life? Check all that apply:

( ) Infancy   ( ) Early adulthood
( ) Early childhood   ( ) Middle adulthood
( ) Middle childhood   ( ) Later adulthood
( ) Adolescence   ( ) Old age

Answer at the end of the chapter.

The first question you might ask is what is "successful," "optimal," or "healthy" aging, and who gets to decide what this really means? Is it a matter of simply coping with one's current age and stage in life, adapting to more limited circumstances without complaint or resentment? Medical professionals, for instance, would define healthy aging in terms of one's functional abilities to meet basic needs, continue mobility, and make sound and rational decisions. But perhaps it instead involves something far more encouraging and satisfying than merely maintaining health and mobility in which the person is truly still growing and flourishing in daily life. This would mean that learning and intellectual development are still a priority, as well as deep engagement in intimate and satisfying relationships. It would include feeling productive and involved in some form of meaningful "work." It would also involve acceptance of the things that are not within one's control, instead focusing on choices that matter the most. It would involve a generally positive, optimistic outlook that makes each day feel like a gift. For most older adults it also encompasses opportunities to pass along knowledge, experience, and wisdom to subsequent generations, whether as a grandparent or resource for the family and community.

According to developmental theorists like Erik Erikson (Erikson & Erikson, 1998), the primary goal of this latter stage of life involves resolving the crisis between maintaining one's integrity in the face of despair after a series of successive losses, coupled with the realization that the time remaining is so finite and limited. It is, after all, a period of dramatic changes that are no less significant than any others that occur during an earlier stage of life. People retire from their jobs and leave their careers behind, after which they may feel "invisible" in many ways. I recall interviewing an older woman, a prominent professor and scholar, for a previous book about adaptations to aging (Kottler & Carlson, 2016). She was at a social event when someone asked her, "Who did you *used* to be?" In other words, she was no longer considered a useful citizen with an identity other than as a retired person, "retired" in the sense of being essentially out of the way. This is all the more shocking when you consider that throughout history, and still in many parts of the world, the elderly are *revered* for their wisdom, experience, and level-headed decision-making. They are relied on for guidance, coaching, and leadership by the younger generation. They are treated with honor and respect rather than being relegated to institutions for basic care. In one sense, through their mentoring, teaching, guiding, and grandparenting, they are absolutely critical for the survival of their families—and the community.

In many ways, the last stage of life is indeed a time of losses that must be accepted and processed. There are losses of optimal functioning since an older person must deal with certain limitations now in place. There are so many physical changes taking place. Sleep is disrupted. Appetite and metabolism slow down. Vision and hearing are compromised. Every system in the body slowly winds down. Friends have died or relocated. Colleagues and coworkers have moved on in their lives. It can certainly be a struggle for older people to find or create meaning in their lives once they leave their work and major responsibilities behind. In many cases they may shift into different "jobs" as grandparents, caretakers, volunteer assignments, or even move into a completely different career, however that is imagined.

In addition, the elderly must deal with a host of other changes taking place in their bodies and minds, all of which lead to new and different challenges in order to define success and prosperity. Numerous adaptations may be required to deal with declining health, chronic pain, reduced mobility, and other health issues. With all that acknowledged, it must be pointed out that this is also the time in which people are *most* satisfied and content in many ways (Kutubaeva, 2019; Levitin, 2020). Even more surprising, 80% of seniors report that they are happier than they were at any previous time of life (David, 2017). Of course the results may be a bit skewed since many seniors with serious health difficulties and meager financial resources, those who were miserable and dissatisfied, have since died (Hudomiet et al., 2020).

It is certainly the case that older people have far more realistic expectations than during their youth. They have long ago abandoned goals that were hardly ever within reach, and eventually shrugged of such disappointments. They have a lifetime of experience dealing with setbacks and challenges and so can more easily take them in stride. For those who are grandparents or mentors in other contexts, they have an opportunity to apply all they learned earlier in life to avoid certain mistakes and function at even higher levels of caregiving. Yet they must also come to terms with dreams that were never realized and aspirations that were never reached.

Given the assortment of different descriptions of what it means to age optimally, there have been very different models within our culture that we are encouraged to emulate (Castel, 2019).

On the one hand there is someone like Jeanne Calment who lived to be 122 years of age (plus 164 days!) and claimed to have never been ill a single day in her life. Yet her daily routines, rituals, diet, sleep, and wake patterns were carefully (compulsively) controlled. Billionaire philanthropist and industrialist Warren Buffet is another model of supposed optimal aging, not only because he lasted until his 90s but also because of his financial success. He attributed his longevity and career success to spending most of his time reading, plus drinking a six-pack of Coca-Cola every day. But of course just because you live a long time and become wealthy doesn't necessarily translate into a "good life."

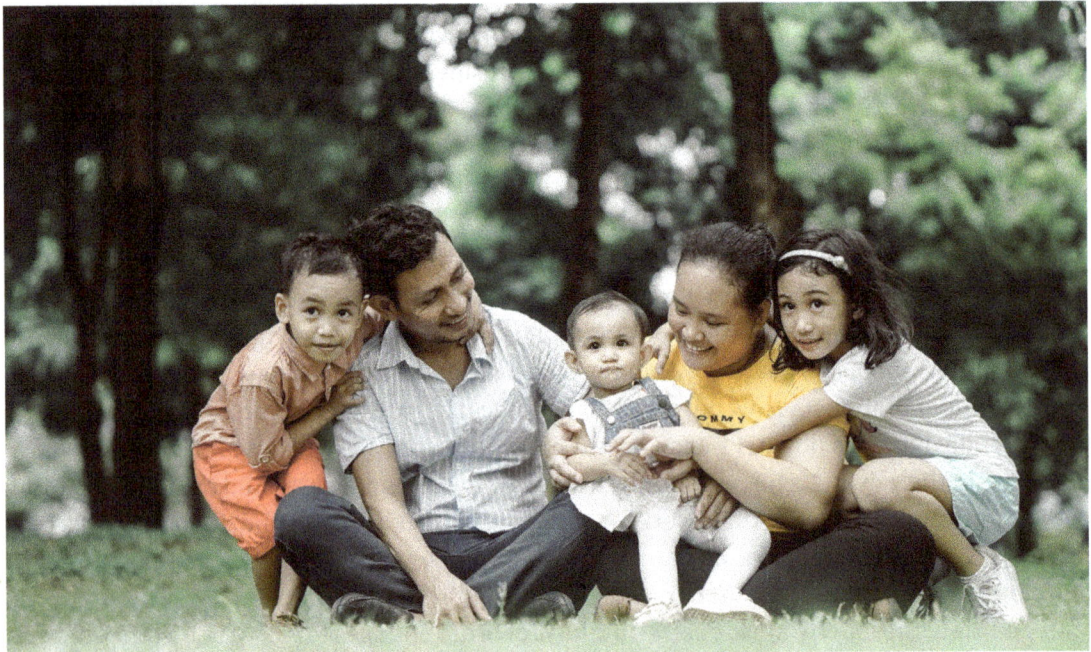

FIGURE 1.1   There are over 100 different definitions of healthy or successful aging, most of them insisting that optimal development is best characterized by physical and external factors such as stable health, mobility, financial security, and meaningful work. However, it is also critical to consider intimate relationships with family members, neighbors, close friends, and grandchildren. In addition, one's positive attitude and commitment to continued growth and learning play a key role in promoting joy and a sense of purpose to one's existence—even when physical health is failing.

One of the interesting differences between the various conceptions of healthy aging is that while some of the hallmarks specified are so difficult to achieve that few people ever attain this distinction, others offer conceptions that are within the grasp of almost everyone who has sufficient interest and motivation. Perhaps one way to sort this out is to bring to mind someone you have encountered who appears to embody all that you admire, respect, and wish to emulate related to aging optimally.

Several writers and philosophers, who lived well into their 80s and 90s and claimed (or were alleged) to live a satisfying, productive, and fulfilling life, chimed in with their own ideas about what it means to age well. For novelist Henry Miller (1977), it was about the ability "to fall in love again and again," insisting that "if you can forgive as well as forget, if you can keep from going sour, surly, bitter and cynical, … you've got it half licked." Bertrand Russell spent the last years of his life musing about what it means to grow old well and concluded that it was mostly about allowing "the walls of the ego" to recede. Rather than fearing infirmity and old age, Russell (1956) viewed death as a sort of gift that forces one to treat every moment as precious: "The man who, in old age, can see his life in this way, will not suffer from the fear of death, since the things he cares for will continue. And if, with the decay of vitality, weariness increases, the thought of rest will not be unwelcome. I should wish to die while still at work, knowing that others will carry on what I can no longer do and content in the thought that what was possible has been done" (p. 44).

A well-lived life indeed.

Adapting Successfully to Changes in the Body—and Others' Perceptions of Aging

When reviewing the developmental tasks and challenges that are encountered during old age it is easy to appreciate how resilient and remarkable many older adults must be in order to roll with the punches and yet still maintain a sense of peace, prosperity, and satisfaction (see Table 1.1). In many cases, their losses and daily struggles better equip them for their current roles that involve caregiving for others, whether family members, grandchildren, or volunteer choices within the community. As such, resilience is among the most important markers of healthy aging, allowing for flexibility and adaptation in one's core identity (Wilson et al., 2021).

TABLE 1.1   Challenges for Healthy Aging in Later Adulthood

- Disengaging from previous responsibilities, obligations, and work
- Creating a new and different identity and sense of personal meaning
- Maintaining a degree of independence and self-sufficiency
- Negotiating, expanding, or contracting forms of social support
- Dealing with declining health, chronic diseases
- Adapting to reduced energy, stamina, and cognitive adjustments
- Taking on new roles as mentors, grandparents, and elders within community and family
- Counteracting discrimination, marginalization, and ageism
- Recovering from grief and losses of longtime friends and partner
- Coming to terms with impending death

While it is certainly true that older people think, process, and reason more slowly (or at least differently) than when they were younger, many have also learned to compensate and adapt to these changes by relying on other internal resources that have been honed from experience. This includes demonstrating greater patience, enhanced intuition, learning from previous mistakes, and the ability to synthesize and make sense out of complex data and discrepant information.

This, in fact, is one of the hallmarks of the older brain in that it has "learned" to become far more integrative over time, making connections that younger versions would never have recognized.

In spite of the losses, challenges, and limitations, the great majority of older adults function quite well in their daily lives. They have learned to accept and manage the things they can't control related to their cognitive decline, health issues, reduced social network, and other issues. As mentioned earlier, many such individuals report that this is the best time of their lives, especially if they have a degree of financial stability and resources (which is not always the case). They feel like they can do whatever they want and go wherever they like. In fact, one of the universal changes that take place with aging is that people become far more selective in their choices. They prefer to spend more time with family and a few close friends, declining invitations that no longer have much meaning to them. With limited time ticking away, they tend to be far more intentional about their choices. Such determined focus helps explain some of the extraordinary achievements that some people have made in the last stage of their lives (see Table 1.2).

TABLE 1.2 Extraordinarily Creative and Productive Elderly Individuals

Name	Age	Activity
Ruth Bader Ginsberg	88	Served on the Supreme Court of the United States for 30 years, maintaining a busy and productive schedule even after numerous bouts with cancer
Sigmund Freud	83	Continued his active clinical practice, research, and writing, completing his last and most controversial work (*Moses and Monotheism*) just prior to his death
Betty White	97	Acting career spanned 80 years but didn't really find her stride as an actor until old age
Chuck Berry	90	Early pioneer of rhythm and blues and rock and roll music who was still performing on stage into his 90s
Jane Goodall	88	Primatologist whose groundbreaking studies of chimpanzees in their natural habitats continued her grueling fieldwork studying her subjects
Queen Elizabeth	97	Carried out royal duties for over 60 years
David Goodall	103	Scientific investigations of measuring ecological changes
Loraine Maurer	94	Has worked at the same early shift (5:00 a.m.) at McDonald's restaurant for over 40 years, showing up every day even when not on her schedule
Walter Bingham	93	Holds world record as oldest radio talk show host
John Lewis	80	Congressman who was active in supporting the civil rights and voting rights movement, having once marched along with Martin Luther King
Anthony Mancinelli	106	The world's oldest barber has no plans to retire any time soon
Frank Lloyd Wright	91	One of the greatest architects in history continued building his masterpiece, the Guggenheim Museum, until his death
Manoel de Oliveira	106	Portuguese screenwriter and director, whose career began during the silent film era and ended during the digital era
Clive Cussler	88	Bestselling author of over 80 bestselling books
Mastanamma	106	Social media celebrity and Indian YouTube star with over 1 million viewers on her cooking channel

In spite of the contributions and achievements of elders throughout history, and the critical leadership and caregiving roles they have played as a result of their experience and wisdom, nowadays many older people report feeling like their contributions are not sufficiently valued and respected. As grandparents, they represent free labor and cheap kid sitters who show up when needed, but otherwise are expected to stay out of the way. Except for drug commercials during the nightly news (who else still consumes news on television?), more than 95% of advertising is aimed at those younger than 50 years old (Beer, 2019). Anything that *is* promoted to the elderly tends to be either health insurance or pharmaceutical products, as if they are barely hanging on to life by a thread.

Just as there are stereotypes for every age group, the elderly are subject to more than their fair share, describing them at either of the extremes of being lonely, reclusive, bitter, living in the past, or else that they are loving, kind, proud, nostalgic, and mostly living in the past. Of course none of these conceptions are accurate, leading to "ageism" and mostly negative overgeneralizations (Gendron, 2022). There is an assortment of examples of how this plays out during everyday interactions when older people are told things like, "You look great *for your age,*" "I can't believe you are *still* driving/working out/dancing," "I guess that was a *senior moment* when you forgot about that." Then there are all the anti-aging cosmetics, diets, elective surgery, hair implants, hair coloring, assisting older people to deny their age and feel shame about it unless they can make themselves appear younger.

There are so many myths associated with aging that just perpetuate the discrimination, marginalization, and prejudices toward the elderly (National Institute on Aging, 2022). Older people are often portrayed as essentially hapless, confused, forgetful, stubborn, and handicapped, both in their cognitive and physical functioning (see Table 1.3).

One of the reasons older people may have difficulty attaining greater satisfaction with their position in life is that they buy into the myths related to aging that are perpetuated by our culture in such a way that it marginalizes those who are not the perfect picture of youth. One example of this is that younger adults and teenagers often assess their popularity and social satisfaction in quantitative terms, how many "friends" they have on social media, the number of "likes" they receive, how expansive their social circle is, the relative status of their group, the number of invitations they receive to social events, the number of different people they interact with throughout the day. As mentioned earlier, elderly people are far more selective in the choices they make regarding who they want to spend time with. They are more inclined to limit social contacts to just a few, intimate friends along with family members, and often feel particularly committed to spending time with grandchildren. They are no longer willing to "waste" their limited, precious time left engaged in relatively meaningless social encounters or spending time with those they don't value all that much.

Interestingly, an older person's health (or anyone else for that matter) is not just an objective state but is determined by one's attitude and beliefs. Those who view their health as good, or even satisfactory, regardless of their actual physical condition, are much more satisfied with their lives. After all, if you *feel* sick, infirm, or disabled, that's exactly what you will be. It would therefore appear that healthy aging throughout the life span, and regardless of age and stage,

TABLE 1.3   Myths About Growing Older That Are Unsupported by Research

- *Genetics and family history determine one's health and life span.* In fact, researchers have found that 60% of the factors that influence longevity and health correlate with lifestyle, such as diet, sleep, exercise, and self-care.
- *With age you become weak, unstable, and frail.* This may be true for those with serious health conditions, or who don't engage in regular exercise, but it is the exception in most cases.
- *You lose your mind and memory in old age.* Very few adults over 70 develop dementia, although the risk of memory loss increases with age.
- *Older people are rigid, risk-avoidant, conservative, and resistant to change.* Some are—and some are not; many have prepared their whole lives to finally do things that weren't possible earlier.
- *It is no longer possible to learn very much of significance because of difficulties in memory retention, entrenched habits, and resistance to change.* It is true that the speed of learning, and its retention, diminishes with age, but the capacity for learning on a more global scale, making connections between varied sources of information, is actually enhanced.
- *Sex is over.* Three quarters of the elderly say that romance and sex are still important to them; it may just require adaptations but is still considered enjoyable and satisfying.

- *Less sleep is required during old age.* They still need about 8 hours; it just takes a different form with more frequent awakenings.
- *Productivity and contributions to the community come to a close.* The elderly frequently stay busy with volunteering, family support, and other jobs.
- *Older people lose their creative spark.* Many inventors, creators, artists, writers, scientists, and innovators have done their best work after their 80s.
- *Old age leads to depression and helplessness.* It is actually the stage of life when most people experience their greatest satisfaction and contentment.
- *The elderly are lonely.* This is really the stage in life when people feel *least* lonely since they rely on fewer friendships and have more realistic expectations.
- *They will eventually end up in nursing homes.* Only 2.5% require or choose assisted-living facilities, with another 4.5% residing in nursing homes (Institute of Medicine, 2010).
- *Exercise and active lifestyle are no longer safe.* At age 72, I still hike and run 8-minute miles, and last year I climbed a 19,000-foot Himalayan peak.

involves several important actions (American Psychological Association, 2017): (a) staying physically active through regular exercise and direct engagement with meaningful activities, (b) maintaining a healthy lifestyle related to diet, drinking alcohol in moderation, avoiding addictive substances, and regular self-care, (c) seeking regular medical care, not only to treat ailments but also for prevention of future problems, (d) viewing oneself as an "interesting" person, someone who is knowledgeable, inquisitive, articulate, capable, and experienced, (e) recruiting, maintaining, and cherishing intimate, trusting relationships with a handful of close friends and family members.

FIGURE 1.2   At the age of 77 Jeanne Socrates became the oldest person to sail around the world, solo, nonstop, and unescorted. After returning from her voyage, the grandmother said, "Age is just a number, it is your health and mental attitude that matters, not your age" (Mitchell, 2019, para. 8).

When we talk about healthy aging in action we are referring to particular behaviors, personality traits, beliefs, and attitudes (like resilience) that lead to optimal functioning and contentment, if not feelings of pride and achievement. Of course, these change over time, just as the developmental tasks of each stage of life require different coping strategies. Many of the characteristics, however, remain powerful distinctions of healthy aging throughout the life span. Motivation and desire are key features of this process, triggering passion, commitment, energy, and interest in one's interactions with others—and the world at large. Also considered significant is a "growth mind-set," a determined belief in one's own capacity for change, transformation, and adaptation no matter what challenges are faced in life (Yaeger & Dweck, 2020).

Distinct and Different Stages of Old Age

It has been clear for some time that one's actual physical age and developmental life stage are not necessarily equivalent given the increased variations in functionality (Arnett et al., 2020). The researchers cite as one obvious example how the decade from 20 to 30 used to be identified as the stage of "young adulthood," the period typically designated for finding a mate, selecting a career, and becoming self-sufficient and fully independent. After all, that's the way it has been for thousands of years. Nowadays, however, this time of life is no longer identified as a marker of adulthood, nor is it really a kind of extended adolescence; it is something else entirely.

The same is true with respect to "old age," which, in the past, has been conceived as beginning about the age of 60, although today this is more accurately a part of "middle age" since most people are expected to live another 20, or even 30 years. With better health, improved medical care, more active lifestyles, and a significantly longer life span, many people don't really hit their prime until their sixth and seventh decade of life.

Much of this literature has treated "old age" or the "elderly" as if this is a singular developmental stage when this time of life may more accurately and appropriately segmented into three distinct stages! Furthermore, each of these developmental stages presents unique challenges and satisfactions. It is clear that being a member of the "young-old" stage (55–65 years) includes developmental tasks somewhat different from that of the "middle old" (66–85 years) which, in turn, may be quite different from those who are "very old" (86–120 years). Even these demarcations are changing after new advances in medicine, health, and lifestyle breakthroughs that not only continue to extend life but also address issues that may have once been debilitating or fatal.

The reality for these later stages of life is that memory training, cognitive stimulation, and physical exercise significantly help to improve brain functioning, prevent neurological atrophy, and improve decision-making. Advances in technology (ocular surgery, hearing aids, virtual reality, medical implants, other sensory enhancements) counteract some of the physical deterioration that inevitably take place. Older people (baby boomers in particular) are far more willing than previous generational cohorts to seek mental health services and counseling for personal problems, leading to better adaptation and emotional regulation. Social media, online meetings and groups, and virtual interactions, all make social engagement more accessible.

There are indeed many losses, adjustments, and physical limitations that accompany advanced age, many of which do make tasks and activities more challenging in some ways. And yet there are still many opportunities for continued growth, development, learning, and significant contributions for those who embrace the stage of life they have earned through such hard work throughout their lives. Resilience and hardiness are not just ideals for those who are recovering from trauma but also traits that assist older people to make the very best out of their supposed "golden years." For those who remain physically active, feel a sense of mission to accomplish something meaningful, and have several close confidantes, whether friends or family, the last stages of life are among the most fulfilling and enjoyable. It appears to be particularly important that older people feel a sense of purpose in later life, most often as a mentor to younger generations.

Late Bloomers and Creativity Among the Aged

Despite broad generalities about so-called "normal" or "typical" aging and what *usually* happens during development, there are always some notable variations, if not exceptions. If we take creative innovation as an example, another one of the myths of our culture is that creativity and invention exist primarily within the domain of the young and spirited who are more likely to pursue adventure, exploration, experimentation, and risk taking. This dominant narrative of innovation presents stories of visionaries like Wolfgang Mozart, Marie Curie, Pablo Picasso, and Orson Welles, all child prodigies whose creativity blossomed in their youth. Likewise, tech wizards such as Steve Jobs, Mark Zuckerberg, and Bill Gates all made revolutionary contributions to the birth of Silicon Valley during their 20s. Our culture is fascinated by these stories of precocious youth, celebrating individuals who showed such early promise during the critical stage when such talent blossoms.

Yet there appear to be at least two cycles of creativity during the life span, one for young geniuses like poet T.S. Eliot or novelist Herman Melville, and the other for old masters who don't find their stride until well past middle age (Weinberg & Galenson, 2019). Poet Wallace Stevens was an insurance salesman until his 50s when he discovered a latent talent for writing poetry. Ditto with Maya Angelou who wasn't recognized for her writing until her 60s. Some of the most influential political figures of the last century—Golda Meir, Winston Churchill, Nelson Mandela, Ronald Reagan, and Joe Biden were into their late 70s, supposedly well past their prime, when they served in office. Alfred Hitchcock never achieved excellence as a film director until he was past 50. Johann Wolfgang von Goethe began writing *Faust* when he was 59 years old but didn't complete this seminal work until he was 83. Similar trajectories are evident as well in the lives of Julia Child, Daniel Defoe, and so many others (see Table 1.4).

TABLE 1.4   Late Bloomers Who Achieved Greatness

Pablo Picasso	Igor Stravinsky
Frank Lloyd Wright	Martha Graham
William Carlos Williams	Willem de Kooning
Robert Frost	Wallace Stevens
Alfred Hitchcock	Daniel Defoe
Mark Twain	Paul Cezanne
Sigmund Freud	Benjamin Franklin
Nelson Mandela	Julia Child
Mother Teresa	Mahatma Gandhi
Grandma Moses	Maya Angelou
Giuseppe Verdi	Charles Darwin
Henry Ford	Bertrand Russell
Frank Lloyd Wright	Coco Chanel

It has only been relatively recently that neuroscientists have discovered that brain plasticity continues well into old age, making possible continued growth, development, and learning until the very end of life. In some cases there are even certain abilities that don't come into full fruition until much later in life, especially those that require sufficient life experiences to fully synthesize what has been learned over time. Young people are known for being notoriously impatient and impulsive, for instance, while older adults eventually develop a far better sense of appreciation of timing, reflection, and thoughtful, measured responses. The problem seems not so much related to one's potential abilities as it does involve people over 60 buying into many of the myths and underestimating their own potential to continue growing, learning, and creating (Touron, 2015).

Who Gets to Decide What Optimal Aging Is?

It is interesting how the particular context, environment, and culture in which one resides has such a huge impact on how we describe and experience "optimal" development. Whereas in North America we usually provide caregivers or sitters for children under the age of 10 when they are alone, in other parts of the world, like rural Nepal, a 5-year-old child may be expected to take primary responsivity for the care of younger siblings while the parents work in the fields. Optimal development is thus defined differently, depending on what is most needed for the community to flourish. In some cultures, the stage of adolescence is abbreviated, forcing young people into adult responsibilities during a time when in our culture they are still treated as dependent children. Or consider historical traditions from the past when it was fully expected that a 14-year-old was sufficiently and optimally developed to hunt prey, find a mate, and leave home to begin a new family.

The question we are really exploring is who gets to decide what is considered ideal or desired development? It is not like we are all on the same page, or that we all agree about what is in the best interests of an individual, family, community, nation-state, or future of the planet. For example, during the worldwide coronavirus pandemic each nation, state, region, or city defined the optimal development of coping skills for the crisis in very different ways, whether vaccine mandates, social distancing, face masks, isolation, or complete denial were practiced—and to what extent these norms were consistently enforced by elected officials.

Optimal or "ideal" development has usually been described as mastering age-related developmental tasks or resolving the successive psychosocial stages of development during a particularly sensitive period of life. In the case of young adults, for instance, this would mean the ability to engage intimately with others, to maintain meaningful friendships, construct and maintain healthy romantic relationships, prepare for a meaningful career, and so on. In Erik Erikson's terms, it means resolving the conflict between the urge for connection with others while counteracting the desire for self-protection and isolation. In the case of Jean Piaget's cognitive development theory it means mastering so-called "formal operations," or in Lawrence Kohlberg's conception of moral development it means reaching higher order, sophisticated moral reasoning.

Some of the greatest thinkers have postulated certain considerations regarding what it means to reach peak potential. Abraham Maslow created his "hierarchy of needs" to plot the progression of satisfying our most basic needs for sustenance, shelter, a sense of belongingness, and autonomy, all the way to the top of the pyramid to reach a state of self-actualization, a goal that he believed was the ideal to which we should all aspire. For existential theorist Victor Frankl, optimal development related to the task of finding meaning in one's life, an overriding purpose for one's existence. He believed it takes a certain amount of courage and boldness to pursue such a meaningful life, one that is only possible for those who feel empowered, who have discovered ways to deal with tragedies, trauma, disappointments, and suffering in their lives by using those experiences for personal gain. He disagreed with Maslow that self-actualization was even possible "for the simple reason that the more one would strive for it, the more he would miss it" (Frankl, 1959, p. 115). Frankl preferred instead to think of this goal as a form of "self-transcendence."

Optimal functioning is usually defined as being the best you can be, so to speak. Whether at school, home, work, the playground, or social arena, it implies reaching the highest potential for growth attainment. Although often associated with achievements and accomplishments, the ideal also applies to one's sense of satisfaction and well-being, meaning that it includes a degree of self-compassion, especially after perceived failings, mistakes, or disappointments.

There is considerable disagreement among experts, much less the public, about what might be considered "optimal" as far as one's growth and development. Some scholars argue there is already *way* too much pressure on children, beginning in preschool, to start building a competitive portfolio of exceptional experiences and achievements in order to gain admission into the best schools. Adolescents are more stressed than ever before because of so many uncertainties related to the future economic, environmental, political, and social conditions. Performing at one's best, attempting to reach maximum potential, is certainly a desirable goal, but it is also mostly destined for ultimate disappointment and failure. After all, it is virtually impossible to reach a point of proficiency in almost *anything* such that you can't continue to improve, learn, and grow.

It is also confusing and problematic to settle on who determines what "optimal" really means in the context of an individual life. A medical patient may believe that this can only be attained by a full and complete recovery, while the health professional is thinking more in terms of 50% increased mobility. At the other extreme, a student is willing to settle for a "generous B-" in a class as being an absolutely wonderful outcome, while the instructor was evaluating this performance as quite marginal. It is hardly unusual in medicine, counseling, teaching, leadership, coaching, or any other helping endeavor, that there is a significant disparity between how the various parties view "optimal" functioning once the experience is completed. We see this discrepancy frequently in coaches' attitudes and philosophies related to children's sports involvement. Is optimal development really about winning a game or championship and developing exceptional skills, or rather is it more related to having fun, making friends, learning new things, developing a degree of competence?

Finally, there are the questions, "When is 'good enough' good enough? When is it 'optimal' to become satisfied with moderate (or even) minimal effort?" Given that time, energy, and commitment are all limited commodities, it is important to focus passion and devotion on the selective things that matter the most. None of us function optimally in *all* situations and circumstances. No matter how spectacular you are as a physical specimen, how brilliant as a thinker, how emotionally sensitive and responsive, there will always be domains of life in which you function far less than you prefer. Sometimes the most useful goal involves coming to terms with that reality.

It is more than a little paradoxical that it is precisely those times when we are most dissatisfied with the way things are going in life, when we feel vulnerable, that we are also most amenable to moving toward what has been described as "quantum changes" (Kottler, 2014; Miller & de Baca, 2001). These are *big* spurts in growth, major transformations that can lead to a cascade of other changes. Such a developmental transition can begin with a choice or action that is relatively small and insignificant, a "keystone behavior" that spins into something much more powerful over time. For instance, if academic development is falling off and performance is suffering, that may require a push to a new and different way of thinking about your job as a student. Waking up 15 minutes earlier may seem like a worthless, insignificant thing to do when it feels like the world is crashing and disaster is around the corner, but sometimes little things can foster major development in other areas. When families eat dinner together, for example, this habit can result in children developing better emotional regulation, more completed homework, higher grades in school, lower risk of obesity, addiction, eating disorders, teen pregnancy, and greater intimacy among members (Fishel, 2015, 2022). Another example that is even more dramatic relates to engaging in regular exercise, even just walking for 10 minutes a day. Once exercise becomes habituated behavior changes in other areas related to diet, mood control, sleep, memory, energy, cardiovascular efficiency, immune function, pain tolerance, and self-discipline. Is if that's not enough, exercise also prevents the onset of 40 chronic diseases!

So, what might be concluded from this discussion? It would appear that optimal functioning refers to the kind of development that increases one's competence, if not mastery, in those behaviors, skills, and knowledge that lead to greater productivity, satisfaction, and success. There are indeed critical or sensitive periods during which we are biologically predisposed to have an easier time mastering certain abilities. These windows of opportunity are enhanced during the time when sensory systems first go "online," such as the first few hours after birth when vision starts to kick in. And yet, certain kinds of "optimal" or "peak" development can occur at *any* stage throughout the life span, as emphasized by the number of adults who report their most extraordinary functioning as spiritual beings, or enjoying interpersonal connections, wasn't reached until later life.

What's Grandparenting Have to Do With All of This?

As you will see in the chapters that follow, among the more than 9 million species that occupy this planet, there aren't more than a single handful of them that survive beyond the procreation years to become truly "old." Most animals perish soon after their reproductive functions have ended. As far as evolution is concerned, their job is completed and it is time to make room for the next generation.

Then why has nature allowed older members of the human race to continue existing, taking up space, accessing valuable food and equipment, even though they can't produce any more offspring? In some cases, the aged become a significant burden for the family and community, squandering valuable resources and opportunities that might be better directed toward the most virile members of the group. It turns out this is one of the most enduring mysteries of the universe, one that has driven evolutionary theorists crazy trying to find some answers (Kottler, 2022a).

When attempting to describe what it means to age healthfully, in ways appropriate for one's age and stage of life, we have reviewed several of the standard criteria by which this condition is attained. Although certainly avoiding illness, disease, disabilities, and mental deterioration are a big part of the picture, so too is active engagement with loved ones and the community.

In a comprehensive review of the factors that are most associated with successful aging in later life there is one other factor that stood out above all the rest—"psychological adaptation" that encompasses one's core beliefs, attitudes, and ability to adjust to significant changes that are inevitable (Kim & Park, 2017). In other words, it isn't just about remaining physically active and healthy but also feeling like one has an overriding purpose to life, one that involves a deep commitment to leaving the world better off than when one first arrived. For the majority of older people this typically involves their role as grandparents, whether with their own biological offspring or else in alternative contexts with young people they are teaching, supervising, guiding, or mentoring.

As an example of healthy aging in action, we will study the nature of this peculiar phenomenon, particularly honing in on the various functions, roles, and critical purposes that older people serve, most notably as grandparents and mentors. As a result of their continued existence, more of our children survive birth and childhood, the community has access to their knowledge about valuable resources, and they indirectly continue their procreative functions, not by producing more children but rather by ensuring that those who already exist receive better care, protection, and preparation for all that lies ahead.

Devoting one's latter years to the care and support of young people may seem like a selfless gesture, but such "healthy aging in action" is associated with a number of benefits that accrue to grandparents and other devoted caregivers. One factor that seems to matter, however, is the nature and extent of one's responsibilities, which can either be experienced as a burden or a source of great joy and satisfaction (Danielsbacka et al., 2022). In many such cases, especially with "noncustodial grandparents," a committed role has been found to reduce chronic pain, as well as feelings of loneliness, depression, and isolation, generally boosting mental health. Their caregiving role encourages the elderly to remain not only more physically active to keep up with their charges, but also more mentally focused and stay current on the latest trends in technology, social media, and cultural developments. In addition, general cognitive functioning is improved and life expectancy is actually increased by several years to the point that grandparenting has been described as the "ultimate evolutionary mechanism that has contributed to the increase in human life expectancy" (Hilbrand et al., 2017, p. 397).

With all that said, it is clear there are a lot complex, mysterious, and interesting forces operating within our biological systems and cultural contexts that have "permitted" us to grow old even though we can't any produce more offspring after midlife. The study of grandparents opens a foggy window to widen the viewpoint by which we better understand the nature of healthy aging in action, not only as a matter of functional abilities but also a meaningful life.

ANSWER TO THE QUESTION AT THE BEGINNING OF THE CHAPTER

◇◇◇◇◇◇◇◇

In response to the question at the beginning the chapter asking which stage(s) of life lead to the most significant changes, you probably guessed "infancy" without much thought since during these first few years of life the brain develops the most and leads to all the important life skills—walking, talking, and so on. But you may have found it surprising that the *other* time in life when people change the most is "old age." This doesn't mean just health issues, or failing memory, but rather this is when personality undergoes the most dramatic changes.

QUESTIONS FOR REFLECTION OR DISCUSSION

1. Here's a disturbing thought to reflect on and talk about: Create a timeline that illustrates how long you think you will live. As an example, here is a lifeline for someone who believes they will live to be about 86 years old and are currently 20 years old.

   Birth _____ X _____ 86

   When you glance at the figure it looks like it will be a *very* long time until old age and death becomes anything that you really have to consider. But then remember that none of this is guaranteed, and even if it was, your life would already be one quarter over—*if* you are fortunate not to die prematurely in an accident, violence, or a disease.
2. Project yourself in the future to a time when you are well into your 80s. What do you imagine your life will be like?
3. Compare two different elderly people you know (or have known), one of whom remained extremely active, engaged, productive, and energetic while the other person seemed to surrender to complacency and disengagement. What do you think most distinguished the two of them in terms of the ways they dealt with their situations?
4. What are some myths you held about aging that have been dispelled as a result of the discussion in this chapter?
5. What do you consider "healthy aging" means within the context of your current stage in life and the tasks that lie ahead of you?

Figure Credits

Fig. 1.1: Source: https://www.pexels.com/photo/photo-of-happy-family-4205505/.
Fig. 1.2: Source: https://www.youtube.com/watch?v=0X2jyYeMoUE.

CHAPTER 2

Why Do Older People Even Exist?

For most of the time that two-legged animals inhabited the planet there was no such thing as being "old." *Homo sapiens*, in particular, were subjected to an early death—if they managed to survive birth and childhood given their feeble defenses against predators. With no sharp claws, fangs, blinding speed, or brute strength, humans and their ancestors were fortunate to live beyond their 20s. Almost *anything* could kill you—an impacted tooth, infected wound, virus, accident, disease, plus the dangers of starvation or violent encounters.

A relatively brief life span was hardly unusual since it was never suspected that any creature could live beyond their childbearing years. Typical of this belief that wild animals aren't capable of surviving until "old age," biologists and naturalists from the previous century were convinced that such an existence always ends in premature tragedy (Thomson, 1942). As such, the very existence of "grandparents," as a phenomenon in nature, is a relatively recent "invention" that didn't occur until about 30,000 years ago, at least among our species. It has been suggested that once older people appeared on the scene as life spans doubled (and tripled), their experience and expertise became the driving force for the development of new tools, weapons, art, cultural traditions, and territorial expansion (Caspari, 2012). This may very well be the most significant distinction between *Homo sapiens* and Neanderthals, who almost never lived beyond their mid-20s. And it is most definitively a distinctive difference from the great apes, our most closely genetic relatives with whom we share 98% of our DNA.

Among all the mysteries related to the evolution of our species, one of the most perplexing puzzles relates to why old people exist, or rather why nature permits humans to survive beyond childbearing years. After all, what use are the elderly once they lose the ability to produce more offspring, which nature commands is the ultimate purpose of existence? And we are not just talking about a few years beyond post-reproductive life but many decades. This has led biologists to wonder what menopause is for in the first place and why it ever evolved once eggs can no longer become viably fertilized.

There have been many debates among cellular and evolutionary biologists trying to make sense of this phenomenon. After all, if there is some functional purpose for the continued survival of individuals after childbearing years, then why don't other species beyond orca whales, elephants, and humans develop this capacity? It is indeed a puzzle but surely related to the unique cognitive and social abilities that make mutual cooperation and support so endemic to the survival of human communities (Croft et al., 2015).

One of the reasons this is all so perplexing to scientists is because it has been so difficult to study the life spans of animals, not to mention that there didn't seem to be much economic benefit to doing so since humans are only interested in eating sources of protein when they are young and tender. It had long been observed among many species that there didn't seem to be very many examples of animals that lived much beyond early adulthood. Among those who might have appeared old, methods of accurately determining their age had not yet been developed. Nevertheless, it had long been suspected that since a few animals, like humans and whales, do live to become old, there has to be a useful reason for this, one that improves the survival prospects of our species (Dagg, 2009).

Flipping an Evolutionary Switch

Why on earth, or at least in nature, would evolutionary forces keep animals around who can no longer do their essential jobs of reproducing? If they were to die on schedule older individuals would save valuable resources and food for their younger relatives who are still breeding actively. This leads to speculation that there must be some compelling reasons to keep them around.

Among pilot whales it was discovered that one quarter of the females were well over 3 decades old and yet no longer became pregnant. What functions and roles could they possibly be serving that justified their continued existence? When investigated further it was found that, first, they were still able to produce milk to feed the young, but even more importantly, they could lead the pod to reliable food sources that had been visited previously during such a long and fruitful life span. It was only after abandoning her reproductive pressures that she could focus on other tasks and responsibilities that better ensured the survival of all the calves with whom she was genetically related. It is almost as if a genetic switch was turned on once pregnancy was no longer a viable option, setting in motion a host of post-reproductive actions (Ellis et al., 2018).

There is considerable debate among evolutionary theorists and biologists as to whether menopause was deliberately designed, so to speak, to cease reproduction in order for some other strategic advantage that benefits the individual or, more likely, the larger group (Bone, 2018). There are others that believe this is just a byproduct or accidental side effect of increased life span since it isn't possible to remain fertile indefinitely. Regardless, there are similarities between the value that matriarchs serve among long-toothed whales and elephants, which should immediately come to mind related to our own species. Here are just a few of the crucial roles that we will explore throughout the book.

FIGURE 2.1   Orca whales are among one of the few animals besides humans that have an extended life span to serve other functions after post-reproductive life. Grandmother whales not only serve as babysitters and supplementary nursing sources of young calves, but they also often lead the pod since they are already familiar with the best places to search for reliable food. This helps explain one of the reasons the elderly continue to exist even though they can no longer produce offspring. Instead, their continued presence increases the likelihood of survival of all the other youngsters.

1. Elders command authority based on their experience, expertise, and wisdom. They hold a piece of the collective knowledge within a family and community, providing guidance, mentoring, and instruction in basic skills and core values.
2. They assist with childcare that frees up parents to take care of other responsibilities, as well as better ensure the safety and well-being of the children.
3. They have a more global, synthesized view of how things work in the world, or within the culture, that allows them to think more deeply about issues and make more reasoned decisions.
4. They provide additional resources to the family, whether gifts, inheritance, supplemental food, transportation, and babysitting.
5. They share stories, anecdotes, and narratives that provide a sense of continuity and history from one generation to the next.

It is clear from this abbreviated sample of contributions that without the input, support, instruction, and wisdom of our most senior citizens, the rest of us would be stumbling around in the dark trying to reinvent the same things that were already developed previously.

Life After Menopause

There are surprisingly few animals that go through menopause—and all of them, with the exception of humans, live underwater (four species of whales). Although scientists don't yet understand why this feature of evolution applies to such a small number of creatures, marine biologists still marvel at the accumulative benefits for the pod in the case of orca or pilot whales, and the family structure for *Homo sapiens*.

When reproductive hormones abruptly shut off to the point that females can no longer produce viable eggs, this sets in motion some uncomfortable symptoms and biological processes that weaken the system. With the reduction of some protective immune responses, older individuals are more vulnerable to infections and diseases such as osteoporosis, arthritis, Alzheimer's, and coronary disease. "Going through menopause is almost like having polio," one researcher said, "even the survivors bear the scars and are at greater risk for the rest of their lives" (Westreich, 2018).

It is interesting to consider that the menopausal phenomenon appears to be both intentional and strategic on the part of nature in order to reduce the number of weaker elderly people who could become a crushing burden on the community. This was especially important during ancient times when hunter-gatherer tribes were always teetering on the edge of survival as a result of starvation, diseases, and predators. Evolution ensured that only the strongest elders endured long enough to pass along their collective wisdom and knowledge to the next generations.

Among those individuals that do attain advanced age it is obvious they must have some extraordinary capabilities. Indeed, they must have excellent genetic material that they have already passed along to future generations. They would also display certain traits (patience, conscientiousness) that are greatly admired. But far more than that, they hold critical intelligence and information that is useful to others, knowledge about sources of food and water, territory ideal for settlement, historical events that are part of collective identity. If nothing else, they are survivors, having endured droughts, disasters, famine, conflicts, wars, and other catastrophes. They are mentors and teachers with valuable skills, role models whom others within the group would wish to emulate.

For anyone who seriously questions the intrinsic value of the elderly, one would only need to look at the various roles, functions, and responsibilities within Indigenous communities. Among their various contributions elders have comprehensive and vast knowledge about the best territories that are safe to inhabit, as well as hidden water sources. They often take on roles as teachers and mentors, helping young people to master the essential skills of hunting and gathering food necessary for survival in such a harsh, unforgiving environment. They are also the healers of the group, having developed expertise with various herbs, potions, and medicines that can be derived from local plants. They often become the spiritual and religious leaders of the tribe, sanctioned with authority to perform sacred rituals designed to bring peace and prosperity to the group. Their accumulated wisdom after a relatively long life makes them excellent advisors for group decision-making. As if this devotion and commitment to the well-being of the tribe is not enough, among some cultures like the Inuits of the Arctic region, they are even prepared to sacrifice themselves by leaving their igloos to freeze to death in order to save others when food is in scarce supply.

Obviously, older people in more developed and Westernized countries no longer depend on the aged to serve these various functions, preferring instead to assign specialists (priests, doctors, nutritionists, supermarkets, armies, the internet) for targeted assistance. This may very well be one reason why the elderly in these places are no longer treated with great reverence, adulation, and respect. Instead, younger people may only feel resentment and annoyance while they are trying to establish their own reputations and solidify their upwardly mobile careers: "Why won't those old dudes retire already, and get out of the way to make more room for me, someone with fresh ideas for a change?"

Even the medical establishment during previous eras viewed aging as the loss of essential vitality, leaving a kind of empty, withering vessel composed of wrinkles, stooped posture, feebleness, and gray, lifeless hair. Older people were warned to conserve what little energy they had left, avoiding any exertion or excesses or else they'd risk a host of inevitable symptoms including headaches, vertigo, faintness, heat flushes, plus moral perversity and eventually insanity (Coughlin, 2017). The great psychoanalyst Sigmund Freud (1912), who remained professionally active well into his 80s, still insisted that "old people are no longer educable" or suitable for psychotherapy because of their inflexibility (para. 15). It is best to warehouse these old people in special places called sanitoriums or "old folks' homes" so they don't bother anyone with their annoyances and burden.

Contributions and Achievements of the Grandparent Generation

Most of the attention and credit for humankind's dominance has been attributed to ancestral males whose hunting, toolmaking, and exploration led to dramatic advancements in technology, food production, territorial expansion, and improved quality of life. Less understood and recognized have been the achievements of post-reproductive females, the grandmothers, whose contributions have been just as significant. It is these "indirect" effects and influence on reproductive success that led to the "grandmother hypothesis," one popular explanation for prolonged aging (Peccei, 2001). The prediction is relatively simple: If a grandmother lives within commuting distance of her family, the mother will tend to have more children, and they are likely have a better chance of surviving until adulthood (Hawkes, 2004). There is also evidence that this "grandmother effect" not only provided additional expert childcare assistance for the family but may very well have led to some of the most unique and signature qualities of our species—pair bonding and social cooperation for mutual benefit (Hawkes, 2021). It has even been suggested that this dramatic increase in longevity associated with grandparenting functions is also responsible for the radically increased brain size of humans that was needed to retain a lifetime of experience and knowledge (Finlay, 2019). This makes sense when you remember how helpless humans are after birth and how they have just a decade to learn almost everything they need in order to survive.

There are some who have challenged the value of the so-called grandmother hypothesis (Callaway, 2010; Driscoll, 2009; Strassman & Garrard, 2011; Watkins, 2021). Although there are some who have questioned its explanatory power, the theory does partially account for the reasons women live to a ripe old age, double or triple the life span that had existed much earlier in time. However, it does not explain why elderly men continue to survive since they are also no longer able to reproduce. This leads critics to speculate that once humans practiced monogamy, paternity certainty became more reliable, thus allowing males to become more invested in the care and safety of the couple's children. Secondly, once more sophisticated tools were invented, it allowed less physically developed males to compensate for their small size or meager strength and compete with others within the tribe on equal footing. It is theorized that the combination of these factors permitted sexual partners to produce offspring that gradually and dramatically increased their longevity.

FIGURE 2.2 Physical proximity and accessibility to grandparents, or elder caregivers, is a key factor that affects the accumulative learning, influence, and effects that take place. Whereas parents tend to focus their efforts on helping children learn basic life stills, grandparents tend to offer different perspectives on moral and spiritual development, as well as background on family history and life stories.

Who Are Grandparents Anyway?

It must first be acknowledged that identifying who qualifies as a "grandparent" is based on self-reports rather than any kind of biological marker or confirmation. Most of the research on the subject simply asks older people if they are grandparents, and if so, how many children there are among their brood. Given the number and variety of divorced marriages, separations, remarriages, same-sex marriages, stepparents, step-grandparents, formally (and informally) adopted children within families, let's just agree it is complicated to sort out who actually qualifies. Nevertheless, attempts have been made to settle on reasonably accurate data to at least determine what it means to *be* a grandparent—or not. (Hank et al., 2018).

In just a few years it is estimated that there will be more people over age 65 in the United States than there are children and adolescents, estimated to make up 21% of the population (U.S. Census Bureau, 2019). Among the aged, more than three quarters of them will become grandparents, and many others surrogate mentors and caregivers in a volunteer capacity. Although the average age for transitioning into this stage of life is the mid-50s, the range for first-time grandparents can span anywhere from 30 years old to 110. This is usually perceived as an exciting time in life but also quite stressful and worrisome, just as would be expected after such a dramatic shift in identity and responsibilities. Most grandparents spend an average of about 8 hours per week engaged in childcare (Bradley, 2020), but those who have custodial responsibilities treat them like a full-time job—one without any compensation. In reality, most grandparents also make significant financial investments in their families, providing supplemental income, paying for school and leisure expenses, and contributing to household resources.

It has been observed that this is an age of grandparent "expansion," not only because there is such a significant increase in elderly people, but because there is increasing demand for their assistance over a much longer period of time. Whereas 150 ago, with life expectancy in the mid-50s, children might only know their grandparents for about 3 years, but with increases in longevity it is now common that this role could last for more than 40 years. Or to state this another way, in the United States a century ago only about 5% of 10-year-old children had four living grandparents; now that figure is close to half (Feldman, 2019).

Demographic changes and fractures in the nuclear family all point toward even greater involvement of the aged in family and community life. There are even some groups, such as Pacific Islanders, where almost half the children are cared for by older adults who are *not* their biological parents (Sokolovsky, 2020). This leads to the conclusion that the meaning of "grandparent" takes on different forms within various cultures, just as does almost everything else.

Families are obviously structured differently across the world. Whereas in Western countries it may be common for an individual, couple, or nuclear family to live within their own separate dwelling, separated from extended family and grandparents residing across the globe, in much of the rest of the world it is far more common that three or four generations live in the same household. This results in very different notions about the role, functions, and responsibilities of older adults and will be discussed in later chapters.

Genetic Investment Is a Mathematic Calculation

Remember that as far as evolution is concerned there is only one overriding purpose to life: to pass along one's genetic material and then expire. That's why most creatures die soon after giving birth, or at least immediately after launching their young as self-sufficient beings. It is not only highly unusual in nature, but very peculiar, that humans, and just a few other species manage to continue existing long after they are fertile. But if you do the math, it is also easy to calculate that if you help to raise just two grandchildren (or four nephews and nieces) you are essentially meeting the desired genetic quota—or at least breaking even, so to speak. It would then appear that it is highly adaptive for older individuals to cease producing more of their own children, many of whom may not survive in congested conditions, and instead devote time and energy to helping those kin who are already in existence but need lots of help to survive until adulthood. As we will discuss repeatedly, when grandparents are actively involved with the children, the family will have more offspring and they will more likely survive the trials and dangers they will face.

A study by Engelhardt et al. (2019) of birth and death records in Canada during the 17th and 18th centuries found that among the over 50,000 grandchildren included in the review, if they had a grandparent (especially a maternal grandmother) who lived within 200 miles of the family, the kids had a 30% better chance of reaching the age of 15 years old. In addition, the mother would have more kids because of supplementary expert childcare that was available. Interestingly, if the grandparents were deceased, unavailable, or lived a greater distance from the family, those effects disappeared (Engelhardt et al., 2019). Also interesting and contradictory, if the *father's* parents resided with the family, grandchild survival actually *decreased*, probably as a result of extra burdens on the parents and even more limited resources to take care of everyone (Chapman et al., 2019).

The relative causes, influence, and effects of older adults within the family and community are difficult, if not impossible, to sort out because of all the potential factors involved, although computer simulations have been undertaken with ambiguous results (Thouzeau & Raymond, 2017). Does post-reproductive life exist for reasons other than providing additional caregiving for the children, or is this just a side effect of increased longevity of *both* sexes as a way to help protect young mothers during their most vulnerable stage of life? We may never know the answer to that question because it is so challenging to determine the interactive connection between increased aging, menopause, and the benefits for children.

The Differential, Specialized Power of Grandmothers and Grandfathers

Patriarchal "cultures" within the animal kingdom (and queendom) tend to focus on the superior physical and hunting skills of the alpha males. Such "families" tend to be smaller (think gorillas) because of the alpha's sexual jealousy, unwilling to tolerate any competition within the troop. On the other hand, matriarchal cultures tend to be far more collaborative, socially cooperative, and much larger, since the grandmother in charge emphasizes mutual support in such a way that extended families can grow well into the hundreds of members without major conflicts. Interestingly, if the grandmother (or great-grandmother) matriarch dies, most often by hunters, poachers, or attempts to cull the herd, chaos ensues without a commanding leader who can organize their journey and activities. All the previous levels of harmony fall apart, and even the most basic decisions about which direction to head next become a point of endless dispute, potentially putting all at risk.

Most behavioral and evolutionary scientists throughout the ages viewed very clear differences between the development and primary roles of males and females. Among our own hominid ancestors it has always been assumed that men were "designed" to bring home the bacon, so to speak, providing the most critical survival tasks to feed the family and tribe with their superior strength and guile. Although this hunting behavior has received a lot of attention in the literature, media, and popular films, it has been considerably overrated and exaggerated considering that hunts with primitive weapons (spears and bows and arrows) were typically unsuccessful 95% of the time, requiring supplementary food sources in order to meet daily nutritional needs (Hawkes, 2016).

Historically, women have been portrayed as "useful" harvesting food but much less than males since they stayed close to home caring for the children and gathering and preparing food within the immediate vicinity. These were activities that weren't considered nearly as heroic. One outcome is that this may very well have been the impetus for pair bonding within our species since both partners increased their chances of survival with their respective skill sets, as well as producing viable offspring who would be protected and well fed.

It is obvious within our own species the different styles of leadership evident in male-versus female-dominant organizational cultures, the former characterized by a far more autocratic, threat-based enforcement of norms (Kottler, 2018). As you've no doubt noticed, men are more likely to lead via authoritarian commands and control, focusing on directives and task achievement. This actually works quite well in terms of efficiency, especially during crisis situations, even with undesirable side effects such as feelings of oppression, resentment, and rebellion. This is in marked contrast to female leadership within most animal groups in which members are urged to work cooperatively. Among human cultures, this is often characterized by more open communication and supportive behavior, as well as collective decision-making.

Although it might appear at first as if one signature style is better than the other, they each have distinctive advantages. During emergency situations, when optimal performance is critical, it may very well be best to take a highly controlling, directive style, at least until the crisis is past. That's one reason why some First Nation tribes of North America favored *two* chiefs, one during times of war when decisive action was required, and another during times of peace when it was far more important to work together cooperatively and democratically in order to relocate camps or locate food sources.

Just as optimal leadership within a group depends on the context and situation, gender specialization appeared to evolve as a means to adapt to changes in the environment and climate. Once upon a time, when hominid ancestors lived in the forest, they relied primarily on fruits, nuts, and plants for nutrition, easily accessed by their longer arms and ability to climb trees. Nursing infants, carried on the backs of the mothers, were able to share and consume the same foods even though they were still dependent on nursing. However, once climate changes forced them to abandon the forests for the open savannah, it led to a host of evolutionary adaptations, among them the ability to walk on two legs, shortening the arms that were no longer required to reach fruit among the trees, stabilizing the head in an upright posture, and expansion of the cerebral cortex (Lieberman, 2013). Unfortunately, a lot more effort, energy, and territory were required in order to find suitable food on the open plains. This, in turn, led to the invention of fire for cooking, once again changing the anatomy of the mouth, teeth, and jaw since softer foods could now be more easily consumed. In addition, the life span was significantly increased to provide more opportunity for the young to learn essential survival skills from their elders.

The males of advanced age were no longer able to hunt, limited to teaching the boys basic skills, but the older women remained accomplished and successful foragers and food preparers, essential for the welfare of the tribe. And it was precisely because their fertility had long ended that they could concentrate their most productive efforts exclusively on caring for others. The tribal groups of early humans thus transitioned into far more cooperative, sharing strategies, even with respect to breeding and childcare in which the older adults reduced the burden of biological parents so that they could devote time to other critical tasks (Hawkes, 2020a).

While doing research among the !Kung Bushmen in the Kalahari, one of the oldest hunter-gatherer cultures in the world, I casually and innocently asked a woman playing with a baby whether that was her child. She looked at me with a confused and curious expression, even after multiple attempts to translate the query. Every time I repeated the question, she just shrugged. Finally, the translator explained to me that they don't really know who the children actually "belong" to, nor do they care who gave birth to them, since *all* the women in the tribe view themselves as the mothers and grandmothers of all the children; it literally takes a village to raise a child, any child.

As we will explore in later chapters, grandmothers and grandfathers have also functioned in very different traditional roles throughout their abbreviated existence in history. Virtually all of the research had focused primarily on the "grandmother effect," assuming it was primarily the matriarch's caregiving that was most critical while grandfathers had somewhat marginal or limited economic contributions rather than direct relational effects (Hawkes, 2004, 2021; Williams, 1957). Dramatic changes in gender roles during the last few decades have altered these traditional roles and typical characteristics, both within the family as well as organizations, politics, and corporate settings. The baby boomer generation was among the first in which fathers took on increased caregiving responsibilities, just as women were able to make the first major cracks in the "glass ceiling" that had previously made it so difficult, if not impossible, to attain prominent positions of leadership. Although still only 8% of Fortune 500 CEOs are female (Kaplan, 2022) and grandmothers are still far more active in childcare responsibilities, there is an increased leveling and flexibility of traditional roles. As such, it is problematic to make sweeping generalizations about leadership or grandparenting based solely on gender. Nevertheless, it is absolutely the case that elderly females have been instrumental in increasing the longevity of our species so as to better ensure the safety of the young and prosperity of the community.

In later chapters we will explore in much greater detail how males and females function in sometimes different but critical roles, as well as how these responsibilities are becoming transformed in light of cultural shifts in the ways that gender is defined, identified, and experienced. In addition, with more opportunities for women to work through advanced age, as well as the birth of fewer children, the dissolution of family structures, even the expansion of how "families" are conceptualized, the whole experience of what it means to be a grandparent is becoming transformed.

From Orcas to Humans

We will be circling back and forth between the behavior of the few other mammals that grow to old age, mostly whales and elephants, and that of humans because of some potential insights that can be derived to figure out the evolutionary importance of grandparents and the elderly. For instance, it was observed that when a 70-year-old female orca whale showed up in the vicinity of a maze of islands and waterways, dozens of other younger females took turns swimming next to her for a few minutes before moving out of the way so others could engage her in "conversation." If we had the ability to understand and translate the unique clicks, pulses, whistles, and other forms of echolocation characteristic of their communication, we might hear the matriarch instructing her younger apprentices about local navigation and where to find a salmon run. They were appearing at her side in order to show respect and homage to their elder who had survived into old age, but they were also interested in hearing her "stories" of survival and learning valuable intelligence that might help them in the future. Such is the critical role that elders have played among the few animals that figured out ways to keep their aged engaged and useful.

Within our own species, grandparents have been described as the "ultimate essential workers," though often unappreciated, unheralded, and certainly underpaid. During the COVID-19 pandemic, many families learned hard lessons about what they had been taking for granted once grandparents were forced to quarantine and parents were left to fend for themselves, trying to juggle working from home at the same time they were homeschooling their kids.

What distinguishes our species from any other living creatures, even the few other mammals that live extended lives, is the prolonged, intimate relationships between children and their oldest living relatives who are able to pass along their wisdom and mentoring over several decades. Although it is certainly the case that many grandparents may be distant, rare visitors, or even absent altogether, the majority of families enjoy considerable support and benefits from the presence of experienced elders in the vicinity. Apart from any physical presence, babysitting, custodial care, and the financial contributions that grandparents make to three quarters of nuclear families are a game changer, especially during tough economic times, employment layoffs, reduced income, and other unanticipated hardships. There are also many places in the West where dual-earning couples can't afford the astronomical cost of childcare and so must rely on their own parents for support.

Anthropologist Michael Gurven makes the point that since children are dependent on adults for such a long period of time, as long as two decades until they reach a degree of self-sufficiency, it is almost a necessity to have other, more experienced caretakers around to assist with family functioning. First-time parents are often highly anxious and not very proficient in their jobs. Among many primates, a first-born child usually dies because the mother is so clumsy, indifferent, and incompetent at her job, barely able to figure out how to nurse the youngster.

Human families' structures have evolved over time to become extended, multigenerational tribal units. According to Gurven, grandparents make unique contributions, not just based on economic assistance but rather through their influence on children's moral, spiritual, and emotional development (Berger, 2020; Gurven & Kaplan, 2008). While parents tend to focus on practical, developmental skills, completing school assignments, staying safe, and learning the basic rules of the culture and home, grandparents tend to help children view the larger picture of the world and their potential place in it. It is through the stories that elders share about their own lives, their experiences, their insights about what matters most, that children are able to grasp their linkages to the past, as well as their potential for the future.

QUESTIONS FOR REFLECTION OR DISCUSSION

1. What are some of the reasons that you believe that humans developed the ability to live way beyond their reproductive years?
2. Just as evolutionary theorists have a difficult time explaining how and why peculiar behaviors like laughing, crying, yawning, and kissing developed in our species, what are some other examples of human actions that are difficult to explain?
3. Why do you suppose there aren't more animals that continue to survive beyond childbearing age, expiring soon after they can no longer produce viable offspring?
4. Anthropologist Margaret Mead once remarked, "If you associate enough with older people who do enjoy their lives, who are not stored away in any golden ghettos, you will gain a sense of continuity and of the possibility for a full life." What are some examples of this that you have experienced in relationships with older people?

Figure Credits

CHAPTER 3

What Whales and Humans Share in Common

At first glance, one could justifiably wonder how three such different animals as an orca whale, Asian elephant, and human being could share such a singularly unusual characteristic that is found nowhere else among living creatures. Whereas the average life span of our closest primate relatives, chimpanzees, is about the same as it used to be for *Homo sapiens* several thousand years ago (about 30), toothed whales, elephants, and humans have the capability to live more than eight decades, serving in a unique role as grandparents, or even great-grandparents, for their existing kin.

One example of the value such an elder can have on her family and community is clearly illustrated in the case of one grandmother who was particularly dutiful and committed to protect her rather extensive brood of grandchildren. "Granny," as she was affectionately (and widely) known, was a resident of rural British Columbia in Canada, but she also traveled annually to visit relatives who lived further south in the state of Washington in the United States. Even well into her 90s Granny was still very active in the care of her family; although in later years as she began to slow down a bit, she preferred to travel with her eldest son who was well into middle age himself.

Given the huge size of her extended family, numbering over 75 members during some of their reunions, Granny was quite busy with all her varied responsibilities as the matriarch of her group, babysitting the infants, planning their activities, making sure everyone was safe and well fed, at times imposing strict discipline on those teenagers who would occasionally test boundaries or engage in delinquent behavior that might be dangerous for themselves and others. What's even more interesting and unique about Granny is that she was the oldest living orca (killer) whale ever discovered, estimated to have reached the age of 105 before she mysteriously disappeared into the depths of the Pacific Ocean.

Although Granny was extraordinarily old for a whale, or for any other creature, she was absolutely essential to the pod of whales with whom she was responsible for half a century. She had long ago been unable to produce any more calves, but once motherhood ended she transformed herself into an inspirational leader whose sole purpose and function was to protect her living relatives. In terms of biological calculations, it makes sense that this would be highly adaptive from an evolutionary perspective and seems to explain why just a few species of whales, plus elephants and humans, are able to redefine their roles after they are no longer fertile.

The Critical Roles and Responsibilities of Oldsters

Anyone who believes that oldsters are feeble and all washed up should consider the case of Flo, a 40-year-old chimpanzee who was observed, and greatly admired, by Jane Goodall (1988). Since the average life span of this primate is about 15 years, and the maximum life expectancy about 30, Flo was ancient by these standards, perhaps the equivalent of 90 or 100 in human years. Yet—and this is very big "yet"—she still occupied the role of chief combatant and defender of anyone or anything that threatened the troop, especially the young ones. She was such a fierce adversary in old age that nobody would challenge or defy her. Even more remarkably, she was still *very* sexually active even if she could no longer become pregnant. And when I say "very active" I mean there was one day in which she was observed mating with a partner 50 times! Let's just agree that the experience of old age in many animals is not necessarily congruent with our image of a helpless, over-the-hill creature.

In one sense, the elderly are the ultimate winners, the superheroes of their species who were able to navigate all kinds of challenges—escaping predators, surviving accidents, miscalculations, droughts, famine, and conflicts within the group. They must have inherited exceptional genes, which, in turn, they have passed on to strengthen the stock for the future. They are also the role models for others, able to demonstrate the optimal behavior in order to flourish.

As mentioned previously, there are only a few animals ever discovered that survive beyond their reproductive functions. It is the way of nature: You produce offspring and then die off to make room for the newcomers. Even our closest primate cousins like chimpanzees or bonobos are able to produce offspring until almost the end of their lives (Ellis et al., 2018). The existence of "elderly" individuals, or grandparents, as a phenomenon, is thus so extremely rare it is unprecedented among most any other species.

Besides humans, there are only two species of whales, orca and pilot, plus a few other creatures, that ever "know" their grandparent, much less profit from their wisdom, experience, and contributions. This leads to the interesting question as to whether whales, or any other animal, understand they are actually genetically related? The answer is a pretty definitive no, since by the time most animals are born, their grandparents are long since deceased. Orcas are among the few who do know their grandparents (principally grandmother) intimately over a fairly long period of time (Croft et al., 2017). In fact, a young calf without a grandmother in the pod is five times more likely to die! Extrapolating to our own species, a similar but less dramatic phenomenon emerges in that the presence of a post-reproductive grandmother (but *not* one that is premenopausal) significantly increases the survival of children.

In the context of elephants, the other species known to be completely dependent on (great) grandparents to manage and lead the herd, the presence of a dominant matriarch is also considered crucial for survival of the young. Similar to whales and humans, elephants are known to survive well into their 80as, continuing to grow larger as they age. The combination of their size, maternal fierceness, and enhanced ability to assess dangers makes them particularly well prepared for their leadership roles in later life. Their presence has been known to astronomically increase the survival rate of the calves as a result of their experience and skills finding feeding grounds during lean times, but also their superior social and navigational abilities that keep the group working cooperatively (Lahdenpera et al., 2016). It is also interesting that among elderly elephants the majority have been able to maintain very high levels of cognitive and social functioning with little noticeable decline (Lee et al., 2016).

Because they no longer have to be concerned with taking care of their own infants, grandparents have more time, energy, and commitment to take on the protective role of group defense. Studies have confirmed their superior capability of differentiating various lion sightings, determining which ones require evasion versus aggressive intervention. They thus have a heightened sensitivity to danger, accompanied by extensive experience in fending off predators (McComb et al., 2011).

No Longer a Reason to Exist

In addition to humans, and primates, an octopus is among the most intelligent creature on the planet with one of the most complex nervous systems. Since she is abandoned immediately after birth, and only has a year to live in an environment in which she is among the most vulnerable of prey to predators, powers of reasoning, creativity, toolmaking, and disguise are among

FIGURE 3.1 Most animals are programmed to expire soon after they have completed their evolutionary function to reproduce. An octopus has a life expectancy of just a year, during which time she must learn everything she needs to know in order to survive, find and hunt prey, and evade sharks and barracudas. She receives no instruction from parents she never knew, nor will she ever have a mentor to assist her adjustment. Once she gives birth she will devote almost all her energy and time caring for her eggs, so busy in this job she will eventually die of starvation. This is the most common scenario in nature, that adults perish soon after they can no longer give birth.

her only means of survival. She is capable of evading enemies by changing her color, altering her shape to fit into tiny crevices, or even covering herself with shells, demonstrating a level of curiosity, imagination, and cleverness that is unprecedented among most other animals.

Everything she knows she must learn on the job. And for those one in a 100,000 who do manage to evade the ocean's dangers, their reward upon giving birth is to slowly starve to death. After the first few days they stop eating altogether, becoming listless and erratic in their behavior. They continuously groom themselves, tangling their arms into a chaotic mess. They lose all their muscle tone as their metabolism begins to shut down. After all, what purpose do they serve after they can no longer produce offspring? Like almost all other creatures, once they pass beyond the reproductive stage of life and have passed on their genes, there is no longer any reason for them to exist.

This once again raises the existential question why half the human population has not expired after completing their main reproductive job. It is curious indeed that the creatures of the world appear to be divided into two main groups. The vast majority of living beings have rather compact efficient brains that basically contain almost all the intelligence and cognitive skills they need to survive, either immediately after birth (e.g., the octopus, squid, salmon, or mayfly), or else just a few months of parental instruction thereafter. Many other animals, such as calves, baby giraffes, horses, zebras, and camels, can walk immediately after they are born, already somewhat independent.

Given the lengthy gestation period to give birth to a human infant, plus the more than 15 years of careful nurturance and care required for this child to survive, it is no wonder that nature figured out a way to keep a bunch of wise, older adults around to make sure nobody gets in trouble. Imagine what would happen if, like a lioness, our mothers forced us to leave home when we mastered basic hunting skills, or like an octopus, we became orphans immediately after birth, left to figure out life on our own even though we couldn't even roll over, much less feed ourselves.

What Animals Are Inclined to Do

It would appear as if one of the signature attributes of humans is that we have evolved alternative and complementary forms of childcare that better protect the safety and welfare of children via collective responsibility for offspring. Whether a child contains 50% (parents, siblings), 25% (grandparents, uncles, aunts), or no genetic inheritance whatsoever (adoption) with a caregiver, humans have the ability and willingness to form enduring connections. It is even more remarkable when you think about how rare this is among other animals. After all, infanticide is common among lions, sloths, mongooses, and baboons in which adults will actually kill (and eat!) the young that are not their own offspring. This may seem abhorrent, but in evolutionary terms, it is highly adaptive to ensure that one's own genetic investment is maximized.

It is all the more surprising, then, that some animals have developed the tendency to protect members of their group with whom they are not genetically related. This is not a matter of altruism as much as it is about the imperative to ensure that the community remains safe and viable; otherwise, it doesn't matter how many infants are born because they wouldn't survive very long without adequate protection. Many birds and primates will call out warnings when a predator is in the vicinity, sacrificing itself for the greater good. In the case of older individuals, they may not survive to produce more young, but their already-born offspring will live to see another day, a seemingly logical trade-off.

Of course this self-sacrificial or protective behavior varies considerably, depending on the species. Among elephants and whales, led by female grandparents with sophisticated social skills, the groups tend to be much larger and the responsibilities much more varied than patriarchal species. For instance, in the case of gorillas that are led by the largest, most powerful alpha male, sexual jealousy ensures that the band is kept relatively small with a clear hierarchal system in place.

Similar to humans, both elephants and whales are highly socialized animals that work together as cooperative units. Sperm whales are an interesting example of this since they live in constant fear that the far more aggressive and hostile orcas will pick them off if they aren't careful. But once again, while the parents are otherwise occupied hunting for food at extreme depths that their young can't visit, the elders stay behind to watch over them. The older females form a protective, defensive circle around the young in the event of threats, while the grandfather hangs out along the periphery as an ancillary guard to repel invaders.

Exceptions to the Rule

One additional exception to the phenomenon that animals never "know" their grandparents are elderly langur monkeys in India that have been observed hanging out with their daughters and grandchildren. They act as disciplinarians, intervening during times when play gets out of control. They are also enforcers, defending the troop against enemies and predators. But more significantly, they do recognize their own kin and show definite favoritism toward their grandchildren, even grooming them.

It is indeed perplexing to figure out why just a few species live such long lives even though they can no longer have offspring. Adding to the mystery, although elephants are known to survive many decades past their prime, they still remain potentially fertile in later life. It is only orca whales that are similar to humans in that the protective effects of grandmothers occur once menopause begins and their sole focus involves protecting and feeding the young within the pod, most of them genetically related to her. This is not at all the case with elephants since a matriarch's sons may very well go off on their own separate journeys, never to see the mother again. In this situation it would appear as if some altruistic motive might be involved in protecting the herd since genetic connections are not a significant variable in the calculations of potential investment.

Although elephants and many primates enjoy a relatively long life, without the hormonal disruption that occurs during menopause among whales and humans, they are handicapped by comparison because they still have active reproductive functions. As one illustration, there was a remarkable case of a female Japanese macaque that pulled off a coup among her troop, battling four different male competitors before dethroning the previous leader to take charge as the queen of more than 650 companions. This hostile takeover was not only highly unusual, but her reign continued for close to a year, during which time she sought to solidify her position. Once she had managed to calm things down and resume business as usual, the middle-aged still-fertile macaque entered the mating season and all hell broke loose. Without menopause to end her reproductive cycle, she was in danger of becoming dethroned by another alpha male who could take advantage of her otherwise distracted, chaotic, vulnerable position.

This example demonstrates quite clearly the value of menopause, ceasing that reproductive stage of life, in order to better adapt to alternative roles that are highly valued for survival of the group. That's why whales and humans, above all other animals, have been able to take on the roles and responsibilities of grandparenting and mentoring during the later stages of life, and do so with such influential consequences.

As mentioned, throughout their life span, even after their reproductive days are long over, elephants continue to grow larger. Although not technically a (great)grandmother since she is not necessarily related to the others in her herd, the matriarch is nevertheless critical to their mutual survival. She may be "retired" from having more calves, but she becomes the disciplinarian for them when one gets out of line. She settles disputes between herd members, decides in which direction they will travel each day, and pass along their "cultural" knowledge that controls social behavior. Among her many jobs, she is also the preschool teacher, informing youngsters about which plants are safe to eat and which are poisonous, how to avoid dangers, and what is considered appropriate social behavior so that everyone gets along.

In one example of the older matriarch's protective role, Buss (1990) describes how an elephant herd was drinking from a waterhole when the elder spotted a crocodile ready to strike one of the calves. She grabbed the huge, 1,000-pound vicious predator with her trunk, lifted it above her head, and smashed it against a tree repeatedly before stomping on it until it was crushed into pieces. Although the eldest among her companions, she is the first one to put herself in harm's way in order to protect the others.

Here's the bottom line: When an elephant herd is led by a relatively healthy senior great-grandmother, the females will have more calves who will have a much greater chance of surviving their childhood. Because of her superior "social skills," she can recognize the "voices" (contact calls) of over 100 individuals and keep them cooperating in highly functional ways. She teaches the young the local "dialect" of the pod so that they can easily recognize one another, as well as identify the calls of potential competitors. If she is killed by hunters, or "harvested" by game officials, the herd will fall apart; they will become aimless, dysfunctional, and confused (Dagg, 2009). Given that they must travel tens of thousands of miles each year in order to find sufficient nourishment, their ultimate survival depends on the knowledge, experience, and abilities of the elderly leader.

How Do Older Animals Mentor and Guide the Young?

Over time humans have invented a number of ways to protect, safeguard, and teach children the basic skills they need to defend themselves, survive, become self-supporting, and follow the social norms that keep the community viable. There are schools and universities that provide education, books, and online instruction that hold wisdom and useful data, social and news media options to disseminate information and knowledge, after-school programs and babysitting services to assist with childcare, and religious and moral instruction to instill a sense of responsibility and compliance to cultural norms. Then there are experts, tutors, coaches, sages, philosophers, psychotherapists, and grandparents, all of whom offer additional mentoring and guidance as needed. It is clear that we have outsourced many of these roles and functions to designated institutions that are considered specialists.

What is a self-respecting, dedicated parent or grandparent animal to do if the goal is teach the young essential survival skills? There are several instructional methods favored in the wild, many of which are recognizable within our own species (Caro & Hauser, 1992; Langley, 2016). Instead of classrooms or instructional materials, the most obvious method is referred to as "opportunity teaching," in which older adults provide a youngster with a chance to experiment with new behaviors such as providing wounded prey to toy around with as a precursor to hunting skills. Whether among big cats like lions, or other meat eaters in land or sea, older adults will present opportunities to gradually learn the skills of stalking, approaching, and dispatching prey. Initially this occurs via observation of the more accomplished expert tutor, followed by attempts to follow this lead, usually awkwardly and unsuccessfully. Positive reinforcement (encouragement) and punishment are then used to reward or discourage behavior. Whether among primates or elephants, the matriarch can be continually observed either encouraging persistence with a reluctant youngster or whacking a rebellious juvenile on the side of the head.

Imagine the challenges of a black bear that gives birth while she is in hibernation, unconscious and oblivious to the birth of her cubs. She awakes for a few minutes from her 3-month slumber, repositions her body so the infants can access her milk, and then returns to deep sleep. Meanwhile the cubs are left to fend for themselves, at least until the mother awakes and finds herself in the desperate situation of not only literally starving to death after losing half her body weight but she is also now stuck having to teach these little ones everything they need to survive. She's got just a few years to teach them how to locate edible grazing spots, stalk and hunt prey, and protect themselves. Most of this instruction will take place by live demonstration, followed by practice sessions.

Some of the strategies favored by elderly mentors rival those we could witness in any excellent human learning environment. One representative example was described by Payne (1998), who spent much of her career studying elephants in their natural environment. She observed the older matriarch attempting to dig a well in a dry riverbed in order to provide water for the herd. Yet as soon as she started to dig deep enough to form walls in dirt, an infant would be entangled in her legs and then mischievously knock down the walls. The patient grandmother gently pushed the youngster aside, yet the child persisted to the point that the elder kept pushing him aside. When that didn't work, finally in exasperation she led the baby to another spot some distance away from her construction project, where she created a "play pool" for him to engage in his behavior. This allowed her to finish her job at the same time she created space for him to experiment with his own digging behavior. This type of coaching is typical of the kind of teaching that is favored by grandparents across the animal species.

Payne describes another example of how the matriarch sees her job as teaching and guiding younger, clueless mothers who don't seem to know what they are doing. In one situation a young mother had already lost three of her infants due to birth defects or parental negligence. With her fourth child she was also similarly incompetent, unable, or unwilling to nurse the young one. The matriarch had seen quite enough and decided an intervention was required, attacking the mother in anger, after which she took over parental responsibilities for a bit until the mother came to her senses.

This doesn't seem to be an unusual phenomenon among young animal mothers who have been described as "notoriously inept" (Dagg, 2009). Dagg describes another case of a baboon mother who was so incompetent she held her infant upside down, bumping her head along the ground, once again requiring intervention from an older female who could better take charge of the care. There is overwhelming evidence that in spite of the potential health challenges among older parents they are far more skilled and effective in the care and nurturance of the young. They tend to wean their infants much later, giving them more time to adjust. They have longer intervals between their pregnancies, also providing more time for intensive care. And they tend to engage more actively with their last offspring, providing better quality interactions because they recognize this is the last opportunities.

Many of these examples of significant contributions by the elderly members of pods, herds, and tribes, provide some degree of greater clarity regarding our central question: Why do old people in general, and grandparents in particular, even exist? It has been evident thus far that the reasons are varied and complicated, encompassing not only natural selection that contributed to increased life span, but also an abrupt cessation of reproduction via menopause. Remember, there are only a handful of animals that ever experience the trials and tribulations of such hormonal cessation, four types of whales (orca, short-finned pilot, beluga, narwhal), plus humans. It was mentioned previously that it is not yet clear whether this is a side effect of increased life span, or whether this biological process began as a way to reduce competition with younger specimens in their sexual prime.

It makes sense that older individuals would change their reproductive strategy in such a way that they refrain from birthing more children, especially during times of overpopulation and limited food. Instead, they concentrate on making sure that those offspring already in existence have the best possible chance of surviving to adulthood. It all seems to relate to the dramatic increase in longevity that has been bestowed upon us during more recent times, the subject of the following chapter.

QUESTIONS FOR REFLECTION OR DISCUSSION

1. If you've ever had a cat or dog, what have you noticed changes about their behavior as they grow older, not just reduced energy and similar aging effects, but rather the ways they learned to operate in different ways to compensate for changes that have occurred?

2. What is an idea from this chapter about whales and elephants that seems useful to you in making sense of human behavior?

3. Among your own mentors and teachers, what have you found to be the most effective means they used to teach you some essential skill that remains precious to you?

Figure Credit

Fig. 3.1: Copyright © by damn_unique (CC BY-SA 2.0) at https://www.flickr.com/photos/damn_unique/8093376393/.

CHAPTER 4

The Evolution of Longevity and Birth of Grandparents

When we tell the story of aging, we typically divide the life span into two distinct components—when we are young and when we are old. Throughout the ages the definitions of these states of being have changed dramatically. During the Bronze Age (3000 BC) attaining the age of 25 years old was a distinctive achievement for such an elderly survivor, especially since most people died during infancy and early childhood. Today, most 25-year-old adults are still considered so young they are barely given any responsibilities or authority in their jobs. The times have certainly changed in terms of how long one can reasonably expect to occupy this world.

Until this century it was believed that each person was born with a finite allocation of "vital energy" that is gradually exhausted over time. This wasn't presented by the medical establishment as a metaphor but rather as an accurate description of the critical fluids contained in various reservoirs within the body. Some people squander this limited fluid while others more slowly waste away, depending on their wardrobe, sexual practices, diet, and activities. When the tank eventually becomes empty, there was thought to be a fairly quick demise of this wasted shell of a human being. Until fairly recently, this transition from being "young" to "old" typically took place around age 50 or so, a time we now think of as "middle age."

In order to preserve one's health and longevity, it was recommended that everything be done with moderation, whether food, drink, or any strenuous activities. Nonprocreative sex, especially with someone other than one's spouse, was seen as a particularly dangerous choice. Physicians during this era were trained to look for "climacteric disease," a condition that was believed to afflict people over 50 with white or gray hair, wrinkles, stooped posture, and cognitive decline. There was no cure for this disease, of course, but these aging symptoms signaled that it was time to immediately cease any activity that might require a modicum of effort or energy. Otherwise, this wasted-away patient would likely experience increasingly disruptive problems, including headaches, vertigo, irritability—followed by moral perversity and insanity (Haber, 1985). It was at this point an older person over 60 was advised to just rest and stay out of the way until the end that was soon to follow.

Being old has thus been associated with all kinds of maladaptive, miserable conditions, at least among industrialized countries during the more recent past. It was mentioned earlier that even Sigmund Freud, who was 48 at the time, insisted that it was a waste of time to attempt psychotherapy, or for that matter, *any* form of education, on anyone over 50 because they lack the capacity for flexibility and change—this from a guy who continued his clinical work, groundbreaking research, and writing, well into his 80s.

What we now understand, of course, is that "being old" is quite different from "feeling old." Depending on one's health, beliefs, attitudes, meaningful work, and cultural and family context, age is very much a state of mind. This incredible diversity of the ways that old age is defined and identified makes it difficult to settle on a consensus as to when it begins and what form it takes in this stage of life. Even more perplexing is what scientists have called the "longevity riddle," attempting to explain how and why old age has evolved in such few species. This has been described as the single greatest achievement of our species—to have extended life 30 years in a little over a century (Olshansky & Carnes, 2019).

The Rise and Fall, and Rise Again, of Life Expectancy

Human life expectancy has increased dramatically during recent times. In the previous decade alone it added another 6 years to a worldwide average of 74 years. This is all the more startling when considering that most people were fortunate to survive their 20s during Paleolithic times. It has even been predicted that in the years to come it won't be unusual for people to live well into their hundreds of years, perhaps even reaching 130 (Pearce & Raftery, 2021).

We might get the impression that human life expectancy has advanced at a consistent, gradual, and uninterrupted pace, but that has not really been the case at all. Throughout history there have actually been times that the rate of people dying significantly increased even if the previous trend had been to increase longevity. Some of the life span shifts have been counterintuitive. For instance, one would expect that the invention of agriculture would significantly improve health with the increased convenience and reliability of food sources. In addition, with nutritious sources of protein and plants so close by it was no longer necessary to risk life and limb during hunting expeditions. Yet, surprisingly, this adaptation actually led to a number of unanticipated dangers, risks, and health hazards. Once humans lived so close to their animals they risked over 100 contagious diseases (diphtheria, cholera, influenza, anthrax, yellow fever, rabies, bubonic plague). Now overly reliant on grains (wheat, barley, corn), the human diet became less diverse and varied, leading to increased health problems. In addition, famines, wars, plagues, and the slave trade all contributed to a catastrophic fall in the average life span.

Even after steady increases in life span over a period of tens of thousands of years, mostly as a result of improved diet, medical procedures, and health policies, there have been some significant, dramatic drops as events of the era exerted their influence. For instance, about 300 years ago there was a confluence of circumstances (wars, violence) and diseases (cholera, smallpox, tuberculosis) that reduced the average life expectancy to just 16 years old. Three quarters of people alive at the time were lucky to reach 25. It is staggering to compare that to today in which most children born in the last 20 years will likely live to be 100.

It is important to point out that when we talk about human longevity there is tremendous variation depending on where someone lives, their ethnicity, gender, job, and their socioeconomic status. In Britain, for example, the *average* life expectancy may have soared into the late 70s or early 80s, but there are parts of Glasgow where residents are lucky to hit 55, much less than someone in India. In a similar vein, Bryson (2019) points out that that a 30-year-old African American male living in Harlem is at much greater risk of dying than a similar-aged person in Bangladesh, one of the poorest countries in the world. Furthermore, this risk is not the greatest from drugs, murder, or other acts of violence, but rather the Black male would be more likely to die from a heart attack, stroke, cancer, or diabetes. Bryson finds it all the more remarkable that the United States spends three times as much money on health care for each citizen than any other nation, representing a staggering one fifth of all the money that Americans earn.

The explanation for this peculiar state of affairs is related to all the unhealthy lifestyle choices and habits that Americans are fond of pursuing with abandon. The accumulative effects of overprocessed foods, excessive fat, sugar, and salt in the diet, drug and alcohol use, lack of physical activity, stress at work, reckless driving, and especially widespread gun ownership, all take a bite out of the prospects of long, healthy, fruitful life.

To be clear, these are hardly problems limited to Americans since on a global level most people are no longer dying from the things that killed us a century ago. Nowadays, people are more likely to meet a premature, unexpected demise as a result of a car crash, heart attack, cancer, addictions, emotional disorders (depression and anxiety), or lack of exercise.

It is also interesting how even one's religious affiliation or cultural identity has a profound effect on life span. For instance, Seventh-Day Adventists actively and passionately promote healthy aging by prohibiting their members from smoking, drinking, and abusing drugs, while encouraging a vegetarian diet and regular exercise. As a result, they have been found to live an average of 8 years longer than the general population (Fraser et al, 2020).

Suspected Reasons and Causes of Increased Longevity

When exploring the human body, or any other object or phenomenon, there are ultimate limits imposed on its capabilities depending on its physical composition. There are restrictions on everything that we do, how fast we can run, how high we can jump, how many languages we can learn or achievements we can earn. Likewise, it is hardly surprising that there are ultimate limits on how long we can live no matter how much brown rice you eat and colonic wheatgrass enemas you try.

It is important to consider that reproductive functions don't just cease once a child is born. In the case of our species, it takes two decades or longer to successfully launch offspring into the world in such a way that they will actually survive for the long haul. It therefore makes sense that parental life span would have had to be extended significantly to make certain they were around long enough to feed, teach, and protect the young until they become self-sufficient. Because this continual burden of childcare restricts movement and other critical activities, other older adults, especially those with some genetic connection, must also become involved.

I mentioned the "grandmother effect" as one possible explanation for human (and whale) extended life. Once the instrumental value of older people became the centerpiece of survival for a group because of their superior knowledge about foraging and supplemental childcare functions, life span gradually and incrementally increased—at least to a certain point. The complex and huge human brain comes into existence only half completed, requiring many more years to develop fully. This required considerable collaborative efforts on the part of *all* adults within the family and community to keep children safe and teach them most of what they need in order to survive. This, in turn, leads to the incredibly intricate social networks and collaborations that have become the hallmark of our species and a primary reason for our dominance on the planet (Hawkes, 2020b).

According to this theory, it is also suspected that human pair-bonding in an exclusive, monogamous relationship began as a result of these evolutionary changes, coupled with the invention of weapons that made hunting a full-time job for males (Hawkes, 2020a). Since climate change had forced groups to leave the fruit-rich forests for open savannahs, men now took on the role as hunters to provide sufficient food for the tribe. This meant they'd have to leave children behind for prolonged periods, requiring partnerships between males and females to work collaboratively to provide for their joint offspring. This resulted in what we now recognize as the division of labor negotiated between couples since game hunting only rarely resulted in a successful endeavor (less than 5%), requiring the family to depend more often on the mother—and grandmother's—gathering of edible plants, fruit, and nuts. This also led to greater cooperation within the group since individuals would now work on behalf of the whole tribe to provide stored resources during hard times. This is also one reason humans are considered among the most successful "social animals" that required a longer life span in order to fulfill inherent biological imperatives.

There are several other reasons offered to explain this unprecedented acceleration of evolutionary development, the most notable of which is improved diet to a certain extent, although now that is leading to diminishing returns since the greatest health issue on the planet today is not starvation but rather obesity. The number of people around the world who are considered significantly overweight has tripled during the past 40 years, making overeating one of the leading causes of death, exceeding car accidents (World Health Organization, 2021b).

As we will explore later, there is a huge difference between the length of one's life span versus the actual quality and condition of that life during later years as a result of diet, lifestyle, and level of activity that shapes one's body. The "story" of how and why humans doubled, then tripled, their life span begins during ancient days when some of the oldest members of the tribe, usually females, began to share extra food with their grandchildren, better fortifying them with enhanced nutrition. This, in turn, led to their greater survival rate, as well as their future opportunities to mate and have children who would also be in better physical condition to tolerate the inevitable droughts, famines, and other challenges of daily life. They would thus pass along their grandparents' healthy genes through natural selection, gradually extending the endpoint of life. This extension became necessary once the human brain evolved, along with the size and shape of the skull, requiring significantly more time for children to develop and become reasonably self-sufficient. What used to take a single decade for a human child to launch herself into the world as an independent being now extended to a lengthy adolescent stage that added another decade of parental care required. Once elders retained their health to enjoy a much longer life span they could become even more involved in family life and caretaking responsibilities, once again ensuring that more children were successfully launched.

We can still observe this phenomenon of healthy aging in action among traditional cultures in Southern Africa where the oldest members of the hunter-gatherer tribes, usually in their 50s or 60s, are strong, wiry, fit, and highly active, especially as food gatherers. According to one researcher who studied their behavior, they "forage the longest hours, dig deeper for tubers, and spend more time gathering berries and processing food than any other category of forger" (Hrdy, 1999). These contributions are believed to be responsible for the kind of bolstered food supply that ensures that the children will survive and flourish, thereby slowly increasing longevity for the larger species.

There have been many other influences, causes, and developments that have contributed to the unprecedented extraordinary increase in human longevity, some of which have saved millions, if not billions, of lives during the past few hundred years alone (Johnson, 2021). First, there were scientific innovations that led to the invention of the microscope, imagery, and similar instruments for more accurate diagnosis of diseases. This was followed by an assortment of medical breakthroughs, including everything from anesthesia, pacemakers, robotic surgery, artificial organs, radiology, and kidney dialysis to the use of blood transfusions and bifurcated needles for injections. Then there are all the drugs that have protected humans against devastating diseases—antibiotics, insulin, antimalarial medications, and especially vaccines. Life spans have also been significantly affected by public health organizations like the Federal Drug Administration (FDA), Centers for Disease Control (CDC), and World Health Organization (WHO) that have helped organize local, national, and global policies warning the public against smoking, obesity, alcohol and drug abuse, teen pregnancy, gun violence, and similar threats to the community welfare. This also led to the introduction of health safeguards like chlorinated water, pasteurization, public innoculations, and sewer and waste processing systems. Other public policies related to child protection and elder abuse laws, combined with media dissemination about health warnings, have all increased awareness of health dangers and increased optimal behavior. Similarly, greater attention to diet, regular medical checkups, and increased monitoring of bodily systems via smart watches and wearable technology have also had an impact. Altogether, there are hundreds, if not thousands, of small, incremental changes, as well as huge breakthroughs, that have slowly added decades of additional expected life even if those benefits have hardly been equitably distributed based on gender, ethnicity, and geographic location.

FIGURE 4.1   There are obvious inventions, innovations, and breakthroughs that increased human life span significantly, such as vaccines, medications, and public health policies. But just as influential has been greater attention to safety issues by advocating the use of seat belts, helmets, and protective equipment at work. More than anything, greater awareness of health hazards that can be prevented have led both medical professionals and the public to alter behavior in such a way to prevent premature death. This was readily observed during the worldwide COVID-19 pandemic in which people attempted to protect themselves with masks, vaccines, and social distancing.

Even with all that we have learned about the nature and progression of the human life span, one enduring mystery is related to the gender differences in life expectancy. There has never been a time and place throughout the history of our species in which men live as long as women. Certainly wars and violent conflicts have taken their toll on males, but none have ever died giving birth, nor was it expected that they would be the ones to nurse the infectious sick. Even with reasonably similar access to health care, a significant reduction in armed conflicts around the world, and women gaining increased opportunities for equality (and stress) in the workplace, there are still imbalances in life expectancy, with women living an average of 5 years longer. In addition, males and females more often die for different reasons: Men tend to fall apart because of their cardiovascular system while women are at far greater risk for inflammatory diseases (Crimmins et al., 2019).

The Birth of Grandparents

It has been stressed that grandparents are a relatively recent evolutionary "invention" that pretty much didn't exist until about 30,000 years ago. Of course in those days, when many people barely survived infancy and relatively few ever reached 30, there was little possibility of three living generations. Once our species managed to invent new tools and technologies, improve diet, and remain in one region for longer periods of time, population density and complexity significantly increased, as well as life expectancy. Larger populations led to faster evolution, resulting in new advances in tools, technology, art, trade, and the domestication of plants and animals.

Researchers have been trying to narrow down the time parameters when those of potential grandparent age first began to emerge. It was during the end of the Paleolithic Era that the ratio between young and old inhabitants began to increase significantly, five times what it had been previously (Caspari, 2012). Within a relatively short period of time, there were now generational cohorts of children, young adults, and older adults closer to 40 years of age. How and why this abrupt change occurred is still subject to debate with consideration of both cultural and biological influences. What we do know for sure is that something changed within human cultures that made it possible for far more advanced aging. As discussed earlier, it may very well be as a result of ideas like the "grandmother effect" and the elevation of elders as wise sages, able to teach the younger generations critical lessons to avoid poisonous plants, weave a basket, locate water sources, or make an arrowhead. This cross-generational communication would have, in turn, increased population size, thus leading to greater interpersonal engagement and cultural complexity, all of which would have also accelerated the pace of future evolutionary development.

Grandparenthood may be joyful for most people, but it is also a mixed blessing, representing a transition to a state of being that is often denigrated and disrespected. As we've reviewed earlier, the immediate associations with old age and grandparents are typically viewed in terms of deterioration, mental confusion, losses, annoyance, suffering, and ultimately impending death. There are movements to change some of these perceptions, especially considering the increased economic power and social influence afoot as a result of the so-called "graying revolution." Terms like *positive aging*, *successful aging*, and *healthful aging* are examples of attempts to recast the latter stages of life and grandparenthood as just another adventure and opportunity for reinventing one's identity.

More recently, beginning the middle of the 20th century, grandparenthood attained status as a legitimate "occupation" worthy of respect and significance. It was during this time that research studies were undertaken to investigate the impact, effects, and nature of grandparent–grandchildren relationships (Neugarten & Weinstein, 1964). For the first time, this role was viewed as far more important than merely an obligation to babysit when called upon and instead was broadened to explore the joys, satisfaction, fulfillment, and personal meaning of the experience for all the participants. Until this point old age was typically painted as a period of disengagement, retirement, and sitting around in a rocking chair. Now it had the allure as a time of special promise, privilege, and perhaps the most joyful time of life (Kahana et al., 2019).

Of course the opportunities and possibilities that came with the job were quite different than they are today. Grandparents during the 1960s were more likely to assume the more traditional, "formal" role that was often portrayed in movies. This was a time of self-exploration, reinvention of identities, and experimentation with alternative social roles. While their children may have gone to Woodstock, their parents immigrated to the Sunbelt for better weather and leisure activities, significantly less involved in their families than we might see today. Now that those of grandparent age are living so much longer, with much greater physical abilities and better health, the potential options for family involvement are so much more diverse.

During the last few decades a number of changes have taken place, both within the family structure as well as the larger community. Families became far more varied and diverse as a result of dual working couples, divorce and remarriage, gay partners and marriages. The life span was further extended to the point that there were not only more grandparents alive but also *great*-grandparents. It is actually predicted that in the future there will be far more four-generation families and multifamily households, the result of increased life span and greater lifestyle flexibility. There is indeed a special legacy that great-grandparents are able to pass on to their young family members, more than just inheriting their property and savings to include their accumulated wisdom and knowledge (Schuler & Dias, 2021).

There are other legacies that are also passed on to family members. They may include significant events in the history of the elders, how they came to immigrate, members who sacrificed themselves in wars, and others who disappeared for reasons unexplained. There are also darker legacies passed on that warn of future mental illness, violence, alcoholism, drug abuse, disabilities, as well as family secrets that may threaten to erode trust in future generations (Boszormeny-Nagy & Spark, 2013). Finally, both grandparents and great-grandparents pass along legacies related to religious and spiritual beliefs, core values, and ultimately what it means to be a member in good standing of the family, whether that involves good deeds, a successful career, multiple children, or accumulated wealth.

Charting Longevity

Living creatures vary tremendously in their assigned life spans. Whereas mayflies last less than a day in which to mate and die, Greenland sharks don't even hit adolescence until their second century of life, eventually reaching up to 500 years of age. Jellyfish do even better since they are essentially immortal. Humans are at the top of the heap as well, living twice as long as our nearest primate relatives.

There are all kinds of charts, graphs, statistical calculations, and algorithms that have attempted to explain and predict this unusual human longevity. Variables have been taken into account related to socioeconomic status, ethnicity, geographic location, profession or job, level of stress, and lifestyle choices, among others, each of which tries to account for why some people live longer than others. We are already well aware of how drug use, smoking, overeating, impulsivity, lack of exercise, and other behaviors take years off of one's life expectancy. But one aspect of these studies is that they almost always describe aggregate averages. According to this perspective, we see human life expectancy practically doubling every few generations, implying that soon we will all live for 150 years or so. Indeed there is always tremendous attention directed toward the latest person to survive until 120 years old, implying the rest of us are well on our way toward immortality.

Of course, there is very wide distribution in these supposed averages. For instance, how do we explain that during a time when the typical age of death was 50 or 60 years, that presidents of the United States, occupying the single most stressful, demanding job in the world, often lived two decades beyond that of their citizens! If we take a brief inventory of presidential longevity we might indeed be impressed with the likes of Jimmy Carter (97), Ronald Reagan (93), and George H. W. Bush (94), explaining their durability as the result of the best possible medical care in the world, plus a very privileged life that helped them to live at least 15 years beyond the average. But how do we explain John Adams (90), Thomas Jefferson (83), and James Madison (85) during a time when most people never survived until their mid-50s?

It would appear that health condition alone is not the only thing that determines how long any of us live, but rather the ways we manage our lives, the choices we make, the attitudes we adopt, the beliefs we hold, and the meaning of our life's work also affect not only our well-being, but ultimately the quantity and quality of our life span. It is also ironic that the dangers that tend to kill us prematurely are not very similar to those in the past. In the early 20th century most people died of influenza, pneumonia, diphtheria, tuberculosis, and diarrhea (plus World War I), none of which are major threats today, at least in the developed world. Compare that to present day when the leading causes of death are heart disease, cancer, accidents, and suicide, either indirectly via drug abuse or intentionally through acts of self-destruction.

Some experts have wondered whether aging is essentially just another form of pathology, a time bomb that is set to detonate at a particular moment but that can be ignited far earlier by various infections, diseases, conditions, and behaviors (Finch, 2010). Regardless of whether it is a feature of evolution, or an unintended side effect, death eventually gets us all, even if it is postponed a few extra days each year. One consequence of this, of course, is that our population is aging dramatically with the declining death rates coupled with reduced fertility among women having fewer children. Countries like Japan and Italy now have one quarter of all their citizens over the age of 65. In the United States, the percentage of old people is just 15%, but that's expected to double in the next few decades (Furstenberg, 2019).

The Value and Legacy of Elders

A case can be made that it is primarily "elders" who were responsible for the success and proliferation of the human species, making it possible to produce more offspring with added childcare options. In addition, elders represented a link to previous generations, passing along crucial knowledge. These elder grandparents were also responsible for the education of children, passing along to them critical information about their group identity, history, and cultural norms.

We've already reviewed some of the contributions and critical functions that older animals serve to preserve the safety and survival of their grandchildren and group. It is also interesting to look at the critical roles that elders play within the cultures of traditional, Indigenous peoples. Among the !Kung hunter-gatherers of the Kalahari, it was observed that Elders are vital in a dozen different domains (Biesele & Howell, 1981; Kottler et al., 2004). Even with certain physical limitations elders have been observed as important participants in the daily affairs of the people, sharing stories about their past their unique cultural identity, settling disputes and conflicts between members, providing practical information about hunting grounds and territories to inhabit, but especially doting on their grandchildren. As such, they not only operate as babysitters when parents are otherwise occupied, but they function as mentors, teachers, and coaches for the tribe. They also serve the important role of spiritual leader, the conduits to the gods who engage in healing rituals. Eventually, they not only pass along their historical legacy but also all their worldly possessions.

Whether among traditional cultures, or more industrialized nations, there are pretty compelling reasons why older people continue to exist. Once the human life span expanded to the point that people could shed their previous reproductive functions, they were freed up to do all kinds of things that benefit the prosperity of everyone else. Once again, among the !Kung people they function as the healer and medical expert, spiritual sage, craft maker, storyteller, and guardian of the precious water.

Should anyone question the commitment and self-sacrifice that elders are willing to make on behalf of their descendants, when the Inuit Elders of the Arctic region felt as if they'd become a burden to their tribe during times of famine, they would intentionally depart the igloo and wander off onto the ice to die so that others might survive. Another example of how cultures differentiate useful versus burdensome elders are the Chippewa, who distinguished between their "old people" who really were a burden at times because they could not easily keep up with the tribe during their journeys, versus "senior people" who maintained respect, vitality, and leadership positions because of their personal achievements. In the case of "senior women," they were considered even more important at times because of their willingness to adopt orphan children who had lost their parents due to disease or war (Dagg, 2009).

Changing Demographics and the Future of the Human Life Span

The reality is that there are more diapers sold to the elderly than for infants in Japan (Livingston, 2015). The changing demographics of the world make it clear that there will continue to be a disproportionate number of elderly people compared to any previous time in history. It isn't just their numbers that will increase the power of this population, but also their economic clout and financial contributions to the family and the welfare of grandchildren, averaging thousands of dollars each year to each child (David & Nelson-Kakulla, 2019).

There are other adjustments expected as a result of demographic changes. One of the most prominent will not only be the increased size of the elderly population but also an increase in single-person households, most led by older women because males die off much earlier. This could also lead to larger extended relational networks if the nuclear family invites grandparents to reside with them, an increasingly popular choice.

Increased longevity will also contribute to far more so-called "beanpole" or four- (or even five!) generation families, permitting great-grandparents to also have a designated role. This, in turn, will alter the ways that being a mother or father are defined and experienced, especially if both partners are working, engaged in a same-sex marriage or cohabitation, or negotiating the special challenges of a blended family consisting of stepparents and step-grandparents. Technological advancements and the worldwide pandemic also led to increased work from home, as well as the ability to conduct most jobs via screens, which will also have an effect on the ways that families engage with one another. Compare all this with the ways a "good mother" used to be defined—a stay-at-home, dutiful wife, whose main jobs are to cook, clean, and look good for the husband when he returns home from a day at work. More of these trends will be discussed in the final chapter about the future of healthy aging.

How long will humans eventually be able to live? It has been mentioned that some scientists have estimated a term limit between 120 and 150 years for the human life span, since cells will no longer be able to repair or rejuvenate themselves. This may be the result of evolutionary design rather than any glitch in the system, intentionally installed to ensure that the natural order of things continues in which the old die off to make room for younger organisms.

The ultimate goal for most people should not necessarily aspire to a long life, but one that extends the *quality* of life over time. For every year of added life that has been added to our life span, only 10 months of that time is actually considered healthy (Lieberman, 2013). Nobody wants to spend their last days—or years—stuck in a "warehouse" for disabled elderly, an intensive care unit, or isolated in bed with chronic pain, cut off from the rest of the world.

What's so great about living to be 100 years old if one's life is dominated by visits to medical professionals, attempting to minimize pain and suffering, and barely able to hobble around? Despite the promise of longer life just over the horizon, there are also studies that indicate that any further advances in life span would have to go up against biological barriers that form an in impenetrable ceiling (Olshansky & Carnes, 2019). Although this indicates a limit to how far longevity can go, it is pretty obvious that older people and grandparents are going to be even more important in the future with more years of shared life with their families, hopefully coupled with changing perceptions of what it means to grow old.

QUESTIONS FOR REFLECTION OR DISCUSSION

1. When you imagine your life once you (hopefully) reach 80 years old, what do you imagine things will be like? Describe a typical day from the moment you wake up until you fall asleep.
2. Describe an important relationship you have had in your life with someone who is "old."
3. What are some puzzles, curiosities, or mysteries that evolutionary theory has failed to explain or account for?
4. What are some of the innovations, inventions, and breakthroughs, as well as the environmental and biological changes, that you predict may affect longevity, for better or worse?

Figure Credit

Fig. 4.1: Source: https://pixabay.com/photos/passengers-face-mask-coronavirus-5711260/.

CHAPTER 5

Models to Explain the Continued Existence of the Elderly

The compelling, overarching question that has been the focus of this book attempts to address the curious and mysterious phenomenon of post-reproductive existence. It is one of those things that we take for granted even though it is actually such a bizarre and unprecedented evolutionary adaptation among living creatures. Everything in nature, even random mutations that occur, do so for reasons that can be both advantageous and deleterious. In the case of our own species, beneficial examples include (a) the development of a protein (Apo-AIM) that scrubs the cardiovascular system to remove cholesterol; (b) increased bone density; (c) resistance to malaria; or (d) development of color vision. There are many other instances of people developing immunities to infections, diseases, or pandemics as a result of mutation of genomes (Williams, 2016). Due to other biological anomalies, that is one reason some people are considered "super sleepers," able to fall asleep on demand, or "super tasters," who have enhanced abilities to savor food and drink more intensely, or individuals who can tolerate great amounts of alcohol without feeling the effects, or those who can get "drunk" on just a single drink. In each case, genetic anomalies within the biological system produce unusual changes in a person's capacities or functioning.

Was it simply a random mutation that first "permitted" a whale or human to survive long after procreative duties were completed, eggs exhausted, or sperm depleted? Or was there some "intelligent design" at work that created conditions for our species to extend life, thereby providing the time, resources, and tools to take over the world? What are the various theories, explanations, and models accounting for this dramatic shift in life expectancy?

Regardless, there are certain facts in evidence to support the postmenopausal value of older people. As discussed previously, the presence of a maternal grandmother in relatively close proximity to the family increases the survival of the children. When studies from a few centuries ago compared sisters who stayed close to their parents, versus those who moved elsewhere, it was found that the ones who were homebound had two more children than those who left; in addition, their children were more likely to survive until adulthood (Engelhardt et al., 2019). Of course, there are also alternative forms of childcare to supplement parenting (schools, babysitters, nannies, playdates, after-school activities) that may reduce the magnitude of effect.

Differential Effects

It is intriguing that when childcare opportunities decline, so too do the future prospects of older women who face a decreased life span. Adding considerable complexity to these interactive effects, when the father's older mother lives with the family, and has compromised health, grandchild survival actually decreases, leading to the conclusion that not all grandparents, in all situations, are very helpful and can, at times, lead to increased family conflicts (Chapman et al., 2019). We frequently see this dynamic played out in popular films, shows, and especially family therapy sessions in which there is cross-generational tension, especially between the in-laws and parents.

One variable that appears to make a difference is the age of the grandparents, since those who are over 75 years old (especially paternal grandfathers who live in the household) can create additional burdens rather than serve as a helpful aid (Chapman et al., 2017). Although these historical studies may not necessarily apply to contemporary life because of advances in health and medical care for the elderly, it is clear that the quality of grandparent care is directly related to the older person's health, abilities, childcare skills, and sense of personal well-being.

The Grannie Effects

The evolution of longevity based on the "grandmother effect" has been described previously because it has been such a popular model that elevates the value of older women as mentors. We've also discussed how puzzling it has been to make sense of how and why menopause developed in humans, given the toll that it takes on the body over time. Almost 100 years ago it was first proposed that evolutionary genetics played a significant role in the extension of the human life span by calculating the relative reproductive value of any individual (Fisher, 1930). This eventually influenced other scientists to develop explanatory models of aging, including the impact of post-reproductive life in older women.

There are several different theories that help explain the ongoing value of older people, including the "grandmother hypothesis" (Pavard et al., 2008; Watkins, 2021). There have also been several studies challenging the value and applicability of this idea, suggesting the importance of considering other explanatory models, including kin selection, parental investment, alloparenting, among others (Bone, 2018). After all, focusing exclusively on maternal grandmothers who live nearby does not come close to revealing the whole story.

As favored as this model might be among anthropologists and evolutionary scientists, critics have questioned how this explains why males also live beyond their reproductive years and clearly do not go through menopause even if their fertility diminishes over time. In terms of evolutionary fitness, however, the model has also been applied in such a way that the increased use of tools and weapons for hunting allowed males to significantly improve the quality of diet for everyone in the clan, including their own expanded life span.

We have already covered most of the features of ancestral grandmothers and their suspected evolutionary impact in post-reproductive life, especially their adaptive functions to help with childcare, food gathering, and transmission of collective knowledge (Hawkes, 2020b). Nevertheless, like most academic theories there are also alternative models that focus on either the limitations of the theory (what about grandfathers?) or other variables that have been ignored or not considered (Callaway, 2010; Peccei, 2001; Strassman & Garrard, 2011; Watkins, 2021).

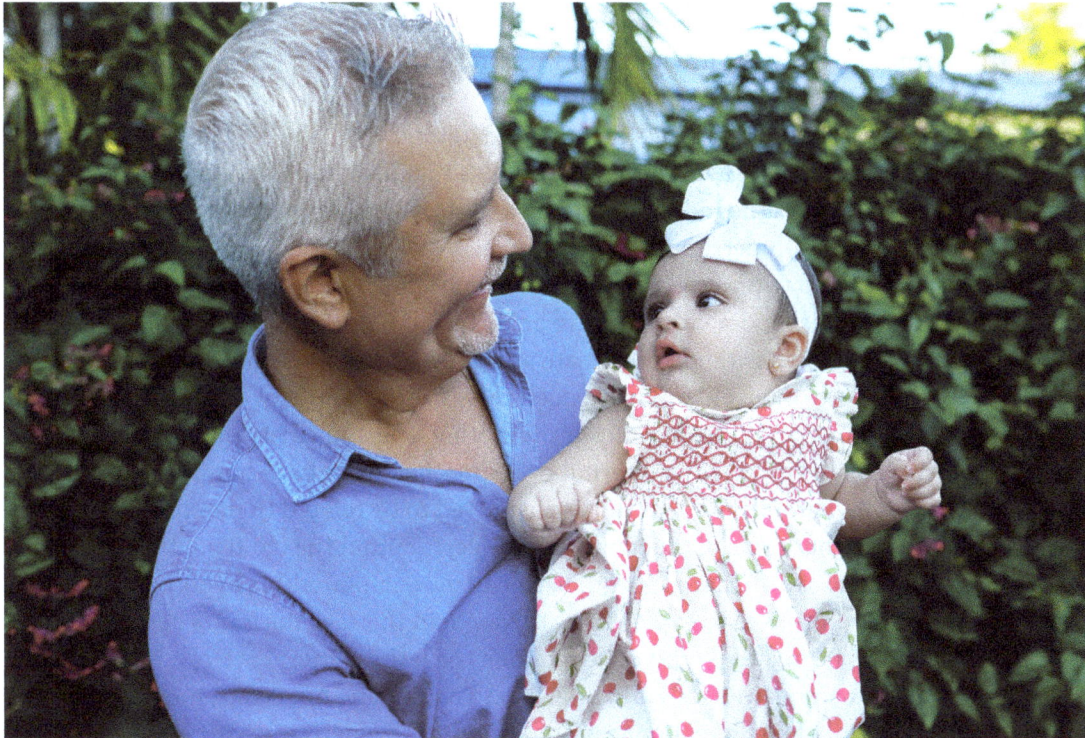

FIGURE 5.1   Historically and traditionally, it has primarily been maternal grandmothers who are given most of the credit for their contributions and influence on children's survival. Reasons for this include their typically closer relationship to their daughters, their greater role in childcare, and their expertise and success in food gathering. Yet during the latest age cohorts, beginning with the baby boomers, grandfathers and older males have taken a much more hands-on role within family affairs. Exceptions thus abound of instances in which paternal parents or grandfathers become more engaged, influential, and impactful within the family.

Let's briefly review the main assumptions and propositions of this influential theory before briefly reviewing some of the other options:

1. As people age, the time and energy they spend continuing to produce offspring falls off since after "middle-age" fertility declines. It makes sense that it is a far better investment to take care of the children that already exist rather than producing more infants who

would likely not survive very long. It has been estimated that a human child requires a whopping 15 million calories provided to them before they become self-sufficient and are able to feed themselves. This quite literally takes a village.

2. Grandmothers, in particular, became the focus of this shift in responsibilities to provide food, support, and expertise for all genetic kin. Since during ancient times everyone within the clan tended to be related in some way, an older adult could protect their own genetic lineage by providing additional resources beyond more children.

3. Historically it was been discovered that if there is a maternal grandmother living close to the family, especially if she's relatively young and healthy, the children's chances of survival until adulthood are increased significantly.

4. Menopause, or the cessation of reproductive life, occurs so infrequently in nature that it remains both mysterious and misunderstood. We have discussed how, besides humans, there are only a few species of whales that also undergo this transformation that virtually forces the individual to expand its role. Mentioned less often, however, are all the potentially detrimental effects of menopause such as hot flashes and reduced estrogen that lead to an assortment of conditions and diseases that would have made older women much more vulnerable to accidents, predators, and other dangers.

5. Once childhood was extended to create sufficient time for full maturity, so too was it necessary to have more older, experienced caregivers to help provide for the vulnerable offspring. Grandparents, especially grandmothers, became instrumental in this role.

6. Interestingly, it is primarily maternal grandmothers who have had the most impact on families and grandchildren. This is suspected to be related to parental investment in that the mother's side of the family can be certain that the child holds their genetic material whereas the father or grandfather can never be sure. This hypothesis of "paternal uncertainty" is used to explain why throughout the ages the mother's mother is far more likely to be involved with children then the father's mother (Hrdy, 2009).

7. Studies have demonstrated that in addition to caregiving functions, the grandmother effect also highlights the economic productivity of the elderly in terms of the resources, food, and knowledge they bring to the family and community.

The grandmother effect is mentioned far more frequently than almost any other theory to account for the extraordinary life span of humans. This is in spite of the fact that the effects vary widely depending on geographic proximity, maternal or paternal lineage, cultural beliefs, and health of the grandparents. Its proponents are so enthusiastic and passionate about the phenomenon that they also believe the power and influence of older women during ancestral times is also responsible for the development of pair bonding, social cooperation, and enlarged brains among our species (Coxworth et al., 2015; Hawkes, 2020b).

Grandmother effects may be one significant reason the human life span has evolved beyond reproductive years, but it isn't sufficient to account for the extreme expansion of longevity 4 four decades beyond what would normally be expected. In addition, this model has been questioned because it doesn't take into account other adults within the family (aunts, grandfathers, uncles, cousins, siblings, and especially fathers) who provide caregiving roles to children. Also, related to older women there are other hypotheses that question whether menopause evolved not so much as the primary biological "motive" but rather as a side effect of other forces at work such as improved diet, cultural influences, environmental changes, and changes in the structure of the family unit.

Perhaps grandmothers were not the only reason for female longevity but simply the need for mothers to be around longer to make sure children and adolescents survived until adulthood with sufficient support and protection. Once again, the undervalued contributions of women are brought to the forefront after so many decades of research undertaken by mostly older male anthropologists who tended to impose their own values on what they witnessed during cooperative behavior within the culture. In addition, their own cultural and political beliefs also seeped into their conclusions in such a way to overinflate the functions of males as courageous, fearless brutal specimens of manliness, while simultaneously denigrating women's contributions—especially older women who were often viewed as enfeebled burdens. For almost all of the historical past it was assumed that once females were done with reproduction they were mostly viewed as irrelevant, "a nuisance," and "physically quite revolting" (Hrdy, 2005, p. 295).

Patriarchal Dominance

Given the widespread popularity of focusing mostly, if not exclusively, on the impact and effects of older women, at least as the reason for increased life span of the species, it also seems reasonable to assume that males, as well, played significant roles beyond simply fertilizing eggs. While hunting by males may have been overly romanticized as a critical function for survival of the family and tribe, it is likely the benefits have been significantly exaggerated considering how rare it was that any hunt was actually successful more than a few times each year. The consumption of meat in the diet was certainly desired and appreciated but hardly the provisions that were relied on most of the time; it was the older women who supplied and prepared most of the food (Watkins, 2021).

It would appear, then, that the actual value of hunting—if successful—was less dependent on just the food collected and more likely an indication of high status and physical prowess as mating signals that communicate "Look at me! Aren't I awesome? Wouldn't you want to make children with me since I can run so far and throw a spear with such accuracy?" This has been described as the "show-off hypothesis" to demonstrate mating worthiness, not to mention that it increases one's perceived value if meat is shared with everyone (Hawkes et al., 2018). Nevertheless, since any potential female mates wouldn't have been present to witness a prospect's hunting prowess, it is been suggested that even this benefit would have been minimal since it would be equivalent to a someone competing in a sports event without an audience (Sterelny, 2012).

Patriarchal dominance offered an alternative explanation that capitalized on the invention of tools and other breakthroughs that made it possible for those who were smart, creative, and highly skilled to overcome some of their physical limitations when competing with others who were much stronger or faster (Marlowe, 2000). No longer would alphas dominate human groups based solely on their size, age, physical condition, or family lineage; the experience, cleverness, and knowledge of older males qualified them for positions of leadership and power. This, in turn, was credited with altering the evolutionary script to lengthen the life span so that males could continue their contributions for the greater good.

This sounds good in theory, but there's still a rather tenuous connection between surviving elderly men and their impact on producing more children who are better fed. That likely is the case, but it doesn't explain the reality that the sperm of older males is not as viable, nor are they particularly desired as mates except for their economic resources. The truth of the matter is that it is still somewhat difficult to explain why males are needed after their reproductive functions are completed, at least from a purely biological perspective. One grandfather (or great-grandfather) role and function that is often ignored, however, is passing along their legacy to their descendants, not just their accumulated wealth and resources, but just as critically, their stories of "who they are," "where they came from," and what it means to be "one of them" (Schuler & Dias, 2021).

The Senescence Hypothesis

As humans and other animals age they become noticeably weaker, less physically capable, and less successful in producing more offspring. They have fewer eggs or newborns, miscarriage more often, and have longer delays before they can conceive once again. Since they are no longer able to give birth, or the intervals between them become much longer, a new adaptive strategy is undertaken that is also considered highly functional in a post-reproductive life span. In other words, they change jobs based on the needs of their group and their accumulated skill set. This switch to new, valued responsibilities is possible only as a consequence of menopause, freeing up time and space for older animals to focus instead on their roles as mentors and caregivers.

Senescence has been described as the loss of optimal functioning among cellular growth, maintenance, and repair that occurs over time. Senescent cells have lost their ability to reproduce or repair themselves, becoming waste, debris, or "ghost cells" that still remain within the body. Unfortunately, although they no longer can divide, they still release proteins that cause inflammation and compromise immunity (Sinclair & LaPlante, 2019). This eventually leads to the deterioration we recognize in old age with reduced mobility, cognitive impairment, and vulnerability to disease, accidents, predators, or starvation because of reduced abilities in self-care. In response to this inevitable, gradual erosion of biological functioning, continued survival was based on the ability and willingness to make oneself useful in other ways beyond producing more babies.

Keep in mind that evolutionary natural selection favors the means by which an individual manages to maximize fitness via adaptation to changes in the body, environment, and culture.

With limited stores of energy and reduced physiological efficiency, older people reallocated their priorities in different but useful directions, all within their capabilities. This is also what is believed to be responsible for prolonging life since accumulative cellular damage can be slowed or even repaired, just like what happens with other organisms like bacteria that are capable of reproducing endlessly. This has led some to wonder if life could eventually be extended for humans indefinitely, although as mentioned earlier, most biologists are convinced there is a finite limit for our species. There is also speculation by some longevity experts that due to natural selection over millions of years, life expectancy has already far exceeded any reasonable expectations and will not advance more than a handful of additional years (Dong et al., 2016; Rizvi, 2021).

Terminal Investment (in Children, Not the Stock Market)

Similar to almost any phenomenon or biological mystery, there are numerous competing theories to explain what is suspected to be occurring. Some of these explanations directly contradict one another, such as creationist versus evolutionist ideas regarding the origin of our species. It turns out that there is another way to account for the presence of older people that ignores senescence in favor of the obvious reality that new mothers are usually pretty inept caregivers for their young. They are learning a novel, very strenuous job during a time when they are feeling most confused and overwhelmed. That's why, regardless of the animal, first-born offspring usually suffer the indignities, mistakes, and cluelessness of parents who really have little idea what they are doing without the assistance of more experienced elders. Parents frequently make jokes about all the mistakes, misjudgments, and overprotection they inflicted on their first children, compared to a far more relaxed style after subsequent births.

This phenomenon holds true with most other species since no new parent is ever really prepared for the responsibilities and burdens that come with the territory, especially the first time they are faced with these challenges. This may explain how, with experience and greater expertise, successful reproduction among many bird species steadily improves over time. They tend to produce many more eggs after conception that are also more likely to hatch successfully. Is this the result of better sexual technique, more effective foreplay during mating, or just more experience?

In studies of insects, worms, reptiles, and other mammals scientists developed equations to calculate the "residual reproductive value" of an individual based on their utility for the group in alternative ways. These additional contributions involve providing resources, food, safety, knowledge, expertise, or other skills accumulated via vast experience. Once the potential for producing additional young is limited it seems obvious that a new and different approach would focus instead on investing more directly in the children who already exist. Since they can't produce young any longer it is advantageous to make sure that one's existing genetic offspring—even if they are only nieces, nephews, cousins, and grandchildren—are well cared for.

Reproductive Conflict Hypothesis

Why would an animal stop its reproductive functions halfway through it allotted life span? Female elephants, for instance, continue childbearing until the very end of their eight decades of life. Some primates as well, with a life expectancy of 50 or 60 years, also continue producing young well into their later years. Why then, do humans (and orca whales) stop producing eggs to be fertilized and continue their biological imperative?

While attempting to unravel the puzzle of menopause and post-reproductive life researchers discovered an interesting phenomenon that older orca whales abruptly stopped producing calves once they could no longer compete with the calves of much younger mothers (Croft et al., 2017). They found that the whales born to older mothers were twice as likely to die before maturity. It would appear that in order to reduce the mother–daughter conflict, given the limited food supply, biological systems operate to ensure only the healthiest offspring survive. It therefore makes sense that older females would abandon their future reproductive functions for the greater good of the pod, while changing jobs to that of navigator and caregiver for the young. This would significantly reduce reproductive overlap between the generations when younger mothers are more likely to produce healthier offspring while the older ones would be more experienced in care of the young.

In the case of our own species, as social engagement became far more interdependent and cooperative, there was also a need to reduce competition between potential mating prospects, especially between older and younger members. This was even more crucial given the amount of food sharing that is characteristic of human groups. Once menopause removed half the pool of candidates from consideration, this increased the reproductive opportunities for younger, more fertile females who were more likely to give birth to healthier offspring. It has since been observed that some human cultures have a "grandmother rule" that prohibits older females from having any more children as long as their daughters are still able to do so.

This conflict reduction model is not so much viewed as an alternative to the grandmother effects discussed earlier, but rather as a complementary one that explains why older females cease reproductive functions yet continue to survive long afterward in order to serve other roles that are not in direct opposition to the needs of younger members (Cant & Johnstone, 2008). Regardless of the comprehensive explanatory value of any single theory to account for post-reproductive life in humans it is apparent that several different models must be combined in order to make sense of such a complex, mysterious biological process.

Embodied Capital Hypothesis

There were fairly radical changes in the environment that occurred hundreds of thousands of years ago, most notably in the climate and weather patterns. Glaciers receded and advanced over time. The planet cooled significantly, then warmed again. Access to fruits and plants changed, requiring early humans to become wanderers in order to find suitable nutrition.

Out of necessity much longer periods of time were required for the basic survival skills of hunting large animals, recognizing and locating edible plants, escaping predators, building shelters, constructing tools, navigating long distances, and negotiating with other clan members within complex social structures. It was thus suggested that humans had to increase their life spans in order to master all of these intricacies that lengthened childhood and the apprenticeship periods.

This may make practical sense explaining why males lived longer, but it has been argued this doesn't account for why females also were allowed to age after menopause since it did not require nearly as much time to learn the basics of foraging. Clearly there is more going on than can be fully explained solely by "grandmother effects."

As an alternative, or at least a supplement to the grandmother hypothesis, it has been pointed out that the most valuable human attribute is the "embodied capital" that is accumulated, stored, and accessed within our extraordinarily oversized brains (Gurven & Kaplan, 2008; Kaplan et al., 2009). It is all the knowledge, skills, and reasoning powers that are stored within that require such a ridiculously long time for the organ to reach its full potential, all of which require multiple caregivers around during this extended learning stage of life that exceeds two decades. It is thus surmised that just as adolescence extended for more than a decade beyond its ancient parameters, so too did it become necessary for older adults to lengthen their life spans in order to make certain the young survived.

According to his theory, both grandfathers *and* grandmothers—plus aunts, uncles, older siblings, and anyone else available—all pitched in to provide sufficient nutrition, safety, and mentoring for the young. It is a collective investment effort on the part of all within the tribe to ensure that their shared offspring not only survive but flourish. While there's something to be said for the vitality, energy, and exuberance of young adults as parents, it is the older adults who are far more experienced, skilled, knowledgeable, and controlled during crises and conflicts, in a much better position to make sound, informed decisions regarding destinations, safety, hunting, or negotiations with antagonists.

Active Grandparent Hypothesis

It is certainly a compelling idea that menopause began, and human longevity increased, as a result of the priorities by older adults directed away from reproduction and toward care of the young. But that isn't the only effect that occurs as a result of this process. Once fertility ends, if an older person maintains high levels of physical activity through food gathering, hunting, or any other form of exercise, energy sources are reallocated away from fat storage and reproductive tissue since they are no longer needed. Instead, they are reinvested in cellular repair and maintenance in such a way that is believed to contribute to increased life span and prevent more deleterious effects of senescence (Lieberman et al., 2021). This research has discovered interesting physiological processes that occur during and especially *after* physical exercise, a phenomenon known as "afterburn." It had originally been believed that the energy used immediately after strenuous activity was just a way to replace oxygen debt and restabilize metabolic rate, but Lieberman and his colleagues found instead that this more likely represents system repair and maintenance after muscles have been torn and strained (Willingham, 2021b). They also point out that voluntary exercising is a modern invention that was never necessary—or even imagined—when lifestyles were far more active and required continuous vigorous walking, running, digging, and lifting.

During the early years of hominid existence, as well as in contemporary hunter-gatherer cultures that still exist, grandparent-aged tribal members have been much more productive in their food gathering than younger people, providing the young with thousands of extra calories each day while saving others from this backbreaking work. Only those who maintained the highest fitness have been able to maintain such a physical regimen that not only strengthens the group with their nutrition but also optimal genetic material for the future that would lead to longer life.

Even today, when investigators measure the fitness levels of older adults in hunter-gatherer cultures, they find very little falloff in terms of their physical capabilities. In the West, as people age they usually take half as many steps as they did when they were younger and they walk 30% slower (Song & Geyer, 2018). We see this so often that it appears both obvious and inevitable; it is what we expect to happen with aging. But interestingly, among many tribal groups in South America or Africa that have been studied, there is very little, if any, difference in walking pace, hand grip strength, or oxygen uptake levels between the young and the old (Pontzer et al., 2015). It seems that with determination and cultural demands older people remain extremely physically active until the very end. It is believed that this superior conditioning has fortified the biological makeup of elderly people in such a way that their life span has been extended.

There are so many health benefits as a result of regular physical exercise, including immunity to diseases, maintaining optimal blood pressure and lipoproteins, decreasing stress, and increasing levels of neurotransmitters that stabilize moods (Langhammer et al., 2018). Not only does habitual physical activities increase life expectancy by at least a half-dozen years, but it is also believed to be responsible for how and why grandparents and other elderly people in the past lived long enough to be of continued utility to the family. Those adults who were most active, strong, swift, and resilient were more likely to produce offspring that carried their biological gifts, gradually strengthening the gene pool to the point that the strongest and most fit grandparents endured.

There is an assortment of other hypotheses, models, and explanations that all emphasize the nature of the unfinished brain when human infants are first launched into the world as completely helpless creatures that can neither feed themselves nor even become mobile for at least 1 year. If these children are to survive until their brains develop to the point that they can fully operate the "controls" of their bodies, then the parents would have to survive long enough to protect them. That's why the life span after menopause is roughly the same as the amount of time required to successfully raise and launch a child.

FIGURE 5.2 When we predict the future of healthy aging, there is one factor that is undisputed as the single most important one that increases life span, well-being, and productivity—and that's physical exercise. Given that machines, technology, and conveniences like shopping online are slowly replacing even the most basic human labor, there's concern this will have devastating effects on the health and morbidity during later life. The active grandparent hypothesis not only explains how longevity increased as a result of continued physical activity but also how even today it is the single best prevention and cure for most of what harms us. The author, at age 70, is captured on top of a 17,000-feet peak in the Himalayas.

Family Structure and Dynamics

Many of the models previously described examine longevity in the context of biological and evolutionary processes, yet there are also explanations that are based instead on the ways that families are organized as an internal system (Allen et al., 2019). This also helps us better understand the roles and functions of grandparents and elders as they operate within various cultural settings. For many years within Western contexts the family was "socially constructed" as a unit composed of a mother, father, and the equivalent of 2.3 children as an average. In light of so many changes that have occurred with divorce rates, same sex couples, increased mobility, greater diversity, longer life spans, dual-earning couples, reduced birth rates, and even ongoing effects of the worldwide pandemic, there have evolved dozens of different and novel configurations.

One of the main ideas of family systems theories is the concept of "circular causality" in which the behavior of any one member not only impacts everyone else but is, in turn, affected by what others say and do. This means that if you hope to understand, much less change, anyone's behavior, you must also grasp the reciprocal consequences. Thus, why grandparents exist, or why humans are permitted to become elderly, must be understood as the functional effects and mutual influence of how it all plays out within the family, as well as the larger culture.

Depending on the attitudes, beliefs, norms, and expectations that are dominant, the aged may be identified and defined in terms of their abilities or disabilities, their valued contributions or their burdens, their critical functions or dysfunctions. These would all shape the kinds of relationships that develop, as well as their parameters and boundaries. For example, social exchange theory posits that relationships are frequently negotiated based on reciprocal favors: I'll scratch your back if you scratch mine (Homans, 1958). We see this phenomenon all the time with respect to offering loans, providing favors, satisfying debts, and the development of coalitions that are formed for mutual benefit. The main idea is that people make choices and behave according to their own best interests: Even if their actions may appear selfless or altruistic, they still bolster one's standing and reputation within the community. Thus, volunteering to help the indigent, donating to charities, working on behalf of social justice are all indicative of altruism, but they also increase someone's reputation and standing in the community.

Applying this reciprocal exchange model, it is assumed that the elderly are willing to mentor, nurture, support, teach, and care for the young because someday, in the not too distant future, the elders fully expect their family to take care of them in their enfeebled condition. This is obviously a rather limited and cynical view of generosity and caregiving, but it does reveal that the underlying motive that is often part of family obligations, not only for grandparents but also mothers, grandmothers, and other female caregivers whose "emotional and relational labors" have been historically devalued. This leads to more feminist models that recognize and explore the ways that power inequities based on gender, race, sexual orientation, and class also influence, if not determine, the relative contributions of older family members.

None of these theories that have been reviewed are necessarily mutually exclusive, squeezing out the others as a legitimate explanation for the continued existence of the aged. It is not only entirely possible, but highly probable, that this phenomenon is influenced by several of the forces mentioned, including various social, cultural, and biological factors—and the role of grandmothers. Once again, however, it begs the question, "Why do grandfathers exist?"

QUESTIONS FOR REFLECTION OR DISCUSSION

1. Review the theories once again that were mentioned in this chapter. Which one(s) make the most sense to you in terms of probable explanatory usefulness?
2. Circular causality was introduced as the way that individual human behavior both affects, and is affected by, how others behave. What is an example of how you've observed this operating?
3. Patriarchal dominance was described as one of the theories that try to explain the continued presence of elderly people after procreative functions are completed. What are some examples of "patriarchal dominance" that you see manifested in the daily affairs of our culture?

Figure Credit

Fig. 5.1: Copyright © 2019 Depositphotos/fotoluminate.

CHAPTER 6

What About Grandfathers?

"Daddy, will you read me a story?"

"Son, I'm busy right now working on a project. Give me just a few minutes to finish up, okay?

"Sure Daddy. But you said that yesterday too, and then you forgot, remember?"

"One second, just let me finish writing down this one point."

The 4-year-old little boy walks away slowly.

I'm reluctant to admit that this brief interaction between a father and child was actually me and my son. I was in my mid-30s, struggling to establish my career, working long hours on research and writing projects, plus an oversized teaching load of four graduate courses all scheduled in the later afternoons and evenings. I was often overwhelmed and could rarely ever seem to catch up. As important as it was to be a good father—no, a perfect father—I often fell short because of other responsibilities and time pressures to get work done. It felt like I was in survival mode.

Now I'm a grandfather. I can't imagine there could possibly be *anything* that could interrupt my attention—except perhaps an earthquake, devastating fire, or hurricane (each of them did, in fact, one time interrupt my attention)—when I'm playing with my granddaughters. It feels like a do-over, an opportunity to be the parent I had always hoped to be. I must admit I was a pretty good parent, but not to my perfectionistic standards. Now, however, it feels like I have a second chance to prioritize what is really most important in my life—no longer work, achievements, career success, accolades—but just being as fully present as I can be with these little girls. I can play with Barbies, assemble playhouses; do puzzles, drawings, paintings; judge gymnastics routines; dance to the music of Mickey Mouse Playhouse; and create culinary masterpieces. I was granted a second chance to become better than I used to be—and that's why being a grandfather is so important to me.

This personal anecdote highlights one of the most commonly stated reasons older males often report that being a grandfather is the single greatest experience of their lives, a chance for a do-over, an opportunity to be even more committed and dedicated to caring for their offspring—in this case, their children's children.

Why Do Grandfathers Even Exist?

Elderly male lions and other predators are not generally known for their patience, compassion, and willingness to tolerate boisterous cubs—after all, they are inclined to actually kill and eat the offspring of rivals so that they ensure their own genetic material remains dominant. Yet there are instances that can be witnessed in the wild in which such males that operate within advanced social structures (wolves, lions, hyenas, primates) do indeed take on mentoring and teaching roles for the young. One dramatic example describes how a rather large ancient male lion, weighing close to 500 pounds, was snoozing in the high grass (Dagg, 2009; Ross, 2001). Although he was pretending to be asleep, it was obvious he was watching out of the corner of his eye as a tiny cub, weighing just 10 pounds, was stalking him in the high grass. This was a kind of "role-play" to teach the youngster the basics of stalking, hunting, and taking down prey. The cub slowly, cautiously approached his target. Every time the grandaddy glanced his way, he slithered down onto the ground to remain what he believed was invisible to his pretend dinner. Finally, he pounced onto the lion, who then toppled over in surrender. This remarkable display of an older male tolerating such annoying behavior may be highly unusual, but it illustrates the role often assigned to the elderly as teachers, mentors—and role-play targets—for the young that are learning basic skills.

Although there is some evidence that the presence of a human grandfather enhances the welfare of children and the family, there are few other male older animals that spend any time—much less quality time—with their progeny. Instead, they are much more focused on producing more offspring than caring for the ones already in existence. This isn't laziness as much as their own biological imperative to pursue a different evolutionary strategy since they have unlimited sperm while females produce only a limited number of eggs during their lifetimes. As described previously, that is one reason this phenomenon has been called the "*grandmother* effect" (Hawkes et al., 1998; Hawkes, 2004).

If evolutionary scientists have managed to settle on a few compelling reasons why women live beyond their years of fertility, it has been far more challenging to figure out why older men are allowed to survive after they are done fertilizing eggs. After all, at least historically and traditionally, they haven't been known as primary caregivers, nor have they been absolutely invested in family affairs, at least in the same ways that women have been. They don't tend to remain as healthy or live as long as women, so their relative absence is far more common.

Among other animals, even our closest relatives among primates, it is also somewhat rare that elderly males remain very engaged and active within their group because of their reduced strength and endurance, as well desire by the young to replace their power and authority. Both female and male Langur monkeys are no longer dominant within their troops, usually marginalized in both small and significant ways, yet the females still command considerable respect because of their vast knowledge about edible plants and fruits. Elderly males, however, may be tolerated, but they are forced to tag along as best they can at the edge of the troop.

FIGURE 6.1   An elderly male lion cannot usually be bothered with annoying, playful cubs since his main job at this stage of life is to protect the family's territory from invaders and fight off any predators seeking the young ones as easy prey. When he's not otherwise "working," he spends a lot of time taking naps and resting up for the battles that may lie ahead. Typically, it is the lioness that provides mentoring, guidance, and teaching for the young. She also does the "lion's share" of most of the hunting. In this photo, a lioness has wounded prey so that the cub can finish off the kill.

Interestingly, the situation is much different with baboons since they more closely resemble our own species in the ways that older males still have an esteemed place within their community. Although a younger, virile, dominant male may attempt to lead the baboons on their daily journeys, marching off in one direction, the rest of the troop will typically wait until the elder decides whether to follow, or else set off in an altogether different direction. Even though this oldster may be scrawny and small compared to the alphas, no longer attractive to females, his judgment is still most trusted because of his experience and ability to survive even with his physical limitations (Dagg, 2009).

It would appear that although older individuals of any species have trouble keeping up with their group and are no longer able to contribute in previous ways, they still retain important skills and knowledge that are highly valued. It is only among humans that those of grandfather age not only earn their keep via the transgenerational transmission of knowledge and wisdom, but during more recent times they have reinvented themselves in the realm of childcare and mentoring.

Grandfather Bias

There are many researchers who believe there is a distinct feminine bias to the literature on grandparents (Barnett & Connidis, 2019; Bates, 2009; Moore & Rosenthal, 2017). It has even been observed by some investigators that while grandparenting is absolutely a core aspect of a woman's identity, grandfathers supposedly don't consider it as such, merely a part-time series of mostly physical activities they share with the children (Mann, 2007). This is clearly an outdated belief based on norms and values that have since been transformed by more flexible gender roles during the last few decades.

The prominence and popularity of the grandmother effect is just one example of the continued emphasis on women's roles in childcare. In fact, almost always in the past when "grandparents" have been studied or referred to by researchers, they are generally talking exclusively about grandmothers. Older males have been largely invisible in the literature, passive artifacts, or else peripheral figures who are only mentioned in passing.

Just as females have been marginalized in the workplace, restricted by the courts or legislatures in the control of their health and bodies, denied equal opportunities in an assortment of ways, so too have grandfathers been mostly ignored and treated as appendages. There are compelling and legitimate reasons for this given the facts in evidence: (a) Women live longer than men, (b) their life expectancy is still increasing at a faster rate, (c) they also become grandparents at a younger age, (d) grandmothers engage in caregiving activities that are consistently valued more than grandfathers' involvement, (e) children consistently report that they are closest to their maternal grandmother than other grandparents, and especially grandfathers (Bernhold & Giles, 2017). In other words, masculine activities like teaching a youngster how to throw a ball are viewed as less important than the more relationally intimate interactions associated with women's contributions. As such, the influences and roles of grandfathers have been largely ignored—until recently.

Many older men say that they have been strongly impacted by their own fathers (or grandfathers) in determining the ways they function in that role. This influence could have been as a result of positive models they wish to emulate, or just as likely, pushed them to become the exact opposite of what they experienced earlier in life if this patriarch was less than supportive, caring, and accessible. It is interesting that each of us either follows the template stamped into us from early experiences as to what it means to be a grandparent, or else we intentionally choose a quite different path that resonates more closely with one's own values, interests, and preferences. Since my own grandfather was the most important and influential adult figure in my life, I've labored to become even close to the inspirational and loving person that he was to me and my brothers. Alas, I continuously fall short.

In one of the earlier studies of how older men experience their transition into becoming grandfathers it was discovered, not surprisingly, that there are very diverse reactions and meanings (Sorenson & Cooper, 2010). The researchers unexpectedly found that early childhood experiences influenced the kinds of fathers they'd been earlier in life, which, in turn, strongly shaped their role as grandfathers. Previously they may have felt so much pressure to support their families financially that they'd not felt able to spend as much quality time with their children as they wanted. This was sometimes based on deprivations they suffered earlier in life, leading them to work harder and longer as breadwinners so their families would have everything they had lacked.

Once they retired from their full-time employment, many of the grandfathers felt a new kind of freedom and opportunity to become far more active and involved within their families, especially with respect to interactions with the children. As such, they reported a degree of intimacy and emotional closeness with them that had previously been unknown to them in previous stages of life. This is consistent with much of the literature on aging and emotions in which many older men become far more emotionally expressive in the latter stages of life, not only the result of biological changes but also evolved masculine identities.

Grandchildren often become the impetus for older men to explore the deep emotional resonance of their experiences, learning for the first time how to truly acknowledge and express their feelings with a youngster with whom they neither feel judged nor criticized for unfamiliar responses that are outside the usual boundaries of traditional masculinity. As we will explore further in latter chapters, grandchildren actually become the change agents that affect their grandfathers as much as they, in turn, are impacted by the relationships (Barnett & Connidis, 2019).

Different Pathways to Genetic Self-Interest

Nowadays it has been estimated that roughly one third of children see their grandparents several times each week, one third see them less than once per month, and one third don't see them at all for a variety of reasons (living abroad, deceased, estrangement). Maternal grandparents typically tend to be more involved in family life, and not just because they might have a closer relationship with the primary caregiver, which is most often the mother. Evolutionary pressures squeeze in once again since this phenomenon is also best explained by genetic self-interest. If you think about it, the father's parents—and the father for that matter—can never be *absolutely* certain (only about 85%) that the child is biologically related. After all, the baby came out of the mother's womb, but who is to say her egg wasn't fertilized by someone else?

Among certain bird species, males have been known to capitalize on opportunities for "extramarital affairs," so to speak. When a pair-bonded male is out on a foraging mission, or simply looking the other way, an unattached rival can sneak into the nest and secretly fertilize the female (Rice et al., 2018). This is a *very* effective mating strategy since the unaware "cuckholded husband" will end up feeding and raising offspring from another bird's sperm. It also reveals the assortment of different ways that individuals discover (or invent) in order to perpetuate their genetic material, even when they can't find a suitable mate.

There's another fascinating study undertaken many years ago that catalogued the most frequent comment made after the birth of a new baby, immediately after the infant is brought out for display to the waiting relatives (McLain et al., 2000). The most common remark, often verbalized by the mother's mother of all people: "The baby looks *just* like her/his father!" Of course that is ridiculous because newborns don't look like *anyone*, except perhaps an alien with a pointed head, compressed face, swollen eyes, and distended torso after squeezing through the birth canal. If you interpret the deeper meaning of that remark, however, you can readily decode the support that is offered to the father in the form of physical validation: "This baby must belong to you because it has your features!" It is also interesting, that for additional reassurance in most cultures, the child takes the last name of the father as another clear sign of paternity and genetic ownership.

We've discussed how, traditionally, grandmothers have been far more important to survival of family offspring, but as gender roles have expanded and evolved over time, as women have been afforded new opportunities for professional careers, older males have also been provided more significant roles for childcare and family support beyond economic contributions. This appears particularly the case with some grandfathers over others, depending on their educational level and cultural background. For instance, within traditional Western cultures grandfathers may be less directly involved in family life than some minority cultures in which elder males play a significant role developing children's sense of ethnic identity (Jackson et al., 2020). It has also been found that grandfathers' education is highly correlated with their grandchildren's academic success in school. And when *both* grandfathers are highly educated, the influence is even greater on academic achievement (Sheppard & Monden, 2018). While this might not exactly be surprising, it is perhaps more interesting that this holds true even when the grandfather has minimal contact with the kids! It is not clear whether this is because of a trickle-down effect to the parents' own educational priorities, or whether there are some legacy effects from having ancestors who valued advanced learning

A Grandfather's Style

Just as males and females tend to parent differently, based on a variety of biological factors and cultural gender norms, so too do grandmothers and grandfathers differ in their approach, style, and preferences. Whereas females are often described in terms of their relational, nurturing, and supportive traits, males have been traditionally held to a standard based on their role as breadwinners and providers for the family. They are often portrayed as disciplinarians, autocratic heads of household, and relatively unemotional—all of which are hardly associated with ideal grandparenting traits. In addition, their particular responsibilities and roles are far less prescribed and regulated (Miller, 2011). In many places around the world, their value is based primarily on their economic contributions rather than any intimate connection to the children.

Complex mathematical models have even been constructed (Watkins, 2021) that attempt to describe and predict the relative contribution of grandfathers, compared to maternal grandmothers, to children's care and survival in light of the underlying reality of "paternal uncertainty." Although grandfathers may have an advantage in terms of physical strength and durability, grandmothers may rely on their previous experiences as prior caregivers. Once again, so much depends on the personal traits of the individual, as well as the degree of commitment to the (grand)parenting role and responsibilities.

It is perhaps because the idea of having grandfathers around, at least for more than a handful of years, is so relatively novel in evolutionary history that the opportunities to define one's role are so varied and flexible depending on the person's interests, abilities, health, marital status, family needs, and time availability. Not surprisingly, there are distinct gendered patterns in the ways that grandparents communicate and engage with grandchildren (Horsfall & Dempsey, 2015; Jensen et al., 2018). Grandmothers are more inclined to talk to kids about their personal concerns, interpersonal issues, and family history, while grandfathers more typically talk to them about their health issues and their own experiences in the past. In addition, grandmothers usually have more frequent contact, spend more time with the children, and report feeling more emotionally close to the children than their male partners. While it is true that older males are more likely to react to their change in status as a grandfather with a certain ambivalence, once the child is born they may feel the same level of joy and excitement that is characteristic of their partners (Lesperance, 2010).

The major priorities of a grandfather's job, beyond safety and caregiving responsibilities, also depart from those of the matriarch who is more focused on domestic functioning within the family. Senior males often view their influence in terms of how it shapes the child's core values, attachment to cultural traditions, and family identity. Although this follows traditional patterns of the past, younger cohorts and generations of grandfathers now feel much more accessible and prepared to engage children in highly emotional and personal conversations about their fears, conflicts, failures, mistakes, and triumphs. This new version of grandfathers also tends to be more reflective and nurturing than in the past, even while expressing more traditional, masculine norms.

The perceptions of grandchildren toward the differences apparent in their grandmothers versus grandfathers change over time based on their age and gender (Mann et al., 2013). For instance, a 6-year-old girl and a 12-year-old boy often have very different relationships with each of their grandparents, the latter of which is more likely to be close to his maternal grandfather. However, as older men have become more "emotionally literate," their influence has expanded across the spectrum. Their traditional "masculine discourse" has been softened a bit, making them more accessible and approachable. As grandchildren reach adolescence and early adulthood it would appear that their grandfathers become even more important to them, just as their grandmothers were closer to them during their early childhood.

It is clear that the grandfather's style is more attuned to masculine traits that involve physical activities and playing sports, as well as teaching the importance of family identity via storytelling. Even though grandmothers are known and portrayed primarily through their nurturing and domestic traits, when grandchildren have been interviewed about their relationships, they are more likely to associate their grandfathers with providing indelible memories that are described as poignant or humorous (Bernhold & Giles, 2017).

One additional contribution of some grandfathers beyond their caregiving or economic contributions is their gift of longevity. In one interesting study it was found that a person's predicted life span is significantly affected by the particular age at which the child's grandfather gave birth to the father. It is certainly no surprise that family history has a huge impact on mental and physical health, but it has also been suggested that the parent's age during which a child is born affects the length, quality, and health of the telomeres that protect the strands of DNA in our system. It appears as if a paternal grandfather's strands of genetic code are passed through the two generations that may actually have a strong impact on the grandchildren's own future health (Eisenberg et al., 2020).

Gender Roles Are Changing

There have been some fairly radical transformations in the ways that gender roles have been expanded during the last few decades. Whereas prior to the 1970s it was somewhat rare for males to attend the birth of their own babies, more inclined to pass out celebratory cigars in the waiting room while the mother struggled in agony, just 30 years later this has become the norm. Beginning with the 21st century males were no longer expected to identify exclusively with their careers as their only means of satisfaction and life fulfillment. Fathers and grandfathers began to speak more frequently about how important it was to spend quality time with their children, taking greater responsibility for their care, safety, entertainment, and education. They viewed this valuable time not so much an extension of domestic work as a significant expression of their (grand)fatherhood (Gray, 2006). Of course even with this evolution of shared childcare, mothers most often assume the majority of responsibility for the children, even when they are working full-time. On the other hand, it is still common that fathers and grandfathers work longer hours than their female partners, leading to complaints that they wish they could be available to spend more time at home. If the worldwide pandemic offered one positive outcome and gift to families it was to make it possible for more parents to work from home.

During the COVID-19 pandemic, the number of stay-at-home fathers increased significantly, just as it did for mothers, launching a worldwide trend that is expected to continue, if not grow significantly. In Sweden, virtually all fathers (96%) stated that they felt themselves perfectly capable of being primary caregivers for their children, and there's considerable evidence to indicate that single fathers (and grandfathers) are just as competent as females in their parenting skills. Although there have been stylistic differences observed between male and female caregivers in the discipline and control strategies they employ, there's little difference between their ultimate effectiveness (Endendjik et al., 2016).

The very idea of stay-at-home dads, or males as primary caregivers in the family, used to be a statement about being unemployed. This just wasn't supposed to be what real men do; they are the ones who take care of their families and leave the domestic stuff and children to the women folk. Yet in spite of this historical tradition throughout the ages and world's cultures, in addition to the pressures of pursuing a career and providing for one's family, 85% of fathers today say they would do or give up *anything* in order to be fully present with their newborn (Barker et al., 2021). Well, that's what they *say* anyway. They also offer a lot of excuses why this might not be feasible due to lack of time, stress on the job, and other responsibilities that seem to take precedent. Nevertheless, the fact that the vast majority of fathers *want* to be more involved in childcare says a lot about the direction that things are heading—especially for grandfathers.

FIGURE 6.2   During the worldwide pandemic, the number of fathers who became full-time, stay-at-home caregivers increased by 25%, a trend that is only expected to continue. This change in gender roles not only freed up more women to pursue careers and become the primary wage earners of the family but also allowed fathers and grandfathers to redefine what it means to care for their children.

As much as we might emphasize gender differences in grandparenting style, the most important factor of all is actually the proximity and frequency of contact with children. Obviously, the more often, and more time, they spend together—assuming it is enjoyable and helpful for both parties—the more likely a close, enduring, and intimate relationship will develop. With that said, it is more likely that the quality of engagement is more important than the quantity since relational ties are bonded by each party's perception of mutual caring, affection, and respect

(Jensen et al., 2018). There are clearly instances when grandparents, or grandchildren, are forced to spend time with one another even though it may feel less than pleasant and desirable.

For older males, the stage of "generativity," described by developmental theorist Erik Erikson, operates as a powerful incentive to pass along family identity, cherished stories, legacies, cultural norms, and traditions, just as has this has been an integral part of that role throughout our history. Perhaps more than few other influences, this transfer of accumulated wisdom and knowledge to the younger generation is responsible for the long-term viability of our species. The good news is that this not only operates to continue the accumulation of knowledge, expertise, and innovation for future generations, but it is also greatly appreciated by the grandchildren who report that their own values and character traits have been greatly influenced by their grandfathers (Mann et al., 2016).

It is readily apparent that the sheer diversity of relationship configurations between grandfathers and their grandchildren is bewilderingly complex, a rapidly evolving phenomenon that has yet to establish clear and universal norms. There are still older men who remain somewhat disengaged from the children in the traditional, formal family structure: They are viewed by the kids as distant figures, perhaps respected but without much emotional connection. More and more often, however, those who were born during or after the baby boom generation enjoy much greater gender role flexibility and may seek much closer, intimate connections with the children in ways that are far more playful and fun.

Support for Grandfathers

It is often difficult for us to identify, appreciate, understand, and respond to major transformations taking place as shifts in cultural norms and people's behavior. Within the span of just a few months during the beginning of the worldwide pandemic it seemed that *everything* changed in our daily lives. All of a sudden we began avoiding one another, washing hands, wearing masks, isolating ourselves at home. Offices were abandoned. Political discourse became far more angry and conflicted. If someone had been in a coma and woke up a few months later they might believe they were living in an alternative universe—which in a sense we had been!

The unprecedented changes in life span, health care, gender roles, family dynamics, and cultural expectations have created new opportunities for older people to continue their valuable contributions way beyond their fertility years. While grandmothers have been recognized for their value-added productivity for centuries, and across a variety of cultures, it is quite recent that the influence of grandfathers has been explored beyond their economic contributions. This is all so novel and new that many first-time grandfathers are both confused and excited about the possibilities that await them when their children have children. After all, there are so few models they've been exposed to of successful healthy aging and adaptation to this relatively new and novel life stage.

One of the factors that has been found to most contribute to healthy aging and effective mentoring is the availability of family and community support. As we've discussed, and will explore in a later chapter, the stressors associated with the "job" can take a toll on one's life satisfaction and sense of well-being, especially for those elders who feel pressure and obligations to do things for which they don't feel much enthusiasm or enjoyment. When family dynamics are chaotic, or relationships between and among members are conflicted, this presents additional difficulties that compromise intergenerational functioning and lead to dissatisfaction with caregiving roles (Shlomo & Taubman-Ben-Ari, 2017).

Just as few parents receive formalized training to take on what could be considered the single most important job—raising and growing children—grandparents are usually even less prepared for what lies ahead. The same could be said when faced with the last life stage and all the changes within the body and mind that will inevitably occur, setting in motion endless adjustments that must be made. Whether related to healthy aging in general, or grandparenting and mentoring in particularly, effective adaptation seems to be a matter of facing challenges with flexibility, a positive attitude, and an open mind.

QUESTIONS FOR REFLECTION OR DISCUSSION

1. What have you observed are the major differences between the ways that grandfathers and grandmothers operate in our culture?
2. Why do you suppose there's been so little attention, exploration, and research focused on grandfathers and their experiences?
3. Project yourself into the future to a time when you are in later life and perhaps a grandparent to one more children. What do you think this will be like?

Figure Credits

CHAPTER 7

Cultural Variations

Cultural context affects and impacts every aspect of daily life, including the ways that children make sense of the world. All of our values, opinions, perceptions, beliefs, interactions, and family relationships are shaped by local cultural traditions and expectations. It is difficult to understand the nature of elder–youth interactions without taking into account intergenerational cultural transmission to pass along what is considered essential knowledge. This usually includes the established and normative "rules" for conduct that exemplify ideal behavior. Within our culture examples might encompass religious beliefs, political allegiances, and core values with regard to morality, ethical choices, and optimal decision-making. A case could be made that the ultimate purpose of grandparents is to share cultural lessons considered most important to navigate daily life (Hayslip et al., 2019).

Within most human cultures elders are assigned responsibilities related to legacy transmission. Although this certainly includes inheritance of resources, valuable commodities, and financial savings, just as important is the legacy of knowledge that is shared to youth. Typically these core values, regardless of location and context, are connected to values related to honor, honesty, humility, faith, and what it means to do a "good day's work." Depending on the nature and closeness of the relationship between elder and child, the depth and extent of influence can take on even far more influence in other areas of performance related to schoolwork, hobbies, recreational pursuits, sports, and social activities.

About three quarters of all those over the age of 65 are grandparents, which is one form of kinship status within a tribe, culture, or family. In addition, older adults take on responsibilities as coaches, mentors, guides, resources, leaders, and volunteers within the community in order to share their experience and wisdom. The assigned or adopted roles, functions, expectations, and activities are almost completely dependent on the local cultural norms and particular family structure. Most of these expectations and traditions have been transformed significantly during the last generation or two as a result of changing gender roles and demographics, as well as much greater diversity in the ways that families are structured and configured. Mentioned previously were factors such as delayed fertility, geographical mobility, fractured marriages, plus technological innovations in communication. Each of these has had a profound effect on the nature and experiences of grandparenthood as it is experienced throughout various parts of the world.

Adding to the complexity of understanding the nature of elder behavior and family involvement has been the dramatic increase in life expectancy, providing unprecedented extended amounts of time between the oldest and youngest segments of society. When life span rarely lasted beyond a handful of decades it was somewhat rare to even know a grandparent beyond the legends that were told; nowadays it is possible such relationships can last as long as 30 or more years. Thus far we have little idea how this will transform the nature of family relationships, as well as the larger community. What we do know for certain is that these relational dynamics will have quite different effects depending on the previous traditions and norms.

Overgeneralizing and Oversimplifying Trends

It is difficult to make sweeping generalizations about how people experience aging and their roles as grandparents and elders, given the vast differences in the ways human communities and families are organized. The standard Western version of a mom, dad, and 2.5 children is hardly any longer the only common scenario. There are "families" composed of one or more partners who have been married, separated, divorced, and remarried a multitude of times, each of which produced a kid or two or three. Extended families living together might encompass an assortment of aunts, uncles, cousins, grandparents, and genetically unrelated "relatives" who have been informally adopted. There are multiple related families that live together in a compound, while occupying separate dwellings. There are single-parent families, even one version with just one person with a cat (or even a goldfish). Then there are families "by choice," originally devised by LGBTQ community to refer to configurations that are not recognized or protected by the legal system. This has become increasingly widespread in many other contexts in which individuals decide to become live-in partners, raising children together, and functioning as a tribal unit. It is also increasing in popularity amount economically challenged people who can pool their financial resources and share expenses together, in addition to creating a sense of belonging (Gazso & McDaniel, 2015).

In spite of this incredible diversity it has often remained common practice to greatly simplify the nature of human behavior by making universal statements about a particular group. Thus, Native Americans, for instance, are inclined to treat elders with reverence and respect. This may, in fact, be mostly the case; however, there are over 600 distinct tribal groups, just within the United States, each of which has their own language, identity, and cultural norms. In addition, the experience of any individual within a group is shaped by their own personal resources, perceived social status, economic clout, political position, gender, and family identity.

There are also some rather unique family structures that have been known to occur around the world throughout history. Consider the prevalence of polygamous marriages (one man married to several women) that was once common throughout Europe and is still relatively common in Central African countries like Mali and Nigeria or other places where females are relatively scarce. Even more rare are polyandrous marriages (one woman married to multiple men) that still exist in parts of China or the South Pacific. Given the increased flexibility of gender roles and identities, there are even now examples of multiple partners of various sexual orientations residing together as a "family."

If any of this seems bizarre to you, remember that throughout human history, almost anywhere in the world, arranged marriages have been the norm rather than the exception. "Love marriages," often fueled by the hormones ignited by adolescent fantasies, were only "invented" during the past two centuries. Prior to that no sane, rational person would trust the whims of young people to make such important decisions. It has always been the elders within the community, or the parents and grandparents of the family, who decide who should be permitted to wed and mate. More often than not such decisions were made based on friendships between the stakeholders, previous family histories, forging alliances between tribes, increasing economic prosperity, or expanding territorial holdings. When all things are considered, this may, in fact, be a far more stable arrangement for the culture given that the divorce rate within arranged marriages is less than 4% (less than 1% in India) compared to almost 50% within most Western, industrialized nations.

Also keep in mind that among our closest primate relatives, families are assembled according to alliances that have been negotiated through mutual grooming and sharing of food. Similar to other species that seek to increase the viability and strength of their genetic pool, the only members of the group that are actually permitted to mate at all are those that have attained "alpha" status. They must represent the ideal of physical capability that has the most advantageous genetic material to pass along to the next generation, thereby improving the stock for future offspring. Along similar lines, human elders have attempted to arrange suitable matches for their children based on similar and compatible backgrounds that would improve the family's future standing.

Complicating matters further, nothing ever remains static with respect to cultural norms. As people become more acculturated and adapted to their communities they tend to shed some of the traditional practices and values of the past, an evolutionary process that occurs gradually over time. Prior values related to collectivism, or even childcare practices, become diluted and altered in light of new and different norms and social pressures to conform. One example of this might relate to corporal punishment and physical discipline of children, which may have been commonplace and viewed as acceptable in a previous setting but is now seriously prohibited as evidence of child abuse.

In one survey of international variations in discipline strategies, parental and grandparental choices varied considerably in response to children's aggressive or anxious behavior (Gershoff, 2010). Depending on countries' dominant religious traditions, economic status, demographic composition, ethnic and racial composition, and collectivist versus individualist values, among other variables, caregivers might rely on an assortment of intervention options that include corporeal punishment, removing privileges, expressing disappointment, shaming and scolding, yelling, time-outs, teaching alternative behavior, or more extreme actions that involve isolation, removal, or abandonment. Regardless of setting, obviously different methods would be employed with a child who is acting belligerently and defiantly as opposed to one who is highly distraught and anxious.

Demographic considerations also significantly impact the ways that grandparenting operates in various cultures. Whereas in the United States, by the age of 54, two thirds of people have at least one grandchild, the situation is quite different in a country like Switzerland where fewer than 20% have attained that developmental landmark (Margolis & Arpino, 2020). Obviously the age at which one takes on the responsibilities and roles of supplemental childcare would affect one's attitudes, interests, capabilities, health, lifestyle, and experiences.

Many of the cultural norms related to grandparenting also diverge from one another based on the relative tolerance of noninterference versus taking charge as the authoritarian figure. In many Asian countries, for example, elders are clearly empowered as the patriarchs and matriarchs of the family; everyone else is expected to fall in line. This is in direct contrast to many Western nations where elders in the family are expected to abide by parental wishes since they are the ones who retain control. One other example of a varied norm is connected to a sense of obligation on the part of grandparents to do whatever is requested—without compliant or criticism. This is perhaps the one area where fractures are most likely to appear.

Additionally, even residing in a single nation individuals have multiple cultural identities depending on their ethnicity, social class, heritage, language, education, profession, hobbies, interests, and sexual orientation. Many of these various identities overlap; some even conflict with one another. A poverty stricken, African American, lesbian grandmother, for instance, may have to negotiate and reconcile experiences of racism with classism, homophobia, ageism, and sexism, all at the same time. This is all complicated further by narrative scripts that portray custodial grandparents as disempowered, fragile, heroic, tragic figures. This makes perfect sense when we consider that the times that grandparents are expected to assume primary childcare responsibilities occur most often as a result of poverty, addiction, crime, neglect, imprisonment, or crisis (Dolbin-MacNab & Few-Demo, 2020).

Just as the case with so many other aspects of life, one's history and cultural legacy affect personal choices, behavior, and caregiving style (Montoro-Rodrigues & Ramsey, 2020). African American grandparents who were subjected to poverty, racism, and oppression would be particularly sensitive to those issues as they educate and mentor youth, just as Mexican American immigrants would have been affected by their own history of discrimination and relocation challenges. Asian American elders may have internalized values of filial piety even if they are at odds with contemporary norms, just as Jewish or Muslim elders may prioritize religious values. In each case, with each family, the core values that are passed on to the children result from extensive negotiation among family members, as well as their own life priorities.

Diversity Is the Norm

It is obvious that family structure, cultural background, socioeconomic status, and geographical region influence both the quantity and quality of interaction between grandparents and grandchildren, in addition to their personal characteristics. Whereas it is common for some ethnic groups to live in the same home as a multigenerational family (with three, four, or even five generations), within the affluent, privileged class, families tend to reside in smaller households and their own dwellings separate from grandparents and other relatives. This would significantly alter the responsibilities and opportunities that grandparents would enact in their roles. In addition, the quality of healthy relationships formed depend on several factors, the most important of which is the cooperation between mother and grandmother.

It clearly matters how well the parents get along with their own parents and in-laws—and with one another. Is the frequent presence of grandparents welcome and appreciated, or rather is it felt like an intrusion? Is everyone in agreement about basic routines, discipline strategies, and interventions? Are the grandparents respectful toward parental preferences? Do they attempt to undermine them in attempts to win favor or spoil the children? The answers to these questions influence whether caregivers function as a cohesive, supportive team or behave as competitors for ultimate control.

We've also seen how grandparents tend to take on different responsibilities and roles based on their own preferences, time availability, and interests, as well as the needs of the family. When they visit, are grandparents treated like honored guests, occasional babysitters, full-time caregivers, coparents, disciplinarians, annoyances, troublemakers, or entertainers? To what extent do grandchildren feel intimate, close, trusting, and adored by their grandparents? Are they loving, nurturing figures, or cold, withdrawn, punitive authoritarian figures? We do know, for instance, that when brain scans of grandmothers are captured while viewing images of their children versus their grandchildren, there tends to be much greater emotional activation with the latter, implying a closer relational connection (Rilling et al., 2021). Finally, is the emotional stability, personality, interpersonal style, cognitive functioning, and health status of the grandparent(s) conducive to family stability? To the extent that *any* caregiver is well adjusted, responsible, dependable, compassionate, caring, moral, and nurturing, the impact is going to be more constructive.

FIGURE 7.1   Beyond their assistance as caregivers, babysitters, and financial resources, grandparents serve significant roles teaching grandchildren critical social skills valued by the culture. It may appear in these photos as if the grandfather is simply teaching an athletic skill, or the grandmother is providing cooking lessons, but it is the conversations and interactions that take place during these encounters that provide emotional support, mentoring, and seminal stories about the family, historical legacy, and the wider world.

Some Specifics and a Few Universals

In spite of the diverse norms that exist in various cultures there are certain life lessons taught by grandparents and elders that could be considered somewhat universal across time and space. Probably the most prominent among these teachings are providing a sense of belonging, instilling a group identity that holds the favored values of the family and community. A main theme relates to the clear goal "This is who we are—and this is how we became who we are." Grandparents are thus assigned the task of teaching young the values that are held most sacred, whether that is having fun, pursuing adventure, achieving success, helping others, or practicing self-care.

It is primarily by sharing stories about oneself, one's experiences and observations about the world and its mysteries, that mean far more than mere entertainment. These narratives help children form coherent ideas to help them make sense of how the present and future connect to the past. In all cultures this is one of the main jobs of elders to pass on collective wisdom, knowledge, and experience so that others may profit from this valuable intelligence. Whether sitting in a tribal story circle, the dinner table, going for a walk, or even cooking a meal together, most activities are accompanied by suitable stories that explain how things came to be the way they are. As a kind of "body of work" the accumulative effects of these stories provide a deeper understanding of one's origins and roots.

The dominant norms of any culture dictate, to a certain extent, the behaviors that are considered socially acceptable, as well as those that are treated as outliers. There are always stories circulating in media about the peculiar parenting practices within certain families in which children are allowed to engage in perceived dangerous behaviors, or else treated and disciplined in ways that are considered extreme and abusive. First, there are institutional policies and laws related to parental or grandparental rights, family-friendly labor practices, economic benefits for children and their caregivers, educational entitlements, retirement benefits, and long-term care policies (Price et al., 2020). There are also norms for gender equality or disparity, dual-earning couples, retirement age, and other factors that either permit or discourage active engagement with the family. For instance, in countries where both partners are expected to work full-time in order to survive, it is absolutely imperative to have additional support from one's own parents, but those same demands would hardly be necessary if one or both spouses are under- or unemployed.

Inevitable Generational Clash of Values

Throughout most of human history there has been conflict, disagreement, and cultural disputes that split generations into warring camps. Elders have often been seen as protectors of the establishment and long-held traditions, many of which are in direct opposition of those of young people. The various generational cohorts (baby boomers, Gen X, Millennials, etc.) have been battling for dominance, just has this competition has taken place forever. Social movements by young people such as the Greensboro lunch counter sit-ins, Vietnam War protests, Tiananmen Square, Woodstock, the civil rights movement, Black Lives Matter, and Arab Spring were led by mostly young activists who sought to overthrow the status quo that was found to be oppressive and outdated, maintained by older people who control the power.

Throughout the past century or so there's been an ebb and flow of conflict between the generational cohorts. During the 1960s, for example, there was widespread disruption, rebellion, and protests sparked by the Vietnam War, institutional racism, and what were viewed as outdated, obsolete views of what our society had become. Nevertheless, pretty much during every era in recent times, three quarters of people, both young and old, see major differences in their basic values. This is most evident in musical preferences, proficiency with technology, and use of social media, but also in work ethic, life priorities, sexual orientation, and moral and religious beliefs. Perhaps most of all are significant differences in political affiliations and preferences (Bialik & Fry, 2019).

When comparing cultural differences in grandparenting it is evident that there are indeed wide variations in the ways that elders are treated and relationships are constructed and managed (Cox, 2018). Filial respect and obligations are a feature of many Latino cultures, but so are language challenges when children are reluctant to speak Spanish outside of the home. African American families have also traditionally demonstrated reverence and respect for elders, especially the matriarch of the family, but once again challenges are also common when there is a clash of values between generations. Chinese American elders also view their primary roles as helping to build moral character, teach appropriate manners, and push for achievement in school, but these intentions may not necessarily be welcomed by the children, leading to ongoing conflicts in the family. Native American elders also see themselves as the stewards of oral history and collective wisdom, roles that may be important to them but also may receive pushback from younger members of the family who are more interested in age-related norms that may defy these traditions.

These few examples demonstrate the inevitable—and perhaps necessary—conflicts and negotiations that take place between the elders who have been in charge and the upstart, ambitious younger generation that are vying to impose their own values and agenda on cultural life. The differences in their respective priorities reflect not only their competing values but also their diverging views of what is needed most for their community and their own individual welfare.

Good and Bad News

Cultural norms and traditions help to bolster and support the role of elders and grandparents as the deputized disseminators of knowledge. Yet despite their best intentions, many of these efforts are resisted, if not rejected, by young people who may find the values inherent in the lessons to be largely irrelevant in their lives, just a fiction of the past. Especially those elders who are not conversant in the dominant language, largely unaware of technological advances, or who are just not "with it" in the sense of being socially clueless, there are inevitable conflicts and stressors that compromise relationships within the family. These generational gaps can act as significant barriers that must be negotiated or else estrangement is likely.

Additional cultural challenges and obstacles relate to institutional racism and oppression over time, leading to chronic poverty and disenfranchisement. That is one reason gang cultures can attract youth in ways that elders within the family cannot compete with their messages of cooperating and fitting in. A lack of legal standing also keeps grandparents in vulnerable positions, unable to advocate for themselves when families begin to fall apart.

Evolution may usually take hundreds of thousands of years before noticeable changes in biological functioning occur, but cultural changes can occur within a few decades, or even years. Think about fashion trends as one example of this, how celebrities or social media "influencers" can imprint their vision on a favored preference, and it can take off within weeks. Yet biological evolutions, even those taking place this very moment, take considerably longer to unfold, such as the origin of blue eyes that is believed to have first appeared about 10,000 years ago.

Of course the two biological and cultural processes are closely linked to one another as we can readily see how increased life expectancy has also led to new and different roles, functions, and expectations for elders and grandparents. It is also evident that, like any other helping relationships, both partners experience reciprocal effects. In some cases, this may result in additional stress and burdens for the elderly, but also opportunities for learning. Aging and life experience alone do not adequately prepare one for becoming an inspirational mentor and guide—such a role requires intimate knowledge and deep understanding of children, as well as an openness for the new insights they can offer.

Grandchildren become teachers, as well as students of the past. They introduce elders to aspects of cultural knowledge, social trends, technology, music, and art that would have previously been beyond their awareness and interest. One of the reasons being a grandparent increases life satisfaction and meaning in life isn't only because of feeling useful but also because of all the stimulation and learning that takes place as a result of this responsibility.

QUESTIONS FOR REFLECTION OR DISCUSSION

1. What are some of the most important cultural lessons you learned from elders or grandparents that taught you where you came from and who you are?
2. What are some examples of generational conflicts and disputes you experienced in your family growing up?
3. How do you imagine and predict that your identified culture (however that is flexibly defined) will continue to evolve in the future?

Figure Credits

CHAPTER 8

Differential Views of Grandparent Influence

P arents define their assigned and chosen roles in many ways, depending on their income, resources, jobs, family structure, lifestyle, culture, preferences, values, the number of their children, and a multitude of other factors. There are stay-at-home moms and dads, work-from-home parents, those who employ nannies and kid sitters on a regular basis, and others who hover over and control their children constantly. Some parents view their offspring as their most important priority, while others only engage them when convenient.

Given the variety of parental styles, it makes perfect sense that grandparents would also take on different roles and functions according to the situation, interests, and family needs. Some grandparents become the most important figures in children's lives, while others remain largely invisible, if not irrelevant altogether. Some visit their grandchildren almost every day, while others might only see them once or twice each year. In some cases, the children may have never met a grandparent who has simply become a mythical figure who is sometimes mentioned in family stories. Given these possible variations, the kinds of influence and impact that grandparents have on the children would also vary depending on the frequency and quality of their interactions.

Although the focus of most of our discussion is on the impact of grandparents on children, there are other older adults who also qualify for this esteemed and privileged role. In some cases, aunts, uncles, great aunts and uncles, great-grandparents, godparents, even elderly neighbors or family friends, assume certain responsibilities on behalf of the family. In each instance, the particular degree and kind of influence often depends less on the genetic connection and far more on the intimacy and trust that develop in the relationships. After all, just because someone is genetically related to you doesn't mean you trust, or even like, them.

The type of assistance offered by a relative or surrogate can take one of several different forms, whether in the guise of financial support, mentoring, tutoring, childcare, or what has been described as "social capital" that includes introductions to influential people or new interests, providing useful advice, or helping to guide educational and career prospects (Mollegaard & Jaeger, 2015). Of course there is always a difference in any helping relationship between delivering what a person most needs versus what you feel like offering in that moment.

That's why the closeness and communication within the relationship are more important than any genetic connection. There are parents and grandparents known to abuse or neglect their children, while complete strangers may be willing to step in and provide major assistance when most needed.

A Choice or Obligation?

There are many reasons people become active grandparents, often of their own volition but sometimes because of circumstances that were beyond their control. This could occur, for instance, when they are drafted into custodial care because of some difficulty with the parents, such as a death, health problem, incarceration, abuse, neglect, abandonment, addiction, or poverty. In most situations, however, there is some choice in the matter, including the extent, duration, and type of interaction with grandchildren. Obviously, choice would make a difference in the ways that grandparents feel about their roles just as that would be true for any other activity that is the result of external pressure rather than a personal decision.

In those cases in which a grandparent is involuntarily recruited, pressured, or forced to take over certain childcare responsibilities, such reluctance may not indicate disinterest as much as lack of capability for this job. It may very well be true that the elder lacks the skill set, energy, health condition, time availability, resources, perhaps even lack of reliable transportation, in order to function very effectively. In other instances, limits and boundaries may not be respected, further pushing the older person into a sense of frustration and sense of helplessness. Unfortunately, in the majority of these situations there really doesn't seem to be any other choice given that one or both parents are out of the picture.

There are, thus, both positive "pulls" and negative "pushes" that affect the ways that grandparents approach their jobs, depending on their attitudes and feelings according to several dimensions. On the joyful side of the ledger are considerations such as love for the children, enhancing one's sense of worth and value, and finding meaning in later life. Yet other factors related to their health, finances, and, of course, the children's own reactions also contribute to any subjective effects. In the case of full-time custodial grandparents, we've discussed how so much of their adaptation, satisfaction, and perceived efficacy relate to the degree of choice and types of decision-making that they were permitted to make. The particular circumstances that led to them taking over childcare, whether a personal choice or forced obligation, matters quite a lot, leading to both positive enticements or else personal disruptions, conflicts, and overwhelming stress (Hayslip et al., 2021).

Some of the earliest investigations of grandparent experiences described the options ranging from a relatively formal, distanced role to that of substitute parents; between the two polarities were also described functions that resemble that of a favored aunt or uncle, as well as one based on sharing wisdom and experience (Neugarten & Weinstein, 1964). It is this last description that most closely resembles much of what we witness today; however, the roles are hardly stable and often change as a result of transitions that occur within the family that may lead to conflicts, separation, divorce, abandonment, or parental death (Attar-Schwartz & Buchanan, 2020). In these situations, grandparent preferences are less meaningful than the particular needs of the children.

Benevolent or Toxic Force

It hasn't always been the case that grandparent caregiving was viewed as a benevolent force in family life. It isn't unusual that one partner or the other may resent the intrusions of "meddling," overcontrolling in-laws or parents. In many television shows and movies grandparents are often portrayed as frail, crotchety, forgetful, fussy figures who, perhaps with good intentions, always seem to get in the way. From the grandparents' own perspective, a remark can often be heard similar to, "Hey, I love the grandkids, but I also love to give them back at the end of the day." This seems to imply a certain ambivalence felt toward the responsibility that seems forced upon them, which is often not the case at all.

During the years of the Second World War, with fathers away fighting in battle, a prominent medical publisher released a series of books with titles like *Grandma Made Johnny Delinquent* (Strauss, 1943). Psychiatrists during the time believed that with grandparents taking on more childcare responsibilities, the children were becoming more unruly and undisciplined. The idea was that rather than blaming the war, the death and injuries to millions of soldiers, the economic restrictions, the fear of imminent attacks, the destabilization of the family with so many fathers away, the uncertainty about the future, doctors blamed the *grandparents* for being too strict. Years later, grandparents were instead criticized for being too lenient and spoiling the kids. Once again, it is apparent that, like every other role in the community and family, there are both boosters and critics.

There appear to be several consistent benefits for children and adolescents when grandparent involvement is considered helpful and appreciated by the parents (Buchanan & Rotkirch, 2020).

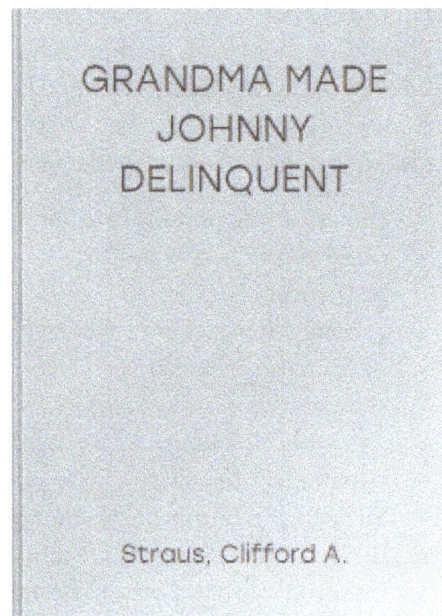

GRANDMA MADE
JOHNNY
DELINQUENT

Straus, Clifford A.

FIGURE 8.1 There are not only cultural variations related to the ways that grandparents are viewed not only around the world but also across time. This best-selling book published during World War II in a psychiatric journal advanced warnings that grandparents were ruining the children while their fathers were away, claiming that either they were too authoritarian and strict, or else excessively lenient and permissive, both of which would lead to lifelong damage inflicted upon them.

Children are likely to have reduced emotional difficulties, as well as demonstrate more prosocial, altruistic behavior toward others. The children are better protected against dangers and risky temptations. They have additional outlets for discussing their personal concerns and seeking advice on matters of significance. They are introduced to activities, sports, hobbies, books, and intellectual pursuits that would have otherwise remained unknown. As discussed in a later section, it is in the realm of educational achievement and career success that the effects are even more impactful (Anderson et al., 2018; Lehti et al., 2019; Mollegaard & Jaeger, 2015). And of course, parental pressures and stress are often significantly reduced with the additional adult supervision available that frees them up for some of their own priorities. This, in turn, often results in smoother relationships within the household.

On the other hand—and you knew the other hand was coming—grandparents who are negligent, incompetent, manipulative, overcontrolling, mean-spirited, or otherwise toxic to the family due to their attitudes and behavior, can become highly disruptive if not dangerous to family well-being (de Becker, 2020). This is particularly the case if these common warning signs and symptoms are in evidence by one or both grandparents or caregivers:

- Undermining parental authority and existing house rules
- Challenging family culture in order to insert one's own values and priorities that may be in direct conflict
- Feeling a sense of entitlement that leads to making unreasonable demands
- Bribing the children with treats, favors, toys, or privileges to earn their affection—or silence
- Being highly manipulative, overcontrolling, or deceitful, perhaps a sign of underlying personality disorder
- Meddling in family issues that are actually of no concern to them
- Blaming, punishing, or criticizing children in cruel or unjustified ways
- Favoring one child over the others in obvious and consistent behavior

Assuming that parents are aware of these issues, which often they are not if the elder is especially careful and secretive (employing blackmail and bribing children), limits must be set to restrict access. It is unfortunately the case that these behaviors may continue even after they are confronted vigorously and the elder is warned to alter behavior. As a last resort, after other avenues are exhausted, no further contact may be permitted.

One of the reasons for much of miscommunication and family conflicts may be directly related to a lack of support that is offered to grandparents. Three quarters of those surveyed mentioned that their caregiving responsibilities compromised their own social life, and one third said that their roles created serious difficulties with their partners. The majority all wished they had counseling available to assist them in their work (Adesman, 2017).

Norms That Influence Roles and Functions

The rules have changed dramatically for what it means to be a grandparent, even if they are variable, confusing, even contradictory. There is a norm, for example, about "being there," meaning being available whenever needed, based on the convenience of the parents. Yet there is also another norm about staying out of the way and not interfering with the established rules, even if they don't make much sense. This is perhaps the most important rule of all—not to undermine or sabotage the parents' relationship with their children. Adding to the complexity and ambiguity of the situation, the parents are still the ones in control, dictating instructions, boundaries, expectations, and especially governing access. Since grandparents have few, if any, legal rights or recourse, it is usually a good idea to comply with the rules established by those in power. One notable exception, of course, is when those guidelines are seriously misguided or dangerous.

In some situations the grandparents may be expected to become replacement parents, custodians of the kids, because of issues or needs within the family. These demands can vary tremendously depending on the cultural context of the family (Buchanan & Rotkirch, 2018). Although we have covered some of these local, situational contexts in the previous chapter it is worth reviewing the most common norms, at least those in most cultures around the world.

- *Filial piety.* Elders are treated with great respect and reverence because of their wisdom, experience, and authority.
- *Social status.* In many places and contexts there is great benefit attached to being the matriarch or patriarch of the family. This is a position of authority and power, not only within the home but the larger community.
- *Multigenerational home.* It is far more common in the world that several generations would occupy the same household and share responsibilities.
- *Obligation for mutual care.* It is fully expected that when the tables are turned, the younger generations will take care of the elderly in their later years.
- *Gender hierarchy.* As in much of the world, males are afforded benefits, rewards, and preferences that are restricted to females. Maternal grandmothers may very well serve as the most common caregiver, but that doesn't necessarily mean they are treated with the respect they deserve and have earned.

Of course, all of these norms for prescribed behavior are not just influenced by the larger cultures but also those that developed within the specific family structure. In cases of parental separation, death, divorce, imprisonment, immigration, displacement, and other traumatic events, the rules are bent accordingly to accommodate the losses and particular challenges.

What Children Think

There's been relatively few investigations of children's perceptions of their grandparent relationships; however, one study from several years ago asked kids to draw pictures of their grandparents, revealing some distinctive trends (Kornhaber & Woodward, 1985). Some of the drawings portrayed the elders as large, vibrant figures, colored with lots of details, and actively involved in some activity, even if just holding the child's hand. Those children who had relatively infrequent contact with their grandparents portrayed them instead as small, colorless, lifeless figures, or perhaps as less than attractive figures. A third group that didn't know their grandparents at all, except as characters in family stories, depicted grandparents in cartoonish or stick figure versions. The idea was to use this simple diagnostic impression to assess the degree of connection between the two generations.

Although frequency of contact is important as an indicator of grandparent influence and impact, so too is the quality of the relationship in terms of intimacy, engagement, trust, and mutual respect. What children mention repeatedly is that they appreciate the opportunity to use their grandparents as sounding boards for their thoughts and ideas, an ongoing process that appears to enhance their own interpersonal sensitivity and relational skills (Hayslip et al., 2019). This appears to take place because of increased opportunities for the children to talk about their feelings, ask difficult questions, and improve their capacity for listening to diverse and different ideas (Freeman et al., 2019).

Some Grandparent Effects and Influences

One of the most well-researched consequences of grandparent influence and behavior within the family relates to educational achievement (Timonen, 2020). Across time, and within almost every cultural group and geographic location, the presence of active grandparents has been found to increase both the health and well-being of the children. Even more impressive is the impact on children's performance in school, whether the result of additional academic support and tutoring, or just as significant among highly educated grandparents, the modeling effects. In one study, for instance, it was found that if one or more grandparents was a member of the professional or managerial class as opposed to unskilled labor, their grandchildren were almost three times more likely to enter such a position themselves. Even more remarkable is this social mobility was evident even among families that had been in the lower socioeconomic class (Chan & Boliver, 2013). In many ways grandparents' involvement appears to compensate for some of the disadvantages and limitations imposed by poverty.

It is clear that grandparents' economic resources do have some impact on the children's own academic achievement, regardless of the parents own characteristics. This makes sense when you consider that affluent elders have better health care, live longer, and provide more resources and opportunities for the family. The magnitude of effect size seems to depend on a variety of other factors related to the location, culture, and characteristics of the people involved (Anderson et al., 2018). Nevertheless, grandparents spend over $2 billion dollars per year on their grandchildren, not just favoring them with toys and gifts but helping to provide for the family so that additional resources are available (David & Nelson-Kakulla, 2018).

There are various kinds of "capital" that elders are able to provide for families that go beyond economic resources to include cultural and social aspects that can all enhance educational success among the children (Mollegaard & Jaeger, 2015). It has also been demonstrated that when a grandchild and grandparent have a close, trusting, intimate relationship, *both* of them are better immunized against depression and other emotional difficulties (Moorman & Stokes, 2016).

Many of the earlier studies on grandparent effects were completed during times when the relationships lasted significantly fewer years than they would today—or certainly in the future. It is obvious that the next generations of grandparents will not only live longer, remain healthier, and retire earlier, but also have more discretionary time available for family matters. Previously limiting factors will be neutralized, allowing for more varied kinds of interactions beyond the traditional invitations to babysit on occasion. If three quarters of grandparents in the previous decade reported that they communicate with their grandchildren weekly via phone or in person, how will the frequency and types of interactions change now that texting, video calls, and soon avatars will allow for other options?

One thing is abundantly clear: Grandparent involvement with children increases their performance, both socially and academically. For every year of shared contact the likelihood of children completing secondary school increases by one percentage point, a significant effect that appears independent of financial status or family resources (Lehti et al., 2019). Besides their value as adult safety custodians, this may very well be one of the clearest examples of elder influence on the growth and development of children.

Review of Functions and Roles Adopted by Grandparents

Three quarters of grandparents describe themselves as "highly involved" with the children in their family, although this is defined in an assortment of different ways (Buchanan, 2019). Whether contact with the children takes place on a daily, weekly, or monthly basis, in person or via screens or phones, there are several significant roles and functions that are in evidence, beginning with that of the family historian, but also including other roles as a mentor, teacher, role model, or playmate.

Family Identity and Sense of Belonging

Who are we, and where do we come from? How are we different from others? How is our family unique? What are some of the critical events of our family history that you should know? What do we stand for? These are just a few of the core questions that elders are best positioned to answer.

Ideally, grandparents support and reinforce parental authority and values rather than undermine them in favor of their own preferences that may not fit well with the established norms. Disputes commonly occur over discipline strategies, eating choices, bedtime rituals, and completing assigned chores. Of course this depends on whether the alternative policies are considered (somewhat objectively) as beneficial and consistent with sound practices. In some cases, grandparents may attempt to redirect, or at least negotiate, alternatives for significant and defensible reasons.

Throughout history and across time, one of the primary roles of elders has been to teach subsequent generations the background, history, values, and unique features of cultural and family identity as distinct from others. This is what creates and maintains a sense of community and provides continuity across generations.

Religious, Moral, and Spiritual Education

Two thirds of grandparents are actively involved with their grandchildren discussing religious ideas. Half of them also say they regularly attend religious worship with the kids. As such, elders are considered the stewards of spiritual development. In addition, based on their own value system they attempt to impart a sense of morality to the young, teaching the differences between "right" and "wrong." Of course this is also defined in a multitude of ways, which can be consistent with community norms or way outside the realm of what might be considered appropriate. That's why parents attempt to closely monitor which lessons might be introduced so as to correct or adjust things that they don't consider suitable. This can also lead to potential conflicts when there are significant differences between the two perspectives. One parent may belong to a different religious tradition than the mother's or father's parents, or perhaps not follow any particular traditional belief system at all.

Storytelling and Life Experiences

It has been observed that human life is not actually composed of atomic molecules but rather is constructed by the stories we live, and those we share (Kottler, 2015). In that sense, we become almost immortal as long as those narratives continue to become passed on from one generation to the next. As has been mentioned, this is far more important than simply regaling children with interesting tales of one's adventures, tragedies, or triumphs, since these narratives eventually become the memories that last a lifetime.

One of the distinguishing features of our species is the ability to pass along valuable cultural knowledge and wisdom to future generations. Long before books, YouTube videos, and blogs were in fashion, this process most often took place in the form of songs, stories, myths, and oral sagas that were featured by elders as part of their jobs. Although parents have traditionally been focused on teaching practical skills like how to avoid a predator or throw a spear, grandparents have been concerned more with the larger pictures of how we fit in the world.

Most people can easily recall some of their favorite, seminal stories told to them by grandparents or other elders. They may include significant life lessons or simply hold amusing, interesting, captivating anecdotes. The narratives often provide a sense of history and continuity, the foundation of establishing a personal identity.

FIGURE 8.2   Sharing stories, whether reading favorite books or sharing one's own life lessons and experiences, is among the most important roles that grandparents and elders serve in almost every culture. This is not only just about entertainment but also one of the primary avenues for imparting values and instilling a sense of family identity.

Life Skills

There are particular abilities and skills that are considered essential to navigate the complexities of daily life. Just this week, my 9-year-old granddaughter was at a reception attended by some community leaders. To prepare her for this event we practiced greeting one another by shaking hands with a firm grip and making direct eye contact. We rehearsed these gestures over and over until she had the basics down. I mention this as just one example of all the different kinds of things that grandparents and elders are inclined to teach children beyond any school curriculum.

Grandparents are known to pass along family recipes, teaching children how to prepare these savory legacies. Other critical life skills are introduced, or reinforced, by grandparents, depending on what is considered most valuable. Sometimes these aren't intentional life lessons but rather the result of modeling certain behaviors that we might admire or want for ourselves, or in some cases, they are simply internalized unconsciously. I am *always* early when I show up for any event, class, presentation, appointment, meeting, or social gathering, all of which follow the template I witnessed in my grandfather's behavior. There are so many other things that we adopt as our own habits, often unaware of their origins that were once modeled for us by elders.

Shared Leisure Pursuits

Whether physical activities, playing catch outside, visiting museums, collecting stamps or coins, baking cookies, doing puzzles or playing games, or even more adventurous endeavors like hiking, traveling, or skiing, grandparents often introduce children to new and fun things to do that create indelible memories. But far more than that, grandparents often teach critical life skills related to cooking, building things, managing finances, mending clothes, and appreciating art or literature.

Many, if not most people, remember their interactions with grandparents as mostly fun engagements that were quite different from other relationships. There are adaptations required by both parties because of age differences and physical capabilities. In addition, whereas such activities might be viewed as mostly a form of play and entertainment, contained within those interactions are often the sort of social support that leads to greater emotional resiliency and prosocial behavior (Moorman & Stokes, 2016).

Core Values and Beliefs

"My grandfather warned me over and over again to never trust White people, never to let them get too close to me. I was told they will always betray me—or exploit me." This was a confession shared with me by an African American colleague I was mentoring in his first academic position. He was the only minority faculty member on the staff and had mostly kept to himself until I initially approached him. It had been obvious to me that he was somewhat cautious and ambivalent about my offer of help. We eventually became close friends, but I found it remarkable that his grandfather's influence had been so powerful and enduring so many years after he left the small town in Georgia where he'd grown up. This seemed like a remarkably clear example of how one's core values and belief system is influenced by family elders, even when the advice itself may not be that advantageous or accurate in all situations. But in this case, the grandfather had felt repeatedly abused by White people throughout his life, so he felt it important to pass along that life lesson to his grandson, who was obviously destined for great things. The problem, of course, was that now he was operating in a world composed exclusively of those he had been warned were untrustworthy. To this day I just can't imagine how confusing, if not terrifying, that must have been for him.

One of the most common ways that children develop a personalized and individualized value system over time is via the stories told to them by their grandparents and other elders. In addition, many of their life and career goals were initially shaped by these conversations (Silverstein, 2019). It is these stories about "what used to be," or "what I wish I'd done," or "what it was really like to be in that situation," that become enduring and influential memories.

Caregiving and Babysitting

This is perhaps the most common practice expected of grandparents, even for those who are very limited in their family involvement. They may be invited once a week or month to show up while the parents are out on the town or busy with work responsibilities. In some cases they become chauffeurs on demand, on call to transport children to various activities when the parents are otherwise occupied. Depending on interest and availability, the practice may become a regular habit, especially if the children treat the visits as a special occasion rather than an obligation (or punishment) they must endure.

Depending on the skill set, interests, and commitment of the grandparents during these childcare occasions, the parents may have to do some damage control afterward to neutralize some of the breaches in norms and rules that have been established in the household. These could be related to relaxing rules related to bedtime, snack choices, or even permitting behavior and activities that have been expressly forbidden.

Protection, Safety, and Health

Among all the roles and functions that elders may serve within the family, perhaps the most critical one of all is preserving the safety of the children and protecting them against dangers, temptations, accidents, and risks that may compromise their health or mortality. Grandparents or other older relatives may be recruited or asked to step in when one or both parents are unable or unwilling to fulfil their caretaking role. Emotional difficulties, drug or alcohol abuse, antisocial or criminal behavior, family conflicts, unemployment, separation, divorce, health problems, relocation, abandonment, neglect, imprisonment, and immigration or refugee status could all be causes of family disruption that require an intervention.

A number of studies reviewed consistently reveal that when there is extra adult supervision and childcare available within the family, there are manifold positive outcomes for the children beyond just preventing them from being injured (Sadruddin et al., 2019). Cognitive abilities, school performance, language and motor development, emotional regulation, and health status are all potentially improved by the presence of competent and dedicated elders. In addition, children are more protected from injuries, accidents, health issues, and other environmental dangers.

What About the Roles and Functions of Great-Grandparents?

By definition, great-grandparents tend to be considerably older than the previous generation, thus a bit more limited in the functions they may be able to serve. For many among the oldest family cohort, perhaps in their 80s and beyond, their roles are minimal, marginal, or nonexistent (Even-Zohar, 2019). For those who are healthier and more physically active, they may sometimes babysit, but they really specialize in sharing stories about the past, about their lives, and about the history of their families.

There have been two very different conceptions of the roles and functions that great-grandparents serve, the first of which, as mentioned, is essentially meaningless except in name only. They may be disengaged from the family for a variety of reasons related to health, distance, cognitive functioning, or just lack of interest. The second model, however, is one that recognizes this as another extension of being a grandparent, a sort of second stage. They may, in some cases, operate as custodial primary caregivers. They may also have financial resources to help bolster the economic stability of the family.

Unfortunately for great-grandparents who wish to have active and continual engagement with the young children, they have to navigate two levels of gatekeepers who control access—first their own children who may resent intrusions into their territory as grandparents, and secondly the parents who would also have their own rules and boundaries. This is likely to become far more complicated in the future as increased longevity creates more great-grandparents, as well as the sorts of blended families that include additional elders from remarriages.

Mutually Negotiated Roles and Functions

Within multigenerational households, grandparents become fully integrated into daily life, providing support (and sometimes burdens) on multiple levels. Reflecting on the diversity of impact in families, one third of Americans can't even name all four of their grandparents, and one fifth can't identify a single great-grandparent. This is in spite of the report that 85% of those surveyed say it is important to know about their heritage. When pressed further about what they would most like to know from their grandparents, three quarters say they want to hear stories about what it was like for them when they were young; two thirds want to know more about their origin and heritage (Haslam, 2021).

The various responsibilities and tasks that elders serve within a family vary tremendously depending on the context, culture, and particular circumstances in which they live. Just as in everything else in life there is a marked difference between choosing to do something versus being pressured or coerced into doing so. When grandparents have been permitted to negotiate roles and functions that are best suited to their abilities, skill sets, and availability, they have consistently been found across the world to provide so much more than babysitting services or inherited wealth. They also provide "social capital" in the form cultural, historical, and social knowledge that is far more enduring and impactful as long-term benefits. But whether grandparents find their roles and functions to be satisfying depends on their own sense of agency and perception of personal initiative, rather than just being slaves to parental whims.

In a massive study of almost 100,000 families comparing grandparent custodial care to that of parental care, it was hardly surprising to find that the children raised by family elders tended to have more developmental problems and more challenging temperaments and produced more aggravation for their caregivers. What was most interesting, however, was that the grandparents appeared to cope just about as well as parents in facing these challenges (Rapoport et al., 2020).

It is clear from our discussion thus far that although there are general statements and inferences we can make about the nature of elder influence and functions within the family, as well as the larger community, it is also the case that variations of these themes are the norm. There are just so many different cultural backgrounds, family traditions, family compositions and structures that broad generalizations lead to multiple exceptions. Then, of course, influential effects are varied according to the particular interpersonal and grandparent style that is adopted, a subject we will take up in the next chapter.

QUESTIONS FOR REFLECTION OR DISCUSSION

1. What are some of the most valuable lessons that a grandparent (or elder) taught you growing up?
2. Take inventory (for better *and* worse) of the ways you have been most influenced, affected, and shaped by elders who were your grandparents, supervisors, or mentors.
3. Given some of the dramatic changes taking place with regard to increased longevity and health of the elderly, plus the greater flexibility of lifestyle and evolving values in the wider culture, what new roles would you assign older people to enhance their community, as well as their own sense of well-being and life satisfaction?

Figure Credits

Fig. 8.1: Source: https://ur.booksc.me/book/57829564/fe694c.
Fig. 8.2: Source: https://www.pexels.com/photo/a-family-looking-at-a-album-8307717/.

CHAPTER 9

Grandparenting Styles

Parents and teachers tend to have very different interpersonal and instructional styles. Some are rather structured, strict, and demanding, while others are far more permissive, flexible, and informal. Some see themselves primarily as expert authorities, while others conceptualize their roles as supportive facilitators. It isn't surprising, therefore, that elders and grandparents also exert influence in many different ways depending on their personalities, abilities, and personal preferences.

Although there are considerable variations in grandparenting styles, it is clear that some approaches may definitely be considered more effective than others. This is especially the case with regard to those that lead to greater cooperation and high functioning within the family. On the other hand, some grandparents can be extremely annoying, meddlesome, neglectful, even to the point that their meddling can undermine family stability. These differences are shaped not only by an elder's personality, values, and social and relational skills, but also the circumstances within the family.

It is hardly unexpected that particular styles of caregiving and parenting produce quite different results and outcomes. What works best for one family or child is not necessarily ideal for others. Individual children may respond best to greater freedom and flexibility, or else highly structured, disciplined, and programmed interventions. Some (grand)parenting approaches are consistently overprotective while others appear somewhat laissez-faire, if not indifferent. So much depends on the quality of relationships that have been developed with the children, as well as negotiated with the parents. None of this occurs in isolation but as part of the structure and dynamics of each family. Far more than that, our species has been described as among the few "cooperative" childrearing species in which biological parents must rely on elders and other members of their "tribe" in order to tackle that lengthy, exhausting, and time-consuming process of raising and launching offspring (Hrdy, 2017; Li et al., 2019).

Styles Do Matter

Just as there are different parenting styles that have been classified, there are also distinct ways that grandparents interpret their roles within the family (Cherlin & Furstenberg, 1985). Two of the more traditional styles within middle-class families, especially several years ago, were the "distant figure" and "formal styles," that are already familiar from portrayals in media. Either because the grandparents live far away, or just don't wish to be actively involved with the children, "distant figures" show up a few times each year or on special occasions. "Formal grandparents" may live nearby but they still view their roles as somewhat limited other than periodic babysitting. They are careful not to become involved in parenting issues related to discipline, schooling, or decision-making.

The exact opposite style of the previous ones mentioned, the "surrogate parent," actually ends up serving this function by taking primary responsibility for childcare, either because one or both parents are absent or work excessive hours. Within some cultural groups grandparents are expected to assume major family authority and take on the roles as "senior parents." Related to this style is the more authoritarian posture in which the grandparent(s) become reservoirs of wisdom and enforce compliance to family values established by them.

The fifth style, the "fun-seeker," is perceived as a source of amusement, storytelling, and playful interactions with children. This is another kind of engaged, active grandparenting, but instead of being focused on strict rules and education the relationship is organized around mutual enjoyment and indulgence. This can sometimes turn out as mixed results for the welfare of children if grandparents are excessively permissive, impacting their diet, weight, and even susceptibility to diseases.

More recently grandparent styles have been studied to determine which ones tend to lead to emotional regulation and a sense

FIGURE 9.1   Styles of grandparenting vary according to a number of factors beyond one's personality and may include health status, interests, generational cohort, gender, cultural background, family configuration, and, of course, the needs of the children. The traditional, formal style that was popular a generation ago has been augmented by other styles in recent years that emphasize more of a companion role that includes informal, fun activities in addition to caregiving responsibilities.

of autonomy versus those that often produce behavioral or emotional problems because of difficulties setting boundaries and enforcing limits (Li et al., 2019). One other model examines how the particular style of grandparenting reflects the extent to which it holds significant personal identity versus meeting expectations of social responsibility (Bone, 2018). In other words, it can be experienced as a joyous, chosen role that provides meaningful satisfaction, or else as an obligation that was required because of family circumstances. These respective situations would influence the extent to which grandparenting is viewed as a relatively minor investment of time or a major source of satisfaction and personal pride. As mentioned earlier, these particular styles would be affected by the older person's age, health, living conditions, financial situation, and personal rewards.

A Brief Review of Physical and Cognitive Changes Associated With Aging

Although the vast majority of people over 65 years of age maintain a high degree of active engagement and cognitive functioning, there are some realities that must also be faced that compromise energy levels and the sorts of activities that are still feasible. The fact of the matter is that some elderly people age quite successfully in the sense that they have adapted to certain limitations and compensated for other losses that allow them to maintain a high level of engagement. There are others, as well, who live mostly in the past, struggle with loneliness and depression, and remain mostly inert.

There are certain inevitable challenges that older people face in the latter stages of life. Their willingness and ability to deal with these changes affects not only their daily functioning and sense of well-being, but also their ability to respond effectively as grandparents or caregivers. The following developmental challenges are most common:

- Disengagement from previous responsibilities, obligations, and work
- Maintaining a degree of independence and self-sufficiency
- Negotiating new and different social support and community
- Dealing with declining health, chronic diseases
- Adapting to reduced energy, stamina, and memory
- Taking on new roles as mentor, grandparent, and elder within community and family
- Counteracting discrimination and ageism
- Recovering from grief and losses of longtime friends and partner
- Coming to terms with impending death

There are many elder politicians, writers, historians, artists, and entrepreneurs who have remained just as successful in later life, even completed their best work after hitting 70 years old. There are many such "late bloomers" who never imagined, much less predicted, they'd end up with their greatest achievements well into old age.

There are, of course, limitations placed on such successes and capabilities in later life. Memory and decision-making are not nearly as efficient. Physical energy is somewhat reduced. Sleep disruption is common. Yet this is also consistently reported as the single most satisfying stage of life, one that allows for reflection, synthesis of experiences, and the attainment of wisdom. To the extent that grandparents have managed to successfully adapt and navigate physical changes taking place they are in a far better position to demonstrate compassion, patience, empathy, and hovering attention on their grandchildren. Their own exuberance and passion for life becomes contagious. Once again, however, the potential and possibilities of one's capability in *any* domain depends not only on interest and motivation, but also adaptation to a style that is congruent with health, energy, and personal characteristics.

Generational Cohorts, Culture, and Context Influence Caregiving Style

The particular type and style of caregiving also depends on the role and functions that are served within the particular family. There is a clear difference in responsibilities between someone who is a full-time custodial caregiver versus another who shows up for a brief visit on occasion for fun and games. There are thus several different types of engagement that are possible.

Part-time grandparents. This is perhaps the most common subtype in many Western cultures in which visitations occur based on need and interest, whether as a driver, kid sitter, or running errands. It is the least demanding and stressful style because activities and choices are usually mutually negotiated in ways that are most convenient. Depending on employment status, social engagements, and other interests, time investment ranges from minimum to moderate commitments.

Multiple-generation household. In this configuration the grandparents live with the family and assume major responsibility and care for the children. It is often the case that grandparents may have serious health or financial issues that require them to live with their own children. Style of engagement with children depends on the degree of mobility and health status of the grandparents as there may often be mutual caregiving taking place in which both the children and grandparents require some supervision.

Grandparent head of household. In this reversal of the previous type the parents and/or grandchildren may be forced to reside with the grandparents because of necessity or financial issues. The grandparents typically retain more power and control since they are the ones providing assistance.

Custodial grandparents. In cases of neglect, abandonment, addictions, death, or incarceration, children may end up living full-time with grandparents as the only willing and qualified caregivers. Half of all such households involve minority groups, and many experience financial hardships and represent the highest levels of stress. The job is considerably more challenging since these grandparents tend to be poorer, less educated, in worse health, more socially isolated, and face more serious discipline issues (Hayslip et al., 2021).

This classification of schemes might highlight the variations in what elders may be asked—or required—to do, but the differences are even more vast when considering individual traits of all those within the family. These personality characteristics and temperament are shaped by both genetics and cultural influences. Given that a grandparent might be 40, 60, or 80 years of age, these imply quite different generational cohorts, each of which reflect different values, interests, and priorities. Their tastes in music and entertainment are different, just as their relative competency with technology may vary considerably. The particular age of grandparents, their gender, race, ethnicity, and health status, would also operate as factors that lead to their caregiving styles.

Just as in any other aspect of life, people most appreciate spending time with others who are generally optimistic, hopeful, supportive, empathic, respectful, and caring. Adding to the mix is that personalities tend to evolve as people age. Some elders have become more patient, accepting, supportive, even-tempered, and easygoing over time, while others changed in the opposite direction, becoming more irritable, impatient, critical, frustrated, moody, even depressed and needy.

Each of us is born with a particular temperament that can readily be witnessed soon after birth. Some infants are fussy, demanding, and quick to react, while others are born relatively calm and easy-going. Such early personality reactive styles have been used to predict emotional problems later in life (Morales et al., 2021), although life experiences, education, parenting, and other factors also exert considerable influence. In the case of older people, those early tendencies and traits become considerably diluted with age, often replaced with other relational habits that have been learned in order to increase (or diminish) one's capacity for empathy, affection, compassion, and caring.

In addition to whatever personality traits are favored, none of them matter very much if the elder or grandparent isn't perceived as truly "available." This is meant not just in the sense of being physically present on regular basis but also truly accessible during interactions. They see their time spent with grandchildren as truly a privilege, as the most important job in their lives that deserves their complete and full attention and mastery. This attitude would necessarily be accompanied by a certain degree of patience and generosity that make anyone more approachable and safe to talk about things that matter the most. This relates to the observation—and brain scans that support the research—that emotional empathy is the key to optimal relational engagement with children (Rilling et al., 2021).

Toxic Grandparents and Challenging Behaviors

There are several common ways that grandparents' behavior can become problematic within the family, all of which reflect a certain degree of inattention, dysfunction, ignorance, malice, or lack of ability. Some of these actions (or inactions) can only be considered annoying while others might be experienced as truly toxic and dangerous. In some cases the children's health and safety may be seriously jeopardized. In other instances, there are increased conflicts, arguments, and disruption in the family.

Undermining Parents

Whether spoiling the children as an effort to win favor or seeking to sabotage existing rules for personal preference, this is probably the single most common breach of goodwill; in some situations this can escalate into more serious and chronic difficulties if left unchecked. It is not only confusing for children when adults attempt to undermine or disrespect one another, but it also sends the wrong message when existing rules are allowed to be flagrantly ignored by those who don't agree to support them.

One of the most consistently ineffectual parenting styles occurs when partners counteract or sabotage one another, allowing children to play them against one another. When grandparents don't agree to abide by the rules of the house, feeling entitled to do whatever they want, it is the children who may ultimately suffer as a result of this inconsistency. This isn't just about slipping a kid a piece of candy or allowing children to stay up a few minutes past bedtime, but rather deliberate, strategic efforts to disrupt the status quo because it doesn't fit with one's own preferences.

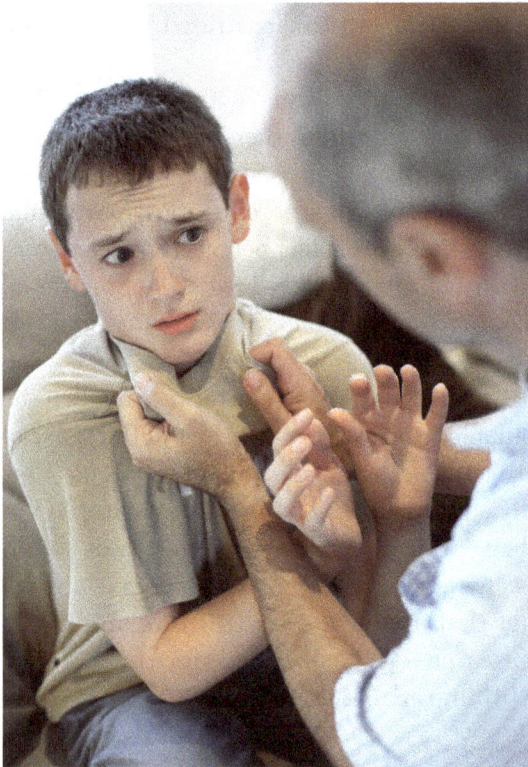

FIGURE 9.2   Among the most toxic behaviors displayed by dysfunctional grandparents is a tendency to be extremely critical, shaming, even abusive toward children when they don't cooperate as expected. Often these expectations are out of touch with reality, beyond the scope of what is truly possible for children to comply.

Feeling a Sense of Entitlement

Age does offer some benefits and a degree of respect, but not to the point that elders are permitted to do whatever they want, regardless of how such behavior fits into family norms. When grandparents are only willing to do whatever is convenient for them it means that everyone else must accommodate their preferences. This can create additional burdens and stress instead of actually providing useful assistance.

In the worst examples of this toxic behavior, grandparents appear to have little interest in the actual welfare of the children and are only concerned with maintaining their own sense of power and control during a time in life when they are slipping away. In cases when they don't necessarily get what they want, behavior escalates into a victim mentality trying to earn sympathy and further attention.

Although these descriptions are focused on the specific actions of the grandparent(s) there is more likely a systemic circular dynamic going on in which other family members are triggered by the behavior, which, in turn, leads them toward increased oppositional behavior. Parents will increasingly argue among themselves, blaming one another for in-laws' meddling or inappropriate behavior. Guilt ensues in which one or both parents, as well as the children, feel like they've done something wrong by setting limits. In worst case scenarios, all of family life can become disrupted.

Manipulative and Controlling Behavior

Some grandparents will attempt to bribe children with favors, gifts, and treats in order to pressure them into doing certain things (chores, homework, obeying rules) or *not* doing certain things (fighting, arguing, making a mess). Even when clear limits have been established for screen time on devices or avoiding forbidden foods, the rules may be suspended, or ignored altogether, so that the grandparents can earn favor. In addition, the children are often spoiled, possibly encouraging their own sense of entitlement when things are denied to them in the future.

Another form of manipulative behavior relates to playing the "guilt card." It is sometimes unconscionable the extent to which a grandparent might say things like, "What kind of hug is that? I thought you loved me!" or "Unless you call me every week, no more presents for you!" Obviously, children are easy targets for such guilt games even as they struggle to make sense of love that is treated as conditional, depending on the extent to which you do what others want.

Playing Favorites

Just as parents love and respond to each of their children a bit differently, so too do grandparents have distinct preferences regarding which kids they prefer to spend time with. Usually there are just minor or subtle differences, but in extreme cases grandparents may make it fairly obvious that one child is clearly favored over others and given far more generous presents and attention. Once again, this can ignite a host of other problems such as increased sibling rivalry and insecurity on the part of the children who are ignored and promoting a sense of specialness in the favored child who receives all the extra attention.

One other variation of this theme relates to another type of favoritism in which one grandparent attempts to compete with the others to become perceived as the favorite. This can occur between spouses in which one grandparent resents that the other receives more displays of love and appreciation, but more often this can lead to conflicts between in-laws when one set inevitably spends more time with the children than the other. This may be the result of geographic proximity, but there is also a marked tendency that the mother's parents are usually granted greater access (Jamieson et al., 2018).

Where will the children go for holidays? Which set of grandparents are invited to go on family trips? Who is consistently invited for dinner or to attend the children's performances or sporting events? There is never perfect equality, and some grandparents can become rather oppositional and resentful about the distribution of opportunities to spend time with the children.

Saying Stupid or Hurtful Things

Regardless of their age and station in life, there are some people who are just plain mean, heartless, clueless, and highly critical—toward everyone and everything. They may be spiteful or have felt wronged throughout their lives—at this stage of life they may feel increasingly ignored and irrelevant, perhaps accelerating dormant, toxic aspects of their behavior. "It is just not like the olden days," is a frequently heard complaint.

Such grumpy, insensitive, even miserable individuals may consistently shame or criticize children whenever they make a mistake or do something considered "wrong." Or such behavior may result from impatience, ignorance, or a lack of understanding about the nature of children's behavior that does indeed appear inscrutable. Under conditions of stress or tension, they may say things that are hurtful and inappropriate. During extreme cases they lose their tempers and become wildly out of control, leading to emotional or even physical abuse, creating wounds that never quite heal.

It is far more commonplace that unwanted advice and opinions are offered that, at first, are only annoying but over time can become disruptive. A message is consistently communicated by elders: "You are doing this wrong! Why don't you listen to me?" Needless to say, any useful input is completely lost in all the noise. In addition, being "right" isn't necessarily appreciated when it is offered in a spirt of criticism and debasement.

Among all these toxic and challenging behaviors that have been mentioned, perhaps the most difficult of all is when the elder is not willing or open to change aspects of their functioning that others find disruptive or unhelpful. It is as if the response from parents or children to grandparent intrusions doesn't matter or doesn't even count: "I'm old. I'm not going to change. You'll just have to accept and deal with me the way I am, regardless of the collateral damage."

Who Are the Most Effective Grandparents?

If there is a clear consensus regarding which elder behavior within the family is most annoying and troublesome, there is also considerable agreement about what is considered most helpful and facilitative. This involves far more than merely being functional or adequate but rather refers to those who are truly exceptional in their ability and willingness to be of assistance in ways that are most appreciated and valued.

As we've seen there are wide differences within families and cultures as to what sorts of mentoring, guidance, and childcare are most needed or appreciated. Depending on the ages and interests of the children, employment and financial resources of the parents, geographic proximity to the grandparents, personalities involved, plus a host of other factors, different things might be expected.

Regardless of these variations there are still a few features and characteristics of optimal grandparenting that are somewhat universal regardless of the particular setting, context, and locale. Just as with any form of relational engagement, whether as friends, partners, colleagues, parents, neighbors, or psychotherapists, being "fully present" is imperative. This means that when interacting with family members, especially the children, the grandparent communicates complete and total involvement in whatever is going on, free from distractions. This means saying in essence, "I am here. I am with you. *You* are the most important person to me in the world right now. Nothing else exists except my focus and attention on you. *That's* how important you are to me!"

This is, of course, much easier to promise than it is to deliver. Nowadays it is so rare that *anyone*, in *any* situation, is willing to put aside their mobile devices and provide unwavering attention to anyone else without interruption or distraction. Nevertheless, it is a hallmark of any influential encounter, or any helping relationship, that the person who is being helped feels heard and understood, respected, and honored during the interactions. This just happens to be the single best predictor of a successful outcome in *any* helping relationship (Kottler, 2022b; Kottler & Balkin, 2017, 2020).

FIGURE 9.3   The hallmark of an effective grandparent isn't just related to adoration by the children but also an elder who supports the consensual ground rules of the home and works collaboratively with the parents.

When family members are asked their opinion about what matters the most to them in grandparent involvement and behavior, the results are pretty consistent across cultures and contexts. Everyone likes to be around someone who is passionate, enthusiastic, and exudes a joy for life. Obviously this is in marked contrast to someone who is always grumpy, critical, pessimistic, and a drag to be around because of their negative attitudes. Both children and parents thus prefer someone who is funny, playful, and enjoyable as a companion.

Although there are gender differences in grandchildren preferences, almost everyone agrees that a key factor is someone who is generally supportive. While males favor the idea of a key advisor and mentor, females prefer to think of their grandparents as companions and friends. In almost all cases, relationship quality was judged based on the degree of subjective emotional closeness and intimacy (Malonebeach et al., 2018). In addition, what appears to matter the most is a willingness to adapt one's style according to the particular needs of the children and unique demands of the family.

Apart from taking care of basic needs related to shelter, nutrition, education, and safety, both children and elders derive the greatest satisfaction from their intimate, loving, mutually affectionate relational bonds. Indelible memories are solidified by the shared activities that were experienced as fun, interesting, or otherwise led to greater closeness and intimacy.

QUESTIONS FOR REFLECTION OR DISCUSSION

1. As you look back on your mentoring experiences by grandparents, elders, or mentors you have known, what did they offer you that you felt was most and least helpful? What did you especially appreciate, and what do you wish had been handled differently?
2. Based on your experiences, what would you recommend to someone who is about to become a grandparent, mentor, or supervisor for others?
3. What are the qualities that you would consider most important for someone who is in a position to care for and mentor young people?

Figure Credits

Fig. 9.1: Source: https://pixabay.com/photos/grandpa-sleep-grandchild-girl-4051229/.
Fig. 9.2: Source: https://www.freeimages.com/photo/father-assaulting-son-2282905.
Fig. 9.3: Copyright © 2020 Depositphotos/photographee.au.

CHAPTER 10

Challenges, Myths, and Misconceptions About Elderly Caregivers

After a lifetime of studying cultural variations around the world, anthropologist Margaret Mead (1972) once remarked that "everyone needs to have access both to grandparents and grandchildren in order to be a fully human being" (p. 282). That is, of course, a lovely take on this significant developmental milestone, but it is hardly a universal experience on the part of every family and elder.

As much as grandparents have sometimes been idealized and romanticized, there is considerable stress and difficulty that many people report serving in those roles. Health limitations, physical disabilities, energy depletion, reduced resources, limited mobility, lack of sanctioned authority, and embedded family dysfunction all contribute to undermine efforts. Probably most challenging of all is often the particular dynamics and relational behavior of the children as far as their behavior, issues, struggles, and attitudes. Some children are reasonably compliant, cooperative, and responsive while others are consistently obstructive and defiant, sometimes even verbally or physically aggressive.

In spite of these possible limitations there are also some cultural beliefs and myths perpetuated in the media regarding the experiences of older adults, most of which are unsupported by research. These include but are not limited to the idea that the aged are more likely to be unhappy when, in fact, this may very well be the most satisfying time in life (Levitin, 2020). Other common myths are that grandparents are often disabled and incapacitated, disengaged and isolated, experiencing major memory loss and cognitive functioning, none of which are true the majority of time (Kottler & Carlson, 2016). Nevertheless, these beliefs and attitudes present one of the challenges that are faced by grandparents when their efforts are sometimes devalued and minimized.

This latter stage of life is often characterized by what developmental theorists like Erik and Joan Erikson (1998) described as "generativity" or the interest, if not passion, in passing along a lifetime of wisdom and experience to the next generation. This has historically been achieved largely through storytelling, teaching grandchildren and others in the community about historical legacies, collective identity, and reminiscences about significant events that have occurred.

As far as the greatest challenges that grandparents must navigate, number one on the list is the overwhelming worry and concern about the welfare and safety of the children. Also frequently cited as obstacles include (a) disagreements and lack of collaboration with other family members (especially parents), (b) feeling little power to make and implement decisions in the best interests of the children, (c) experiencing the legal system as an annoying impediment, (d) lack of financial resources, (e) poor physical health or low energy, (f) dealing with a difficult child, (g) feeling forced or pressured into responsibilities that are not comfortable or desired, and (h) lacking much support (Hayslip et al., 2020). So many of these difficulties are only exacerbated by pervasive beliefs that further compromise and limit the ability of older people to remain productive and useful.

Stereotypes and Myths

Just as there are stereotypes for every age group, the elderly are subject to more than their fair share of soul-crushing attitudes that often describe them in extremes of being lonely, reclusive, bitter, living in the past, or else that they are loving, kind, proud, and nostalgic. Most of these conceptions are extremely inaccurate, leading to ageism and mostly negative overgeneralizations.

There are many examples of how this plays out during everyday interactions when older people hear things like, "You look great *for your age*," "I can't believe you are *still* driving/working out/dancing," "I guess that was a *senior moment* when you forgot about that." Just consider all the derogatory names that have been used to describe older people, hundreds of terms like battle axe, dirty old man, geezer, old dog, no spring chicken, old granny, old maid, codger, crone, old bag, old fart, grave dodger, fossil, and stick in the mud.

As if the verbal slights aren't humiliating enough, there are whole industries devoted to helping elderly people minimize or deny their actual age. First there are all the anti-aging cosmetics, diets, cosmetic surgery, hair implants, and hair coloring, assisting older people to disguise themselves to appear younger. Then the marketing strategies and social media "influencers" all induce people to feel shame about themselves unless they make herculean efforts to make themselves look younger. Finally, added to the mix are the prevalent myths associated with aging that continue to perpetuate the discrimination, marginalization, and prejudices toward the elderly. The accumulative result portrays them as essentially hapless, confused, forgetful, stubborn, and handicapped, both in their cognitive and physical functioning. Some of the most common examples of such myths include the following (Kottler, 2022a).

Genetics and family history determine an older person's health and life span. Although it is certainly the case that we all inherit certain biological predispositions and risk factors based on family history, roughly two thirds of the factors that influence longevity and active engagement relate to one's lifestyle choices, health practices, medical care, diet, exercise, and especially one's attitudes and cognitive mind-set (Niechcial, Vaportzis, & Gow, 2022).

With age you become weak, unstable, and frail. This may be true for those with serious health conditions, or those who don't engage in regular exercise, but it is the exception for people who remain highly active and physically robust and who feel productive in their daily activities.

FIGURE 10.1   One of the popular myths related to aging is that older people become frail, weak, unstable, and confused. The reality is that a small percentage of the elderly do lose memory functioning and mobility, but the vast majority remain vigorous and highly active. Although he was indeed frail as a child, and didn't learn to walk until he was 5, Fauja Singh began running marathon races at the age of 90 and became the oldest person to complete a marathon at the age of 101.

You lose your mind and memory in old age. It is certainly the case that memory and cognitive functioning are not quite as sharp as they once were earlier in life, but very few elderly people ever develop dementia or severe memory impairment. Most people find ways to adjust and adapt to changes that take place in the body and mind.

Older people are rigid, risk avoidant, conservative, and resistant to change. Some are—and some are not. Many have prepared their whole lives to finally do things that weren't possible earlier. Some of the greatest creative achievements took place during the last stage of life. In addition, although it is true that the speed of learning, and its retention, diminishes over time, the capacity for learning on a more global scale, making connections between varied sources of information, is actually enhanced.

Old age leads to depression, loneliness, and helplessness. Surprisingly, this is the stage of life when most people experience their greatest satisfaction and contentment. It is also a time when people report that they feel the *least* lonely since they rely on fewer friendships and have more realistic expectations.

One of the reasons older people may have difficulty attaining greater satisfaction with their position in life is that they buy into the myths related to aging that are perpetuated by our culture. One example of this is that younger adults and teenagers often assess their popularity and social satisfaction in quantitative terms, how many "friends" they have on social media, the number of "likes" they receive, how expansive their social circle is, the relative status of their group, the number of invitations they receive to social events, and the number of different people they interact with throughout the day. As mentioned previously, elderly people are far more selective in the choices they make regarding who they want to spend time with. They are more inclined to limit social contacts to just a few, intimate friends along with family members. They are no longer willing to "waste" their limited, precious time left engaged in relatively meaningless social encounters or spending time with those who they don't value all that much.

The myths and misconceptions about aging in later life are just as prevalent when exploring the status and condition of grandparents. Most of them, for instance, are not necessarily that old, the majority of whom are younger than 60 and many in their 50s or even 40s. There has also been a myth that elders and grandparents have significantly less influence than in the past—which is also not true as we have reviewed in prior chapters: On the contrary, they are not only around much longer because of increased life span, but also the resources, knowledge, wisdom, and caregiving skills are in great demand. More than ever before, grandparents are better educated, more financially stable, and more physically active, capable of doing things never imagined previously.

A Review of Challenges

Although it is well known that parents have more than their fair share of challenges to face in their jobs of growing and launching a young person, the additional burdens of grandparents can take things to a whole different level of difficulty. This is not just the result of more advanced age and perhaps less energy but also the consequence of serving in what has been described as a "counter-transitional" role (Thiele & Whelan, 2006). This means that personal choice is significantly reduced since it is always other people (the parents or the court system) that determine if, when, where, and how often this ever takes place. Most grandparents actually have significantly less power to decide their role in the family since those decisions are usually made by their own children. This leads to a degree of uncertainty and confusion about the type of involvement they are permitted, tasks that may not be consistent with their own expectations and preferences.

Reconfigured Families

The quality of childcare depends, in part, on the cooperation and high functioning of the parenting partners. If there is trouble in the relationship, if conflicts and disagreements are commonplace, then this is obviously going to affect the ways that they coordinate their teaching, disciplinary, and caregiving efforts. Although the divorce rate has generally been diminishing over time, among older couples it has actually tripled (Ganong et al., 2019). This means that the number of elderly people who are now single, separated, divorced, or cohabitating with successive partners has led to multiple configurations of living arrangements, some of them more unstable than others. In addition, increased divorce and remarriages have also resulted in various forms of step-grandparents within families, leading to additional complications and multiple older adults involved. How this is all negotiated and worked out adds a certain complexity to the mix.

There are additional legal obstacles to overcome as families become increasingly blended and reconfigured. Grandparents may have difficulty with access, custody, or guardianship for the children, even when they are clearly the most capable and best options. Their tenuous status in such situations also makes it harder for them to utilize support services within the community.

Children's Behavior and Adjustment

Perhaps the greatest challenge of all for grandparents (and everyone else) relates to children's own behavior, issues, and concerns. For those children who are acting out in extreme ways, experiencing severe mental health issues, struggling in school, abusing drugs and alcohol, becoming increasingly obstructive and discipline problems, stress levels within the family can reach intolerable levels. No matter how patient, skilled, and loving a caregiver might be, there are definite limits to what can be managed when children (especially belligerent, unhappy adolescents!) continue to resist any efforts at control or parenting.

When grandparents have been interviewed about the daily annoyances and hassles that disturb them the most, the item most frequently mentioned involves the children's behavior that is perceived as uncooperative or frustrating. Most of the next sources of stress involve feeling the burdens of too much responsibility or too many tasks beyond what they can comfortably handle (Mendoza et al., 2020).

One of the most frequently cited challenges and annoyances relates to providing a healthy and nutritious diet for the children, a task that is made so much more difficult by the diverse ways that "healthy diet" is defined and practiced (Jongenelis et al., 2021). Adding to potential conflict is the resistance that children often display in response to consuming certain foods that are supposed to be good for you but "taste icky." Clearly grandparents want the children to follow a healthy diet, just as they prefer to restrict unhealthy options, yet they must navigate the complexities of the parents' own rules, the children's distinct preferences and resistance patterns, plus their own opinions about what they believe is in everyone's best interests, which may not jive with those in power.

Another challenge that elders and grandparents often struggle with involves management of interactive media and screen time (Elias et al., 2019). Some of this is based on a lack of experience or familiarity with the technology, but it is also the result of a marked reluctance to set limits when the games or shows are so convenient for babysitting and occupying children's attention.

Parental Gatekeeping

In many ways, grandparents and other adult caregivers can be easily undermined. As we've discussed previously, it is the parents, as legal guardians, who control access to children, a situation that can easily escalate into a power struggle. If the mother doesn't particularly like or trust her in-laws, or favors her own parents to an extreme degree, one set of grandparents can be excluded from access to the family. Likewise, if the father's parents don't approve of their son's choice for a partner, they can also become problematic and disruptive in their behavior.

It is not uncommon that parents and grandparents have different perspectives and approaches to childcare based on their own attitudes, preferences, and prior experience. The older generation may be perceived as having different standards that directly conflict with those of the parents who hold the power. This can sometimes lead to interesting negotiations and discussions, but just as often can lead to chronic disputes and disagreements. Needless to say, when the adults are not functioning as a team, it bodes poorly for the children's ultimate welfare.

In cases of divorce or estrangement within the family, whatever existing difficulties were in evidence are likely to increase significantly. Paternal grandparents may have far more trouble gaining access to the children and, in some cases, may be prevented from contact altogether. As is usually the case, they already have fewer opportunities to interact with the children compared to maternal parents (Barnett & Connidis, 2019).

What are some examples of the mistakes that grandparents most commonly make that drive the parents crazy? One article (Crow & Coleman, 2020) listed more than 60 of them, but the most frequently mentioned include (a) posting photos or stories about children on social media without permission, (b) attempting to raise and discipline the kids exactly the way it was done a generation ago, (c) refusing to follow established safety practices, (d) breaking the rules for bedtime rituals, (e) giving unwanted opinions—over and over and over again, (f) repeating many of the same mistakes with grandchildren that were made with own children, and (g) using screen time or the television as a babysitter. Suffice to say, the list of other annoyances is rather exhaustive.

Ignorance and Obsolescence

There are inevitable intergenerational disputes within families because of a clash of values and priorities based on the very different contexts of their lives. Unfortunately, this is not an equally balanced battle because the ultimate power lies with the parents who are the legal guardians. As has been mentioned previously, grandparents have relatively few rights with respect to access to the children. Sometimes this becomes a tragic and unfair situation in which a family dispute has escalated to become an estrangement that restricts visitation.

In other instances, however, parents decide to restrict or cancel contact because of actions they view as "deal breakers" in the sense that they exhibit inappropriate or even dangerous behavior. If the elder has a history of alcohol or drug abuse, inclinations to become violent or abusive, or a tendency to neglect basic needs, these could be legitimate reasons to block unsupervised contact. In other situations, the grandparent's intentions can be understandable, even admirable, but the actions are based on poor reasoning and judgment, ignorance, or lack of ability to do what is most needed. In such cases the children's welfare and safety may have been compromised, requiring that future safeguards are put in place.

There are certain health risks that are increased when adult caregivers are not familiar with the latest and best practices based on sound evidence rather than myths from the past. In one survey of grandparents it was found that almost half of them still believed that the best way to reduce a child's fever is immersion in ice baths, a practice that has long since been discredited (Brunissen et al., 2020). Another example relates to the belief of one third of grandparents who were not aware of the safest sleep positions for infants to prevent sudden infant death syndrome (SIDS). This use of outdated health practices is further complicated by technological limitations such as being unable to figure out how to use the school website or register online for activities.

Even when warned and reminded multiple times, a caregiver may consistently choose to ignore norms and rules that are considered inviolate. This can either mean the person is forgetful, indicating cognitive impairment, or also just stubbornly refusing to honor the agreement. Examples of this might include failing to use safety restraints or booster seats when driving, giving the kids treats and candy when it is specifically prohibited, or losing track of where the children are playing. In other instances, the grandparents may attempt to "buy" affection by showering children with questionable gifts.

It is important to keep in mind that with any new role or job in life there is expected to be a learning curve in which skill acquisition and competence gradually increase with experience and practice. First-time grandparents thus are likely to make more mistakes as initial ground rules and boundaries are negotiated. Despite parental preferences, the likelihood that the transition is smooth and satisfying for the elders depends a lot on the quality of the relational bonds with the grandchildren. When mutual affection and attachment are strong, many of the inevitable struggles are more easily worked through, leading to greater cooperation among everyone in the family (Condon et al., 2018).

Health Conditions

Anyone's ability to do their job, regardless of the physical, cognitive, or emotional demands, depends on optimal functioning of body, mind, and spirit. If someone is experiencing chronic pain, physical discomfort, unresolved personal issues, or compromised decision-making, then productivity and effectiveness will necessarily be significantly reduced. After all, health isn't just defined by the absence of illness but rather the capability to be fully present and available, as well as physically able to participate in demanding activities typical of children's seemingly unlimited energy (Margolis, 2016).

Age plays a part in the extent to which grandparents enjoy their roles, but the effects are confusing and contradictory (Condon et al., 2018). Some earlier studies found that younger grandmothers appreciate their interactions with children far more than older grandfathers, yet other studies found that grandparents who are older typically have more realistic expectations and are no longer attempting to juggle family responsibilities with their previous careers.

Still other studies found that age didn't make much of a difference. So, there you have it: Age matters, or it might matter, or it doesn't matter at all.

Just as there is a big difference between a full-time custodial grandparent who is 50, compared to someone else who is 80 years old, health and mental conditions will affect childcare outcomes. As previously mentioned if a caregiver is forgetful, distracted by personal challenges, limited in physical abilities, or suffering from pain or discomfort, this will likely lead to additional challenges.

The children, as well, are impacted by a family member's health challenges. When a grandparent is ill, for instance, the children are at much greater risk for depression, anxiety, and uncertainty about the future. When confronting any sick or disabled family member, children are also more inclined to face their own health prospects and mortality in the future.

It is also important to mention that when children are recruited into caregiving roles for their elders, it can teach them a sense of responsibility, as well as to cement closer bonds. Of course, the particular lessons learned depend on exactly what is required of them, how much of a time investment is involved, and how they have managed to make sense of their role.

Mental Status and Emotional Stability

A positive attitude and optimistic outlook are generally associated with higher functioning and well-being in daily life. Likewise, someone who is depressed, highly anxious, lonely, or otherwise emotionally impaired, is not going to be in the best position to take care of others. In cases of advanced dementia of a grandparent everyone in the household becomes at risk for additional life stressors (Celdran et al., 2014). Imagine what it is like for family members when the older person, once so revered, no longer even recognizes anyone.

In the latter stages of life one of the major adjustments is to come to terms with inevitable losses and grief, a process that is sometimes managed with acceptance and grace, but also at times with resentment, disappointment, and despair. There is a gradual erosion of bodily functioning that disrupts sleep, appetite, and vitality. With retirement comes a certain lack of structure and productivity. There are losses related to one's identity. Most of all, there are friends and family members who have died or moved on, even lost to one's memories. To the extent that these losses are processed, replaced with other meaningful activities (e.g., grandparenting and mentoring), there are negligible effects on personal effectiveness. But in some cases older people never quite accept, nor recover, from what they had once been, unable to refashion a new and different identity.

Although grandparenting and caregiving are usually associated with a greater sense of meaning and life satisfaction, if it becomes too demanding, frequent, or intense, the effects can take a turn for the worst. Full-time, custodial grandparents, for example, are far more likely to experience emotional difficulties or mental health issues than those who are part-time caregivers (Kelley et al., 2021). Of course that is also true with respect to any job or activity since optimal functioning is usually the result of a match between the demands of the job and one's ability to complete it satisfactorily. An absence of depressive symptoms, neediness, and cognitive impairment, are correlated with much better functioning in almost any aspect of life.

Elder Abuse

One additional challenge for older people that is perhaps among the most disruptive involves instances of abuse or neglect. This can take the form of verbal aggression or shaming and humiliating an older person, or could involve more dangerous physical threats, withholding food or shelter, or even actual beatings. According to the National Center on Elder Abuse (NCEA, 2021), among the 15% of elders who experience forms of abuse, neglect, or abandonment, the majority of the perpetrators are their own adult children. Sometimes they inflict punishment for perceived infractions, but other instances are related to financial gain.

Those elders who are at greatest risk tend to be those older than 80, manifest cognitive difficulties, and have health problems. Incredibly, half of all elders who have symptoms of dementia suffer abuse or neglect (NCEA, 2021).

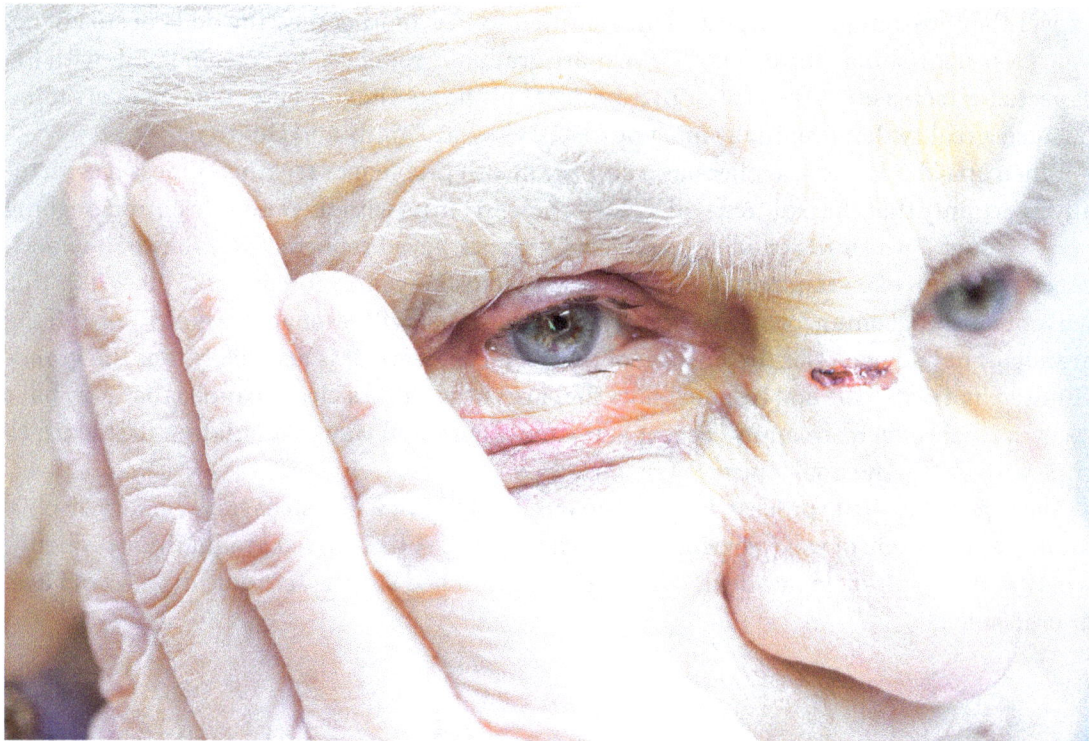

FIGURE 10.2   Although child neglect and abuse seem to get the most attention another crisis relates to the abuse of older people in vulnerable positions. Although the most dramatic examples involve actual physical aggression or complete neglect of basic care, in some cases the motive is not so much fueled by frustration or resentment as financial gains when the elder has untapped resources that family members want for themselves.

It is another type of abuse altogether when attempts are made to deny grandparents access to the children when there is no compelling reason to do so except through pettiness or cruelty. In some cases unresolved resentments of the past are used as excuses to inflict misery onto individuals who are already vulnerable and without power.

Some of the most common warning signs of abuse, besides forced isolation and banishment from the family, include frequent injuries that could be the result of physical abuse (bruises, cuts, broken bones, supposedly frequent "accidents"). Other signs are malnutrition or major weight loss not attributed to a disease, poor hygiene, extreme fear, anxiety, or depression, complete withdrawal from social contact. One final indicator is when family members attempt to extort or steal financial resources from the elder.

Death and Dying

Once someone reaches a certain age and stage in life it is inevitable that issues of mortality and eventual death rise to the surface. Once you hit 70 and beyond, nobody has the right to expect they are actually guaranteed and entitled to live another day. The odds of surviving, much less flourishing, during another year are gradually reduced at a certain point, with life expectancy increasingly uncertain. This may not only be continually on an older person's mind but also a reality that eventually must be discussed with family and children.

When an older family member has a chronic health problem or terminal illness it is virtually a certainty that the children will have to come to terms with their loss, grief, and ongoing bereavement. Two thirds of adolescents who were surveyed reported that they had experienced the death of a grandparent during the previous few years (Yorgason & Hill, 2019). This will obviously become a formative event in their lives that will resonate for many years. If the grandparent had been sick for a period of time prior to death, it is also likely that the grandchildren had some role and responsibility for care of the elder, a circumstance that may have its own ripple effects. In many cases it is the most common way that children first learn to cope with death, the final journey of life.

The type of death, its process, length, and circumstances, will also have an impact on children in a multitude of ways, depending on whether the end occurred gradually or suddenly, whether the result of an accident, drug overdose, botched surgery, chronic disease, old age, or even suicide.

Support and Assistance

One of the most frequent complaints by grandparents and elders is that they don't receive enough support to do their jobs as well as they would like. This is especially true when there are problems within the family, whether acting out or discipline problems with the children, obstructive behavior on the part of other family members, or conflicts with (or between) parents. In addition, there are often role conflicts and confusion within the family, mental health difficulties present in one or more members, financial stressors or lack of resources, or lack of expertise and knowledge about appropriate childcare approaches. There are also specific demographic or contextual factors that make things far more challenging, such as health status, separation of one or both parents, residual disputes over divorce and remarriage, and previous abuse or neglect within the family—either toward the children or the elders.

In such cases, intervention is often required, either from community agencies or professionals who specialize in providing support and assistance to families. It is important to remember that although one must study to pass an exam in order to receive a driver's license, real estate license, even a license to catch a fish or shoot a deer, but nothing at all is required to become a parent. There is no training, educational standard, or even mental fitness test required for the single most important, demanding job of all—raising a child.

In the case of becoming a grandparent, there is even less preparation involved since the transition doesn't even consider one's personal choice in the matter. It is a cruel irony that older family members are expected to enforce rules of the household that may conflict with their own beliefs, agree to a policy of noninterference, and yet are supposed to remain on standby to do whatever is asked regardless of if they have the ability, energy, and interest in doing so. Despite all the attention given to the joys and pleasures of being a grandparent, it remains a challenging role no matter how well prepared one might be for this stage of life. Family support services and professional mental professionals are often important options to provide the kinds of assistance that are often needed. Just as important are opportunities for social support to increase coping strategies for stressors associated with their responsibilities.

There is often a price to pay for the sacrifices that elders make on behalf of their families. This goes way beyond any resources or financial benefits that are passed on to the younger generation. Three quarters of grandparents admit that their social lives had become more limited as a result of their family responsibilities, and one third of the those surveyed said that the relationship with their spouse had been affected unfavorably (Ge & Adesman, 2017). Nevertheless, despite all the challenges that have been reviewed, as well as the myths that have been perpetuated, most studies indicate that the vast majority of grandparents are not only highly resilient and effective in their caregiving but that this role represents one of the highpoints of their lives.

QUESTIONS FOR REFLECTION OR DISCUSSION

1. What are some myths about aging and elders that were *not* covered in this chapter but still seem important in order to understand the challenges that they face?
2. In your own observations of grandparents, whether in your own family or someone else's family, what do you see as some of the greatest challenges that they face?
3. What examples of obsolete or outdated disciplinary or childcare practices can you think of that are still being used?

Figure Credits

Fig. 10.1: Source: https://www.youtube.com/watch?v=gCY0Xx92YvQ.
Fig. 10.2: Copyright © 2017 Depositphotos/ocskaymark.

CHAPTER 11

Reciprocal Effects and Learning

The most satisfying, enjoyable, and intimate relationships are not only characterized by mutual feelings of trust, safety, and respect, but also reciprocity. This means that they are neither one-sided, nor do they typically involve one person doing all the giving, receiving little in return. Of course there is indeed intrinsic pleasure and satisfaction in any form of caregiving, particularly with a loved one, but it is all the more beneficial to both parties when there is an exchange of mutual caring. This isn't to say that an elder expects and demands some form of "payment" for services, but just that there has to be some degree of "reward" that is experienced, even if hugs and kisses.

With that said, it is fairly evident that grandparents do benefit a lot as a result of their family involvement. They are as much students as they are teachers, based on what they learn from their grandchildren about their worlds, not to mention their likely greater expertise with new technology, devices, social media, and other cultural artifacts. That is only one of many reasons why well over 90% of grandparents say that caring for their grandchildren significantly increases the quality of their lives and represents some the most rewarding experiences of their lives (Danielsbacka et al., 2022; Kim et al., 2017).

As one example of this phenomenon mentioned in an earlier chapter, grandmothers were hooked up to a brain scan and shown a photo of one of their grandchildren, something quite remarkable occurred, igniting the somatosensory cortex like a Christmas light display. This is the part of the brain that is most associated with emotional empathy, a measure of relational attachment. Even more surprising, when the MRI scan responses were compared to that of their own children, the grandmothers' level of empathic arousal toward their grandchildren was even stronger (Rilling et al., 2021). This only confirms what is already pretty obvious when you observe almost any grandparent held in the embrace of their grandchild with a grin on their face. There are few more euphoric states than the feelings of love that are exchanged in such a relationship.

Even more intriguing than the feelings of elation, goodwill, and satisfaction that are associated with caring for loved ones who are all the ways that such involvement immunizes elders against loneliness, depression, and other emotional disruptions. The extent of these effects appear to be directly related to the solidarity, reciprocity, and intimacy of the relationships

(Moorman & Stokes, 2016). Humans are indeed social creatures, protected and supported by the affection and caring of loved ones.

Reciprocal Learning and Growth

Research and discussions are typically focused on what grandparents do to help their own children and grandchildren, but what about the value of this role for their own well-being and life satisfaction? It turns out that there are indeed many advantages that include a number of health benefits, including an increased life span. In addition, there is some evidence that older people who provide care for others, even as volunteers, enjoy a boost to their immune systems, better emotional regulation and cognitive functioning, and a greater sense of purpose in their lives (Seegert, 2018). Many of the themes that emerge are similar to those that have been described by psychotherapists in terms of the reciprocal learning that takes place in their work and the things they learn about themselves and the world, all the while they are assisting others with their personal problems (Kottler, 2022b). This includes, but is certainly not limited to, the increased sense of purpose and meaning in their lives, the feeling all they have experienced, learned, suffered, and encountered can be shared with others in the hope it will help them navigate similar life challenges. Similar to any devoted health professional, grandparents and elder caregivers enjoy increased opportunities to grow as a result of what they learn about others, themselves, and the wider world.

There have been interesting investigations that explore the benefits and outcomes that accompany those involved in altruistic pursuits, helping others as relatively selfless acts of service (Dossey, 2018; Kottler & Carlson, 2006; Post, 2007, 2011). People involved in service toward others in need may typically enjoy several benefits that include some of the following:

- Greater sense of well-being and happiness
- Greater appreciation for their own life situation
- Broadened worldview of self and others
- Improved feelings of affiliation and belongingness
- Sense of meaning to life's mission
- Immunity to disease or colds
- Reduced chronic pain
- "Helpers high" (elevated oxytocin and vasopressin)
- Status, trust, respect, privilege
- Spiritual transcendence
- Renewed faith
- Redemption and use of own pain or loss
- Release of guilt and paying something back
- Leaving a legacy
- Opportunity to reinvent self

In a summary of the rewards that accrue to those involved in altruistic pursuits, Mahatma Gandhi once observed that "the best way to find yourself is to lose yourself in the service of others." This is certainly a common report by almost anyone who has demonstrated a commitment to helping others, whether as a volunteer, grandparent, or social justice advocate (Kottler, 2000, 2018; Kottler et al., 2019; Kottler & Safari, 2019).

Whether as a parent, grandparent, or health professional, it is interesting to reflect on the ways that almost all helping roles involve some form of reciprocal influence and mutual learning. Just as teachers, counselors, psychologists, and coaches are often influenced and impacted by those they mentor and help, so too do grandparents enjoy a number of benefits as a result of their intimate involvement in children's lives. It is thus important at life's end to find meaningful work and opportunities to pass along a lifetime of wisdom and experience.

FIGURE 11.1 Successful aging and adjustment to the latter stages of life depends on far more than remaining healthy and free of disease or disability. It is also critical that older adults feel like they are still engaged in meaningful "work," however that is defined. It is all about continuing to feel useful, having a compelling reason to keep learning and growing. That is one reason the grandparent role can become so important to feel productive compared to those who remain passive, disengaged, and lost.

Of course, the desire and commitment to help doesn't necessarily lead to desired outcomes for those in need. Some people have the best of intentions without the corresponding skills, abilities, and patience to actually deliver what is most needed. That's why psychotherapists, for example, endure such rigorous training to put their own needs and interests aside in favor of what others need the most, whether just listening without criticism or judgment or far more complex interventions.

As with everything else in life, whether teaching, mentoring, coaching, or supervising others, there are vast differences in the quality of care and mentoring, depending on attitudes, time availability, interpersonal skills, and qualities such as patience, compassion, wisdom, and dependability. One size does not fit all families and children, so perhaps the most important trait of all is the continued willingness to learn, grow, and adapt according to the particular needs of the situation.

Mutuality is a key feature of any relationship with power imbalances, whether the result of age differences or positions of influence that lead to inequities. In the case of grandparents it may appear as if they act solely out of genetic advantage, or perhaps altruism, but there are many ways that they profit far beyond their family's gratitude (Kahana et al., 2019). We've discussed previously, for example, about the importance during old age to feel productive and useful, and there is nothing more valuable in life than mentoring and guiding the next generation. In addition to feeling a greater sense of purpose and meaning, as well as the deep intimacy and love that is experienced with children, there is considerable satisfaction knowing that one can leave behind one's most cherished life lessons and most interesting stories.

Grandparents also report that the closer family ties they experience provide additional support and companionship. Their interests are broadened as a result of ongoing contact with the children, whether mastering new technological breakthroughs, learning tricks on social media, or exposure to novel forms of entertainment, whether children's favorite shows in media or television, attending sporting events, or fun facts from what the kids learned in school. Finally, there are all the different ways that children reciprocate the support and caring by all the ways they assist their grandparents with chores and tasks that are immeasurably helpful. All of this adds up to enhanced mental health for everyone involved.

Of course as children become older they are in a better position to offer reciprocal benefits to their grandparents and elders in the form of more stimulating and intimate conversations. They are also more likely to provide nurturing roles to those who are frail or require assistance, although if the demands are excessive this support can also take a toll on the children's stress. Typically, these supportive relationships take different forms characterized by a "friendship," "companion," "playmate," or "caregiver," depending on the closeness of the relationship and the kinds of activities that are involved (Matos & Neves, 2012).

FIGURE 11.2   While grandparents introduce their grandchildren to family history, interesting stories, and important life lessons, the influence is reciprocal in all kinds of ways. Young people also teach their elders about current social trends, help them with their technological skills, and teach them new games. Most of all, the mutual support and companionship increases resilience and life satisfaction for everyone involved.

Health and Longevity Benefits

There was an earlier discussion about how grandparent care increases the health prospects and longevity of children, not to mention their safety and welfare. Even more intriguing is that grandparents who take care of kids tend to live longer than those who are not involved in such labor. How about *that* for a peculiar correlation of variables based on evidence? Elders involved in childcare appear to have one third less risk of dying at any age (Hilbrand et al., 2017).

You might imagine that with the added stress, burdens, and responsibilities that accompany childcare this might have adverse effects on health and life span. Indeed, in particular cases of involuntary roles or full-time custodial care there are certain increased pressures that can have deleterious results. Nevertheless, when incapacitating health issues are not involved generally the effects are positive as a result of feeling greater meaning and purpose in daily life.

FIGURE 11.3   One motivation and inspiration for remaining in top physical condition, working out on a regular basis, and engaging in self-care strategies is to remain fit enough to keep up with rambunctious children with limitless energy. This provides additional incentives and motivation to remain in optimal shape, not only for one's own benefit but also for loved ones.

The key factor that maximizes the physical and emotional health of older caregivers relates to operating within their limits and comfort zone. Perhaps that could be said a bit differently since there are often times when going beyond one's imagined limits leads to further growth and breakthroughs. Older people tell themselves all the time that they can no longer do certain things or that they must "act their age," meaning engage in self-restraint and caution. There are times, however, when it is advantageous, as well as freeing, to push oneself a bit to discover new capacities, adaptations, and possibilities. That is one of so many things that children can teach any of us.

Increased Well-Being

Even though the U.S. Constitution guarantees the right to "*pursue* happiness," it is precisely that compulsive quest that leads to such *un*happiness, disappointments, and dissatisfaction in life. The reality is that so-called "happiness" is actually a rather fleeting condition, a temporary state of mind that is subject to one's current mood, situation, and uncontrollable external conditions related to the environment, social restraints, and other people's actions (Kottler, 2023). That's one reason psychologists now prefer to use the term *well-being* to describe the ultimate goal of a well-lived existence. This is a relatively stable condition that is characterized not just by (a) a high incidence of positive emotions but also (b) deep engagement in daily activities, (c) close, intimate relationships, (d) a sense of meaning and purpose to life, and (e) feelings of accomplishment and productivity (Seligman, 2012).

There have been numerous studies that have examined how becoming a grandparent affects one's life satisfaction and personal sense of well-being in a multitude of ways (Condon et al., 2018). As mentioned previously, the magnitude of effects depends on the elder's age, gender, finances, attitude, marital status, family composition, and so on. For instance, first-time maternal grandmothers appear to be affected the most positively, while paternal grandfathers have the most negligible benefits (Gessa et al., 2020). In almost all cases, however, grandparents experience some boost to their spirit in small ways even if the role does not significantly alter their core identity. One reason for this relates to the increased social activities associated with the grandparent role, a significant benefit for anyone's degree of life satisfaction that has also been found to improve a positive outlook on life (Yorgason & Hill, 2019).

Since well-being is known to be bolstered by feelings of achievement and purpose, it is not surprising that grandparents often experience a boost in their own life satisfaction once they take on manageable tasks assisting their genetic kin. This role is intrinsically rewarding, as well as biologically driven. In cases in which the relational bonds are strong, family conflict is negligible, and the role expectations are realistic, older people report among their highest life satisfaction and contentment (Condon et al., 2018). Despite the subjective reports and surveys of grandparents that consistently say that resilience, emotional moods, life satisfaction, and yes, well-being, are increased when providing supplementary childcare, the evidence thus far is still somewhat scant and confusing (Kim et al., 2017). So many of the effects appear to depend on existing factors within the family and the elder's own life.

Another important dimension is the elder's openness and interest in continued growth, learning, and development. There is an assumption, if not a myth, that older people resist change, or any new advancement that renders their previous knowledge and beliefs obsolete. After all, it takes considerable work and effort to master new technologies and "rule changes," so to speak. "I remember the good 'ole days," is the classic refrain that often exemplifies a glorification of the past and denigration of the current conditions.

One of the likely outcomes of spending time with young people is that an elder is exposed to the latest innovations and popular trends that are emerging in music, art, fashion, technology, media, and social movements. Conversations and interactions between the youngest and oldest generations inevitably lead to increased reflections and self-scrutiny about the origins and viability of one's own beliefs. In addition, just as grandparents and elder caregivers have so much to teach youngsters about the nature of the world, so too do these children offer new ideas that can be taken on board and are particularly applicable in the ever-changing nature of contemporary life.

Differential Preparation for the Role

Not all grandparents are well prepared for their renewed roles as caregivers or substitute parents. The world—and the children who now exist—are very different from those who inhabited the household a generation ago. Expectations, norms, cultural expectations, and education have all evolved significantly. In addition, the "job" of grandparent is accompanied by different degrees of power, authority, and roles than that of a parent. Just as parents have likely never received much training, grandparenting is another "profession" in which the key attributes and skills are learned on the job, usually without much supervision or guidance. In addition, because of dramatic advances in technology, there is often reciprocal learning that takes place within the grandparent–child relationship in which the young person is likely far more adept at mastering the intricacies of managing streaming and mobile devices.

If one were to develop a curriculum for grandparent education and preparation, such a program would likely include a number of areas in which it would be highly desirable to learn new or supplementary skills that include, among others (a) teaching children self-control; (b) improving patience; (c) differentiating goals and actions based on gender, age, and cultural differences; (d) discipline strategies without negative side effects like punishment; (e) teaching emotional regulation; (f) monitoring, evaluating, and assisting with schoolwork and learning; (g) assessing risk and preventing dangers; (h) clarifying child responsibilities and teaching time management; (i) teaching moral and ethical decision-making; and (j) evaluating critically and honestly one's own behavior, mistakes, and failures (Strom & Strom, 2017).

Some older people are obviously more interested and committed to further growth and learning than others. Indeed, elders can sometimes become stuck in their ways, resistant to new methods and ideas. Yet it is precisely the exposure to novel experiences and ideas that stimulate passion, excitement, and engagement in daily life. It is not surprising that the youngest generation, attending school every day, constantly exposed to new learning, would bring many of these ideas home, anxious to share fascinating facts with other family members. I recall once asking a third-grader what he learned in school that day, expecting the usual indifferent shrug and rote answer, "Nothing much." Instead he simply said, "pirates."

"Excuse me?" I said, more than a little confused.

"We studied about pirates today?"

"Oh yeah?" I prompted him. "Like how to talk like a pirate? Haaar Matey!"

He didn't think that was very funny. Instead he asked me, "Do you know why pirates wear eye patches?"

"Well, of course! They probably got stabbed in the eye during a swordfight." I was proud of myself that I aced that one.

The boy just snickered at my stupidity. "No! That's not why at all."

"Okay smarty pants, then why do pirates wear eye patches?"

He then patiently and brilliantly explained to me that the reason for the patch over one eye is during battles when then captain had to go down below to supervise the cannons firing he would already have one eye adjusted to the darkness and one eye adjusted to light on the top deck.

You may already know this historical fact, but it absolutely blew my mind. It got me thinking about all the other beliefs that I must have that have been formed by mistakes and misguided assumptions. This little kid not only corrected an interesting and rather minor historical assumption but also unknowingly challenged me to be far more discerning and critical notion about what I think I know and understand. This has been a very big deal for me ever since then, all of it sparked by a child who taught me something I was not even searching for.

To the extent that each of us is open and prepared to learn new things from those around us, even the smallest and most innocent members of our species, life remains an exciting adventure. Even toddlers can teach us so much about the importance and joy of living purely in the present moment, being curious about everything we encounter. This is also what makes interactions with children not only so stimulating and entertaining, but also so exhausting because of their seemingly limitless energy.

It is fairly clear that caregiving roles by grandparents and other elders is at times fairly tiring and stressful, even beyond what can comfortably be managed. This is especially the case if the children have behavioral problems or require major discipline interventions, or if there are entrenched conflicts within the family—especially between the parents or across generations. Yet it is also true that the vast majority of grandparents learn and grow a lot as a result of these challenges, finding new and different purpose in their life's journey.

Depending on their openness to new ideas, elders learn (or relearn) all kinds of important things from children. For one thing they are required to stay current on whatever is going on in the world, or in the local region, so they can carry on meaningful conversations that are triggered by school or life events. Through travel, reading, social media, and other vehicles they work hard to remain aware of new developments, innovations, breakthroughs, and cultural phenomena that may be of interest to the children. In addition, children teach them patience, as well as to listen better to the nuances of communication. They learn the lyrics to children's favorite songs and are exposed to whatever is currently popular to watch on screens. Their grandchildren teach them how to use the remote control, navigate social media platforms, play videogames, download or stream music, and even help them set up their mobile devices or learn the latest tricks.

Health professionals and researchers have figured out that the best way to introduce safer and more hygienic practices for homes in developing countries isn't to educate the adults but rather to reach the preschoolers so they can become the advocates for optimal care. In several programs, 3-year-olds were introduced to the importance of brushing teeth every evening and washing hands after using the toilet. They were given bars of soap and toothbrushes to take home, instructed to teach everyone else in the family about proper hygiene, particularly the elders who were already entrenched in obsolete habits. It is the youngest children who become the mentors and guides for the elders. After all, old dogs (and people) can indeed learn new tricks!

QUESTIONS FOR REFLECTION OR DISCUSSION

1. What are some things that you have taught a grandparent or older person who was a mentor or caregiver for you?

2. How has a close, intimate, trusting bond with a grandparent or elder had a significant impact on your life? How do you believe this relationship also affected this mentor in your life?

3. What are some examples of reciprocal effects and mutual learning that took place in a few relationships in which you were the elder, teacher, or the one with power?

Figure Credits

Fig. 11.1: Copyright © 2014 Depositphotos/budabar.

Fig. 11.2: Source: https://www.pexels.com/photo/a-family-sitting-at-the-table-5960151/.

Fig. 11.2: Source: https://www.pexels.com/photo/a-family-sitting-at-the-table-5960151/.

CHAPTER 12

The Attitudes and Abilities of Extraordinary Grandparents

Determining the effects and influences of grandparent behavior and caregiving would be as varied as doing so with any other group, whether parents, teachers, or psychotherapists. There are good ones and lousy ones. Some demonstrate extraordinary skill, compassion, wisdom, and are essential to the high functioning of the family and the welfare of the children. Others can be as indifferent, neglectful, abusive, or incompetent as any other professional caregiver, leading to a toxic culture within the family. What distinguishes excellence among those grandparents who are exceptionally effective in their jobs?

Three quarters of all grandparents report that they quite enjoy their roles, also claiming that they are excellent at their jobs, far better, in fact, than the parents (David & Nelson-Kakulla, 2019). Of course, relying on self-reports is often distorted and inaccurate, sometimes referred as the "illusory superiority effect" because of the tendency to exaggerate one's own capabilities compared to others (Hoorens & Buunk, 1992). In spite of distorted self-appraisals it appears that for many people becoming a grandparent is the single most satisfying experience of their lives. This is true even when they feel a significant lack of social support, additional stressors, and struggles with their own aging and health issues (Mendoza et al., 2020). It is primarily their reservoir of resilience that permits them to keep depression, loneliness, and frustrations at bay, adopting an attitude that features greater optimism, hope, and caring for others, giving their lives greater meaning (MacLeod et al., 2016).

It is perhaps not surprising that the ability and willingness for a grandparent, or anyone else for that matter, to have a positive and enduring impact on children's lives depends, in part, on the person's deep understanding of the culture and environment, especially via social capital that has been accrued over a lifetime (Mollegaard & Jaegar, 2015). It should be noted, however, that Mollegaard and Jaegar's study took place in Scandinavia, where there is a greater leveling of financial success as compared to other places with much greater economic disparity between people. Nevertheless, in any location around the world, performing in any role or job, extraordinary achievement is often the result of feeling incredible joy and satisfaction while immersed in the activities. This is no less true in the case of caring for children or mentoring others.

One other major factor also comes into play, largely determining an elder's willingness and ability to operate at a high enough level to keep up with the children—and that has to do with adjustments to the inevitable physical changes that take place after about age 60. As any older person will readily inform you, the biological changes that occur within the body appear with increasing regularity. Sleep and appetite habits are disrupted. Vision and hearing acuity are reduced. Aches and pains become more frequent. Fatigue occurs more readily. At the same time that individuals are attempting to come to terms with these dramatic changes, they must also remain sufficiently centered and present that they can manage to help children deal with their own continual developmental transitions.

No One Size Fits All—or Hardly Anyone

When talking about the nature of grandparent excellence it has been clear that the sheer variety and diversity of family situations, contexts, and needs dictates that particular styles will vary considerably. We've previously discussed that the frequency, duration, and reasons for visiting determine the types of relationships that develop over time. Obviously there is a big difference between an elder who is living with the family versus a grandparent who stops by once per week, or even once a year.

The life circumstances of the older family member also determine availability, ability, and essential competence. Some are still working full-time while others are fully retired. Some have achieved a degree of comfort and luxury in their lives while others struggle to make ends meet. Some are wildly satisfied with their lives while others are pretty miserable. Some couples get along quite cooperatively while others fight and argue constantly. Some consider their role as grandparents to be an honored privilege while others see it as distressing burden. Some display extraordinary patience while others are quick to anger. Some enjoy loving and collaborative relationships with their own children while others feel like they are at war. In other words, what it takes to function at the highest level depends very much on a collection of variables that relate to the particular family dynamics, assigned roles and responsibilities, grandparent personality and attitudes, as well as children's own behavior and responsiveness.

Nobody is proficient, much less perfectly competent, in every aspect of caregiving. Some people are better at setting limits and instilling a sense of discipline, others excel at creating fun opportunities for creativity, still others see themselves as life tutors empowered to teach valuable skills. Each one brings something different to the relationship, depending on interests, abilities, and goals. In addition, what any caregiver is capable of doing depends on one's energy level, physical health, and overall fitness, especially when trying to keep up with rambunctious children.

In addition, grandparents, like everyone else, have to deal with many of the distractions in their lives, those that intrude from the outside world as well as their own internal thinking. After all, some people are filled with doubts about their skills, constantly question their choices, second-guess themselves, and feel insecure about their abilities. Likewise, people are trying to juggle the various challenges of their lives, dealing with problems at work or home, as well as in their relationships with family, friends, neighbors, or colleagues. To the extent they have achieved a sense of well-being and reasonable satisfaction with the course of their lives they are better positioned to take care of others, resisting the temptation to become sidetracked by life's many other demands that may compromise their capacity for remaining focused, present, and fully engaged.

It is one thing to talk about the most exemplary cases of grandparent or elder caregiving and quite another to mention instances of complete ignorance of best practices. In one study, for example, 44% of custodial grandparents still believed that the best treatment for a fever was to immerse the child in an ice bath, a practice that might very well make the condition far worse with hypothermia (Brunissen et al., 2020). These are just a few examples of the kinds of health issues that reveal how up-to-date grandparents are on the best ways to introduce discipline and safety practices.

Expertise and Competence

Many of the same skills that make teachers, supervisors, and leaders so effective are just as applicable when caring for and mentoring children. These are abilities and strategies that tend to empower other people rather than control them. They involve deep listening and sensitive responses to others. And they are many of the same things that exceptional psychotherapists do in sessions or that extraordinary teachers do in the classroom, all designed to maximize learning and solidify trusting relationships.

Competence in helping relationships is often based on the *children's* perceptions and experience of the encounters, whether *they* are the ones who feel heard, understood, and adequately assisted. It doesn't matter how satisfied the parent, grandparent, teacher, or therapist feels about the nature of their interactions if the recipient of this help doesn't feel good about what happened. It is the single best predictor of successful outcomes during therapeutic encounters (Kottler & Balkin, 2017, 2020). That's why one of the most important things that any mentor can do is to make certain that the child feels like they were truly heard and understood, regardless of whether the behavior that follows meets expectations.

It isn't enough to merely invite children to report on what happened in school, or talk about their experiences, but to encourage them to explore things they don't understand, to talk about issues that are bothersome, to reveal uncertainties, confusion, and distress about things that may have happened. This doesn't occur by firing off a bunch of interrogatory questions like, "So, did you have a good day in school today?" "Did you get your homework done?" "Did you get a chance to ask that boy for a playdate?" These are referred to as "close-ended" queries, the kind that can be answered with a single word, "yes" or "no," or sometimes just a nod or shrug. Instead, good listeners ask "open-ended" questions, the kind that require detailed elaboration such as, "What was the most interesting thing that happened in school today?" or "What's something that's been bothering you lately that we haven't yet talked about?" These are the sorts of prompts that build deeper communication instead of feelings of intrusion and annoyance.

There are so many other helping skills that are part of the repertoire of anyone who seeks to assist and support another. It is important to restrain oneself so that the conversations are balanced and not overcontrolled. It is always interesting to help the child to dig a little deeper when trying to make sense of something, often by asking for reasoning or evidence to support views. In some situations it can be equally instructive to respectfully challenge beliefs in the hope that this leads to new insights. Most of all it is helpful to clarify their thoughts, express their feelings, and integrate conclusions in a meaningful way.

If it sounds like these are more like the priorities of a teacher, that's exactly the case. But in a very real sense that is what a parent, grandparent, or caregiver does most of the time—not just keep children safe and secure but stimulate them toward further growth and development.

Avoiding Common Mistakes

Anyone who has ever been a parent has regrets about all the inevitable mistakes that were made along the way. Most people are able to put them aside after a period of time, forgive themselves for their lapses, and carry on as best they can after learning from the misjudgments. Once grandchildren are born, and the role of caregiver kicks in once again, it is hard not to relive some of the mistakes of the past. On the one hand there is the opportunity to do things differently; on the other hand, it is challenging not to fall into the same bad habits.

The problem is never about making a single mistake in attempts to impose discipline or manage the children; rather it is about repeating the same mistakes over and over again even though it is clear these gestures are less than useful. Whether in the context of parenting, or anything else in life, it is rigidity and stubbornness that most often lead to trouble, especially during times when you don't learn from the error of your ways. If older people have a reputation of being overly stubborn, unwilling or unable to change, reluctant to adopt new methods that have been shown to be more effective, then conflicts will continue to be prevalent.

If parents, children, and grandparents were each asked to name the most common caregiving mistakes that take place in the household they would likely provide different responses. The parents might most annoyed by attempts on the part of the other two constituencies to undermine their authority or circumvent rules ("Don't worry about the treat. Just don't tell your parents.") During an earlier discussion there were other frequent mistakes mentioned, such as the times grandparents fail to keep track of the children, are lax about safety procedures, or give unsolicited advice that is obviously annoying, even disrespectful. Children would instead be more likely to complain that the biggest mistake grandparents make are their obsolete assumptions and ignorance about current trends, technology, and information ("Grandpa, that's not how we do things anymore."). Grandparents, on the other hand, might be more inclined to blame themselves for just not knowing what to do in certain situations or how to best manage, control, or discipline the children. There are times when it seems like nothing is working and the children are frustrated, crying, angry, or otherwise acting out. It is hard not to blame oneself for feeling incompetent.

What distinguishes extraordinarily resilient and skilled grandparents is not their tendency to avoid mistakes but rather the learning and growth that comes when refusing to repeat them again. If scolding a child when upset only makes things far worse, then it is best to stop doing that and try something else, *anything* else, whether bargaining, negotiating, reasoning, or intervening in some other way that feels less punitive. One grandparent admits he learned this lesson the hard way: "I used to believe I had ideas that were so much better than those that were enforced in the household, much more efficient and time-tested. So I used to make recommendations and offer advice, much of which was never really appreciated. If anything it just made things worse. So I've learned to just keep my mouth shut and follow the rules they've established, even the dumb ones that don't make sense. The hard part now is to stop being critical and judgmental just because they do things differently than I would."

This confession holds many of the most important attitudes and abilities of effective grandparenting. This elder acknowledges the differences between his own beliefs and those of his family, but he also recognizes that his job is to work within their system. To do otherwise tends to create resentments, conflicts, and intergenerational battles that will never be good for the peace of mind of the family members.

Resilience, Hardiness, and Metabolizing Stress

It is well known that people react to crises, stressors, and challenging situations in very different ways. Some people remain calm, in control, and deal with difficulties as best they can. They maintain a positive, hopeful attitude. They draw on resources available to them, internally as well as relying on friends and family for support. Even more impressive, once they survive and recover from whatever crises they faced, they report considerable growth as a result. On the other hand—and, of course, there is another hand—some people experience incapacitating trauma after identical predicaments, and as a result they are never quite the same. They become increasingly fearful. In some cases, they lose the ability to function effectively.

It is more than a little interesting that in studies of how people manage difficulties in their lives the outcomes fall into three very different categories. As would be expected, after a near-death experience, financial catastrophe, health issue, or other trauma, it is reasonable to expect that that adjustment and recovery would take some period of time afterward, often several months. A second group never quite recovers from this experience and may experience symptoms of severe posttraumatic stress (PTSD) for years afterward, perhaps for the rest of their lives. They develop major depression or anxiety disorders, or other mental conditions. Surprisingly, however, a third group of "survivors" not only recover fairly well after the incident or trauma but actually report incredible growth. They learned some significant life lessons as a result of what they endured, often appreciating relationships more, changing their priorities in significant ways, and feeling stronger and more resilient as a result (Schulenberg, 2021; Tedeschi & Moore, 2020).

Resilience has been described as the capacity for successful preparation and adaptation to perceived threats, dangers, adversity, losses, and tragedies. Although it is most typically imagined as bouncing back or recovering to a previous condition, ideally such a position sparks additional development and learning that better protects people for the future. It is not that they don't experience the same kinds of discomfort and disruption that others might, it is that resilient individuals are better able to metabolize what happened and move forward without lingering side effects. In that sense it is not only just a positive attitude one adopts but also a skill that has been strengthened over time. It may also have an inherited component to it since researchers have identified a genetic marker (Nr3C1) that is associated with resilience when it activates chemicals in the brain's hippocampus (Zannas & West, 2014).

With age and experience, one's capacity for resilience actually increases over time, making it much easier to roll with the punches and shrug off disappointments. It is true that what doesn't kill you can indeed making you stronger (as well as weaker). It all depends on how the experiences are perceived, interpreted, and processed. The capacity to adapt and respond effectively to adversity is considered one of the hallmarks of successful aging, characterized by reduced depression, higher life satisfaction, and improved health and longevity (MacLeod et al., 2016).

With respect to older adults, adaptation is the key. There are adjustments to be made with respect to physical changes taking place inside the body, leading to new limitations. There are also innumerable adaptations that must be made in light of one's previous mistakes, failures, disappointments, and life's losses and tragedies. In the case of grandparents, they must also make herculean adjustments to the unique demands and rules of the household, an environment which they no longer rule. Their resilience also comes into play when they are called upon to swoop in for a rescue attempt when parents are otherwise occupied, stressed, or overwhelmed.

In each case, their ability to manage the situation effectively, remain reasonably calm and in control, and even rise to the occasion depends a lot on a few characteristics that include "hardiness," which describes one's flexibility in the face of unforeseen circumstances and unanticipated changes. When this is combined with a hopeful, optimistic attitude, and feelings of self-efficacy ("I've got this!") resilience tends to operate at the highest levels (Musil et al., 2019).

In addition to the reservoir of resilience within any individual there is also a kind of collective family resilience that influences how and why members either come together or fall apart during times of stress or crisis (Vogel, 2017). How are decisions made within the family during times of upheaval? To what extent does the family function cooperatively and supportively? These are important questions because when grandparents or older adults are recruited to offer assistance it tends to be during times of stress, whether a chronically chaotic condition or the result of some acute crisis.

It is important to recognize that resilience is not just a static personality trait but an ability that strengthens over time with experience and practice overcoming types of adversity. Despite all the difficulties and challenges that grandparents face in their roles, the majority do quite well dealing with the accompanying stress. The ability to do so appears to relate to something more than just individual attitudes and skill but also harnesses social support from friends, family members, and health professionals (Mendoza et al., 2020).

Making the Best of Second (or More) Chances

When grandparents were asked what they were inclined to do differently compared to their time as parents, they had a lot to say about the subject (Freeman et al., 2019). Of course there were regrets about the past, even if it was fully acknowledged that the circumstances had been so different earlier in their lives. It was mostly in the type and quality of communication with children that was so distinctively different. First, they considered it far more of a priority to create and maintain space for meaningful conversations without the previous interruptions of work demands or other responsibilities. Rituals and traditions were established to encourage mutual sharing during most encounters, regardless of the tasks or activities that were involved. It is all about creating more opportunities for listening, dialogue, and bonding.

Compared to earlier in life elders admitted that they were now far more likely to talk about deep emotions and uncomfortable feelings than they ever had previously. Likewise, they were more focused on inviting the children to talk about their own feelings of confusion and uncertainty. Many grandparents confessed to even telling their grandchildren about their previous indiscretions, shameful mistakes, and life regrets. Needless to say, such expressions of trust and openness have a contagious effect that encourages children to talk about certain things that they previously kept to themselves. This is just one of the reasons most of the grandparents believed themselves to be much better at taking care of the children because of their increased emotional maturity, improved patience, and acquired wisdom (Freeman et al., 2019).

One example of this relates to the age-old problem of managing children's diet and eating habits. Naturally the food preferences of kids (snacks, sweets, treats) versus adults (vegetables, fruits, reduced sugar, fat, and salt) are often in direct opposition, requiring some degree of oversight and supervision of meals. Whatever diet norms and nutritional standards were considered cutting-edge a few decades ago have since been replaced by newer guidance informed by research. Take eggs as just one example. First they were good for you, then bad for you, then okay to eat the whites but not the yolks, then fine to eat occasionally, now, like almost everything else, it is acceptable to eat them in moderation.

Due to the changes in dietary guidance, as well as strong parental preferences, as well as the children's tastes and tolerances, mealtime can become a battleground. Whereas parents might have instilled certain policies and practices that are considered mandatory it is another thing altogether for the grandparents to enforce these rules. It turns out that this isn't really all about healthy nutrition but also brings into the picture struggles over power and control. Hopefully over the years older adults have learned a few tricks of the trade, so to speak, strategies for deescalating battles over meal preferences. They walk a fine line between trying to honor parental wishes, remain consistent with one's own beliefs, and yet literally feed children's preferences (Jogenellis et al., 2021). Although there may indeed be restrictions of certain forbidden foods, grandparents still retain the right to provide special indulgences without necessarily undermining the system.

One other common challenge that tests caregivers' patience and abilities is relatively new on the scene for grandparents. Perhaps in their day as children, and then parents, there were often restrictions on television viewing habits. That might have been limited to special times of the week such as after finishing homework or Sunday morning cartoons. At the very least there were some limits placed on the amount of time children were permitted to sit in front of the TV, no matter how convenient it is as an auxiliary babysitter. This was much easier to enforce during a time when there were only a handful of stations available instead of the thousands of viewing and streaming options now available. As a result children are inclined to spend hours every day on mobile devices, playing games, listening to music, talking to friends, watching videos or shows, viewing movies, and engaging with social media. This presents a whole new arena of temptations that, collectively, can eat up all of someone's discretionary time with mindless stimulation. In fact, it has been determined that roughly half of all the time that grandchildren spend with their grandparents involves them engaged with mobile devices and screens rather than actually interacting with one another in any meaningful way. Furthermore, the grandparents are often complicit in this behavior, appreciating the ways that screen time reduces their own burdens and gives them free time for other activities (Elias et al., 2019).

This may be a new potential difficulty for grandparents to manage this activity, but it is hardly unique in the spectrum of prior experience. During every time and era there have been parental (and governmental) controls over what children are allowed to do. The current situation of widespread screen use (compulsion?) does indeed introduce other addictive factors into the picture, making this one of the most frequent complaints by everyone involved in the conflicts. Nevertheless, the ways this negotiation and management are handled reveals quite a lot about the underlying quality of the relationships. It has been found, for instance, that when grandparents are effective in helping to manage children's media use, it is not only beneficial for the kids' well-being, but it also reflects well on the levels of commitment and engagement as active caregivers (Nimrod et al., 2019).

That's not to imply that older people refuse to embrace change and new developments, another myth that is perpetuated based on limited anecdotal data. After all, elders' main responsibility is collecting and distributing accurate and valuable knowledge of use to the community. The whole world has undergone a fairly radical set of changes during the last few years that have impacted social relationships, political beliefs, health policies, technological innovation, and family structures. Not wishing to be left behind, whether in their careers or daily life, the majority of elders strive to remain up-to-date on whatever is current on the scene and seek support from others (especially their own grandchildren) to learn new skills and methods (David & Nelson-Kakulla, 2019).

Telling Stories

It is interesting to realize that the human brain has evolved as essentially a "storied organ," a means by which to collect, store, and retrieve valuable information in the form of memorable narratives. Whether as fantasies, dreams, recollections, movies, shows, plays, messages, tweets, or conversations almost all of our daily (and nightly) experiences are automatically converted into stories that hold what we have heard, seen, experienced, and lived. In that sense, any human life is composed of a collection of stories that continue to exist long after we are gone.

Among all the evolutionary purposes we've reviewed about how and why older people exist beyond their reproductive functions, the role of storyteller is at the top of the list. During ancient days, the survival of the community was dependent on efficient and accurate ways of passing along crucial intelligence about hunting grounds, edible and poisonous plants, water sources, habitable territory, and navigation routes. It was important for members to hear about the historical legacies of the tribe, including their distinctive identity, achievements, successes, previous failures, and dangerous enemies, as well as allies. Elders were also considered responsible for telling stories that emphasize the values, beliefs, and norms of the culture: who we are, what we stand for, what we wish to achieve.

Over time it may no longer be necessary to pass along travel recommendations or information on food sources since Google, Apple Maps, Instagram, TikTok, and Trip Advisor have taken over those functions. Likewise, history books, documentaries, biographies, Siri, Alexa, and online searches have supplied us with knowledge on demand. Yet elders and grandparents still remain as living legends of the past, eyewitnesses to historical events and critical incidents that have shaped the world and individual lives.

Similar to extraordinary teachers, psychotherapists, writers, and speakers, superlative elders employ stories in a variety of different ways to serve different purposes (Kottler, 2015). In its simplest form a story may provide basic information of interest to a child, where the elder was born, background of siblings, how the family ended up where they are now. Yet some of the most enduring stories, those that last over time, are those that reveal personal details that make the past come alive. There are themes present in any well-lived existence that highlight themes of courage, resilience, tragedy, and ultimately self-acceptance.

As our contemporary cultures have become far more complex, and as technology from social media, streaming, and thousands of storytelling options remain readily accessible on screens, it would appear as if elders have been replaced as the sanctioned holders and tellers of stories. As a counterpoint to this assumption, there was an anthropologist who was embedded in an African village many years ago when a television was first introduced to the residents. This magical device was a marvel, capable of showing all kinds of entertainment inside the box, even switching between different stories on the screen. It was not surprising that all the villagers flocked to watch this incredible and novel storytelling machine, abandoning the elder who was the designated storyteller. Each night everyone would gather around the fire, and he would regale them with stories about their origins, their identity, and their history.

FIGURE 12.1   Throughout the ages, one of the universal jobs of elders in the family and community is to pass along the knowledge and wisdom of the culture that has been accumulated through the sharing of seminal stories. Among their most important jobs, grandparents talk about the lessons they've learned throughout their lifetimes as well as the most valued stories that reveal instructional themes. Whether watching cartoons on television, listening to stories at bedtime, or hearing family anecdotes, children are exposed to narratives that teach them about core values, dangers to avoid, and clear messages about collective identity—who we are and how we are different from others.

What really surprised the anthropologist, however, was that after a few days most of the villagers ignored the television and instead returned to their usual nightly entertainment around the fire. When the researcher asked the villagers why they did so, one person explained, "Yes it is true that the magical box knows many stories. . . . But the storyteller in our village knows *us*!" It would appear that the power and impact of stories are magnified in the context of a close relationship, especially with grandparents. In other studies of hunter-gatherer tribes in the Amazon it was also discovered that 85% of the stories told in the village were offered by the elders and grandparents (Schniter et al., 2018). It was further revealed that this was actually the job specialization targeted for older adults who were expected to further develop and refine their oral narrative abilities for the benefit of the community. This was not simply for entertainment purposes but considered an essential function to pass along valuable knowledge and experience.

Given that almost all useful knowledge is coded in the form of stories (even numerical data represents a kind of "story") it is just too important to be left exclusively to professional storytellers like writers, speakers, and producers. After all, it is usually not so much reasoning that convinces people to change their minds or adopt a new perspective but rather emotional arousal that cements indelible memories. That's why some of the best stories are those that make us laugh, cry, or become fearful or joyful.

Nowadays "we're all storytellers in the digital world," all producers of content that is distributed to small, intimate groups or else huge, online communities (Rose, 2021). Most people may not have received formal training and instruction in the art of storytelling, but it nevertheless remains one of the most powerful and persuasive tools for influencing others. In that sense, as long as the stories of grandparents and elders remain alive in the memories of their descendants, they become immortal.

QUESTIONS FOR REFLECTION OR DISCUSSION

1. What is an example of extraordinary resilience you have witnessed in someone you know? How did this person demonstrate incredible courage, flexibility, and hope in the face of such difficult circumstances?
2. Think of a time when you faced a challenging crisis, situation, disappointment, or major struggle and recovered quite well, even learned some valuable lessons that have helped you thereafter. What do you attribute to your ability to navigate that situation effectively, as opposed to other situations when you did not rise to the occasion?
3. What do you believe most distinguishes extraordinary grandparents or elder caregivers from those who are only merely average or competent?

Figure Credits

Fig. 12.1a: Source: https://commons.wikimedia.org/wiki/File:Louis-L%C3%A9opold_Boilly00.jpg.
Fig. 12.1b: Copyright © 2016 Depositphotos/pressmaster.

CHAPTER 13

The Future of Healthy Aging

One thing we can say for certain about predictions of the future is that they are often unpredictable. Experts proclaimed with confident authority in the past that inventions such as electricity, cars, telephones, televisions, and computers were just a fad that would soon pass. It was also fully anticipated that aging and death were just inconveniences that would eventually be eliminated by medical advances; we were all destined to become immortal. But make no mistake, age is the single most reliable risk factor for disease, disability, or mortality, much more so than genetics or exposure to environmental hazards (Ungvari & Adany, 2021).

When you recall that the human life span pretty much doubled during the 20th century, from about 40 years of age to 75, one could justifiably wonder what the actual finite limits of aging might be. Of course there's a difference between living a long life and enjoying a lengthy existence that is active, engaged, and free from discomfort. One thing for certain, however, is that if people are going to routinely live to be 100 years old, they are going to have over 30 extra years to continually reinvent themselves. There's only so much bridge, golf, and babysitting that someone can do.

It is indeed a certainty that life will continue to be extended in the future, at least to a certain point. If the impact of vaccines, anesthesia, body scans, microscopes, and similar medical breakthroughs added decades to the human life span, what will happen with new innovations that include biological implants, genetic engineering, artificial replacement parts, 3D printed medications, wearable bio-trackers, exoskeletons, neural implants, nanorobotics, artificial intelligence enhanced diagnostic systems, crowdsourced disease treatment platforms, and other technology? During the middle of the 20th century it used to take over 50 years in order to double medical knowledge and technological innovations. Three decades later, such breakthroughs occurred every 7 years. Nowadays it has been estimated that medical and health knowledge doubles every 2 months (Wooster & Maniate, 2019).

It is apparent that more and more lethal diseases will be eradicated in the future just as polio and smallpox were mostly wiped out more than a century ago as a result of targeted

Parts of this chapter are adapted from Jeffrey A. Kottler, "How to Sabotage Development and End Life Prematurely," *Critical and Provocative Issues in Human Development*, pp. 334–337. Copyright © 2021 by Cognella, Inc. Reprinted with permission vaccines. The likely consequence of these new innovations is that people will continue to live longer lives, although the quality of that existence is subject to debate. Is living longer all that desirable if the quality of that existence is compromised by chronic pain, loss of mobility, and unpleasant side effects from the treatments?

Scientists also wonder whether some form of immortality is truly possible in the future or whether we are doomed to fall apart after our bodily systems can no longer repair themselves. Perhaps, as Johnson (2021) suggests, aging and death aren't really "bugs" or mistakes in the system that can be rectified as much as they may be a design feature of evolution that switches off regular maintenance of our cells so that we vacate the premises to make room for others. This is only one of several mysteries that we will be exploring in this final chapter about what the future might bring.

Living Long Versus Living Well

There's a difference, of course, between one's biological age and how old one feels. Some people become old long before they ever hit retirement; others feel young and describe themselves as vital until their last breath. People have tried all kinds of things to extend their life span, without consideration for the quality and satisfaction of those extended years. Explorers have searched for the "fountain of youth." Wealthy individuals have sought to literally put their bodies into a deep freeze so they might awaken sometime in the future when there is a cure for whatever ails them. Scientists have attempted to slow metabolism, reduce systemic stress, control cellular mutations, conduct genetic testing, program DNA sequencing, and prescribe medications to alter brain chemistry. They have investigated ways to monitor and manage caloric intake, diet composition, body temperature, insulin levels, cellular pathways, and other metabolic changes. There have been approaches to diet, exercise, lifestyle, habits, all of which were alleged to extend life.

As life span continues to grow over time, expected to hit an average of 86 years by the middle of this century, so too does the percentage of elderly people with disabilities (Medina et al., 2020). A staggering 40% of those over 65 years old have some type of disability, whether impairing their mobility, cognitive functioning, or ability to live independently. One third of the elderly disabled are considered obese, leading to the conclusion that so many of these difficulties may actually be self-inflicted (Pintado, 2022). It is clear that living a long life is not nearly the same as living a fruitful and joyful existence. It is also apparent that instead of focusing efforts on extending life perhaps we should instead concentrate on extending health (Olshansky & Carnes, 2019). What use is it to try to steal a few extra years if it just condemns one to continued misery?

It has been predicted that the ultimate finite life span of human cellular regeneration is about 150 years (Willingham, 2021b). Based on a study of aging biomarkers this is considered the upper limit to repair cells that have been damaged over time. It is not as if this should be a goal to double the length of longevity if that means that the last 50 years are going to become a miserable decline into suffering and helplessness. After all, it is not the length of one's life that matters as an indicator of healthy aging but rather the *quality* of life on a daily basis—the joy and satisfaction that is experienced, the achievements that have attained, the intimacy in relationships that were created and fortified, the courage, creativity, and productivity that were attained.

Everyone is trying to live longer, extending their life span any way they can without regard for the consequences. People already fritter away so many of their allocated precious moments worrying about things they can't control, feeling badly about things in the past they can't change, obsessing about all the things they don't have or will never attain, distracting themselves with all kinds of substances, diversions, and habits that actually compromise their health and sabotage their ultimate satisfaction. And yet the one thing we have learned for certain is that it is mostly social support, friendships, family connections, intimate relationships, useful and meaningful activities that truly give life meaning. And that helps explain why elders often find that their new stage of life is actually a period of elevated goodwill and feelings of redemption.

Future of Grandparents

Let's do some calculations. Because people are living longer they are postponing the age at which they seek marital partners. It used to be common to settle down with a mate and have children immediately after high school, then after completing university studies, now it is normal to wait until someone is in their mid-20s, 30s, or even 40s before starting a family. With fertility rates falling, population trends shifting, and older people living so much longer it is apparent that in the future the ratio between the oldest and youngest will continue to increase.

In addition, the structure of families is changing as a result of dual-earning couples, divorce, parental abandonment, job relocations, working abroad, poverty, and global immigration. The whole nature and definition of "family" will continue to evolve over time, leading to serial unions, multiple remarriages, cohabitation of multiple partners, collective housing for reconfigured families, and people who are just "living apart together." These new living and cohabitation arrangements will spark new and different role identities and responsibilities for elders, especially for those individuals who may have missed out spending as much time with their own children when they were so busy with their careers.

Before we could hope to understand what is in store for the elderly we first have to consider what families are going to look like in another half century. One writer imagines more than a handful of intriguing possibilities that could develop as a result of economic, political, social, and psychological forces currently operating (Dvorsky, 2015). Not only will more multigenerational families reside in households together in the coming years, but multiple families will also share living space together for economic and social purposes. This would not only pool resources and create more efficient housing but also meet the increasing interest in a sense of community. In some forms this may lead to more communal, kibbutz-like living arrangements in which dozens of families share childcare responsibilities, recreational activities, and maintenance tasks together.

Technology will also revolutionize the ways that childcare takes place, perhaps even putting grandparents out of business altogether with robotic versions and artificial intelligence. After all, some overprotective parents are already using drones and software to follow their children everywhere and carefully monitor everything they do. Imagine the control that is possible once robotic pets, caretakers, and companions get into the act. Or else what happens in the future when families begin colonizing space, a radically new physical environment that will place a host of new and different demands and challenges on daily life? Or what will be the impact of cryonic technology designed to freeze people and bring them back to life at some time in the future? And will all the innovations in virtual technology lead to our families, physically dispersed around the world (or universe), to remain in contact mostly via screens or avatars?

Even now there are forces in the outside world that will lead to major life transformations, including wars, changes in how work is conceived, even evolution of our biological systems. The COVID-19 pandemic not only killed millions of elderly people but also had a huge impact on everyone's behavior in a multitude of ways we don't yet fully understand. One thing we do know for sure is that as people live longer, as couples split up and reconfigure themselves in new and different relationships, the sheer number of grandparents is going to continue to grow. In Japan, for instance, there are now more diapers sold for older people than there are for infants.

Whereas previously children were fortunate to know a single grandparent during their lifetime, blended families might very well not only have the full complement of four grandparents, but also another set of step-grandparents. Since the birth rate is continuing to go down, this means there will be far fewer grandchildren and a lot more grandparents competing for quality time. Plus we'd have to add to the mix a whole bunch of great-grandparents who may still very well be alive and healthy. This means that although three-generation families are still the norm we are only a few decades away from the majority of families including a fourth generation (great-grandparents) still alive and perhaps active within the household.

In addition, more young adults are moving home for economic reasons than previous generations. Urbanization, economic downturns, population spikes, increases in home schooling, and flexible work schedules will all boost the need for this trend to grow. In at least one sense this is likely a positive trend considering that grandparent involvement with children increases childrens' resilience, pro-social behavior, emotional regulation and mental health, among other benefits (Buchanan & Rotkirch, 2018).

If the biological purpose of all life is to perpetuate our own genetic material, then grandchildren represent the elder's greatest achievement and legacy. We've discussed how grandparents share stories about their lives, what they've learned, what they know and understand, hoping to save their grandchildren heartbreak and disappointments that they couldn't avoid. They want their youngest family members to truly *know* them, to understand and appreciate their background and life experiences. They take pride in feeling like they continue to be useful and contribute to their sense of worth.

There will also continue to be changes in the family structure as a result of demographic shifts, globalization of employment, even global warming and climate changes. This means that, more than ever, grandparents' free labor will only become more essential and valuable in the future. Despite this reality there is still so much we don't really understand about this evolutionary process that has forever changed the ways we "grow" our children.

What About Great-Grandparents?

In the not so distant past, just a century or two ago, hardly anyone ever knew their grandparents. The prospect of ever having great-grandparents must have seemed like science fiction. Nowadays, however, the prospect of a four, or even five-generation family, will become the norm in the future; most children today will know at least one of their parents' grandparents. One of the consequences of this phenomenon is that family legacies will become even more transmissible once the oldest elders can continue to pass along their traditions, history, and stories. This has been considered a major influence building family cohesion and identity over time (Schuler & Dias, 2021).

As already mentioned, one of the most important factors that determine life satisfaction, well-being, and healthy aging relate to a sense of meaning and purpose to one's life, a compelling reason to get moving every day. It is one of the most frequent complaints of the elderly that at times their lives feel empty, boring, without meaning after abandoning their life's work. Regardless of one's age, it is imperative that someone, anyone, feels valued, worthy, and respected for their contributions. Yet older adults say they often feel "invisible," no longer taken seriously the way they were at the height of their productivity. It therefore makes sense that even those great-grandparents in their last decade or two of life still wish to remain useful and productive, still feel the urge to help others to the extent their health allows. In this case, health doesn't just refer to an absence of disease, illness, chronic pain, or disability but also the capacity to engage in physically demanding activities without collateral damage or excessive fatigue (Margolis & Iciaszczyk, 2015).

Although much of the focus is typically on healthy *physical* condition, optimal cognitive and psychological functioning are also critical. By its very nature, caregiving is quite demanding in ways that drain one's energy and patience. Among the oldest of the old, those who perform best maintain a positive outlook on life, are free from excessive anxiety and depression, score high on tests of executive functioning and decision-making, and demonstrate interpersonal sensitivity and responsiveness (Yorgason & Hill, 2019).

Those great-grandparents who are actively involved in family life and caregiving of children report a greater sense of meaning in their lives and greater investment in the family. Yet when close, intimate relationships are forged between the youngest and oldest members there is increasing evidence that everyone profits in measurable ways (Even-Zohar & Garby, 2016). Of course this development is still so novel and new we don't yet understand what the ultimate consequences might be for the future structure of the family that includes four, or even five, different generations.

For simplicity's sake, there have been described essentially two styles of great-grandparenting, based primarily on accessibility and frequency of contact (Even-Zohar & Garby, 2016). Those elders who live with the family, or nearby, obviously will be more influential than those who live far away. They communicate more regularly with parents and grandparents (their own children), typically see the kids at least once per week, and often babysit, take the children shopping, help with chores, and engage them in fun activities. The second style is a far more traditional, formal, symbolic role in which the elder(s) might be present (in person or virtually) only on special occasions or holidays. Finally, there is a somewhat rare third type when great-grandparents become the primary custodial caregivers because nobody else in the family is available or capable. Obviously, these different roles will lead to very different kinds of relationships in the future, not only between the great-grandparents and the children, but also within the expanded family structure.

One additional challenge for great-grandparents, beyond dealing with the difficulties of advancing age and health problems, is that they are even more caught in the middle between "double gatekeepers." They must not only answer to the parents to visit the children, but also to their own children, the grandparents, who may also restrict access because of their own interests and needs. On the other hand, there's also some evidence that regardless of the quality and frequency of contact between the grandparents and the children, the great-grandparents are still able to create, negotiate, and maintain their own intimate and fulfilling connections that are sincerely valued and appreciated (Evan-Zohar, 2019).

How Older Adults Shorten Their Lives Prematurely

The major causes of death vary considerably, depending on one's age and stage of life. At a younger age you are most at risk for accidents, homicide, and suicidal depression. In the latter stages you are most likely to die of heart disease, cancer, or respiratory disorders. Almost all of these threats are avoidable, or at least significantly reduced, if certain behaviors and choices associated with successful aging are in evidence. The greatest risks to health and longevity are those you've frequently heard about already—smoking, substance abuse, unhealthy diet, overeating, lack of exercise, social isolation, among others. One's personality traits and attitudes are also factors in the equation. For example, one personality attribute particularly significant is conscientiousness (Stephan et al., 2019). That is the quality that makes one cautious and selective about taking certain risks, as well as being generally very reliable, responsible, dependable, and likely to pay close attention to warnings and scientific evidence. Such a person would get regular medical and dental checkups and follow whatever sound health recommendations are offered.

There are other personality characteristics that also predict a longer life, most notably an upbeat, optimistic attitude, one in which you try to access and express gratitude as much as possible. It helps to develop a level of hardiness and resilience so that one can bounce back from disappointments, crises, and trauma rather than permitting the deleterious symptoms to take their devastating toll. Related to this is more of an internal skill than a trait but it involves talking to oneself in constructive ways and challenging thinking that is irrational and self-destructive. When someone is diagnosed with a health problem or disease, it isn't just the medical care that determines the outcome but also how the patient chooses to face the difficulties.

Genetic inheritance and chromosomal abnormalities certainly play a strong role in life expectancy since so many of the fatal diseases and health threats are inherited from parents, including the risk of developing cancer, heart disease, sickle cell anemia, Huntington's disease, even obesity and depression. With that acknowledged, there are still vast differences in the ways that people cope with their conditions, how compliant they are to medical advice, how they structure their lifestyles, and again, their attitude toward their condition and prognosis.

Certain habits take years, if not decades, out of one's life span, while others significantly improve the prospects for a longer life. You can surely guess which habits are most dangerous, such as smoking, overeating, alcohol and drug abuse, chronic stress, just as you already know how important physical exercise, a healthy diet, strong family ties and friendships, and meaningful work likely prolong life. It would also be expected that those who live in poverty, or have severe financial problems, would have limited access to good nutritional options, safe housing, convenient transportation, clean water, and quality medical care, all of which would prevent the risk of early death.

There is overwhelming evidence that a healthy diet and regular exercise are among the best things you can do to extend life but that leads to the questions that have also been covered: What *kind* of diet exactly, and what *type* of exercise? There have been all kinds of conflicting advice in the media and by so-called experts who advocate diets either high—or low—in fat, protein, carbohydrates, fiber, macronutrients, high glycemic index.

It is generally accepted by nutritional experts to reduce consumption of sugary, fatty, salty, processed foods and instead rely as much as possible on smaller portions of lean meat, whole grains, nuts, fresh fruits, and vegetables. With respect to exercise, we've explored previously how anything is better than nothing at all, but a balance of walking, vigorous aerobic activities (swimming, cycling, running, cardio machines, fitness classes), stretching and flexibility activities, and weightbearing to strengthen bones and muscles, are ideal. And if all that is far too ambitious, then once again, *anything* you do makes some small difference.

There is compelling evidence that predicts how many years of your life span you lose with particular habits or conditions (Härkänen et al., 2020). Based on the average 30-year-old who engages in the following activities, researchers have estimated how much earlier they will die. Smoking cuts five years off of one's life expectancy, diabetes trims another 5 years. Chronic stress—2.3 years stolen. All total, it appears one can voluntarily extend one's life by as many as *14 years* by avoiding excesses and sticking with healthy lifestyle habits with regard to diet, weight, exercise, smoking, alcohol and drugs, and social life (see Table 13.1).

TABLE 13.1   Predictors of Longevity and Healthy Old Age

- Old parents (genetic inheritance is among the most important variables)
- No history of mental illness in family
- No early trauma or significant developmental delays
- Skills, ability, and persistence to recover from early trauma
- Healthy diet
- Regular exercise and physical activity
- Meaningful work
- Type of work that does not jeopardize health or safety
- Safe, secure, comfortable housing and living situation
- Supportive "family," however that is defined
- A few close, intimate friendships
- Optimistic, positive attitude
- Feelings of gratitude for life's gifts
- Efficient recovery from stressful situations
- Resilience in ability to recover from disappointments, crises, and tragedies
- Regular self-care, including regular checkups with health professionals

In addition to the somewhat familiar factors that predict a long, healthy life there are also some interesting if not peculiar correlations between variables that have been discovered. These are not cause-effect relationships but rather indicators of underlying behavior that are associated with many of the things mentioned previously. For instance, how fast you walk and how firm your handgrip are somewhat reliable predictors of overall health and body functioning, on a par with blood pressure and nutritional habits (Williams & Thompson, 2013). If you think about it, this makes sense as signs of functional behavior, vitality, mobility, and strength.

In summary, geneticist and longevity researcher David Sinclair (2019) reminds us that besides exercising regularly, it is important to not worry about things that are uncontrollable and that don't really matter very much. His conclusion, after several decades of study: "If there is one piece of advice I can offer, one surefire way to stay healthy longer, one thing you can do to maximize your life span right now, it is this: eat less" (p. 89).

On the other hand, if you want to die young, the optimal strategy would be to follow certain prescriptions that are fairly certain to compromise health, reduce longevity, and reduce functional abilities (see Table 13.2). These are precisely the attitudes and behaviors that have been found to be associated with deleterious health outcomes, regardless of the setting.

TABLE 13.2 Prescriptions for a Premature Death

1. Smoke or vape throughout the day to help you relax and boost energy.

2. Eat all the rich, fatty foods you can find until your weight balloons to the point you can barely fit inside a chair that you remain in most of the time.

3. Try to make up for nutritional deficiencies by taking vitamins and supplements even though there is no compelling, reliable evidence that they help very much.

4. Don't trust other people; in fact, go out of your way to be mean and insensitive to others.

5. Broadcast your sense of privilege and specialness until people ignore you—but don't worry, just tell yourself that this is for the best and you are better off alone.

6. Drink excessively and spend more money than you can afford to soothe the depression you sometimes feel.

7. When the booze stops working then supplement it with opioids, weed, and other drugs.

8. When you are eventually and inevitably struggling with anxiety, depression, sleep disruption, and chronic stress, tell yourself that you don't really need help since you can just deal with this on your own.

9. Maintain a pessimistic outlook toward life in general.

10. Critically judge everyone else's behavior that doesn't conform to your own beliefs, and make sure you tell people what you think about them any time you are reminded of something that would make them more like you.

That should just about guarantee that if someone doesn't kill you first, or if you don't kill yourself, then you'll likely die prematurely of heart disease, a stroke, cancer, or just chronic misery.

The Future of Healthy Aging

One important question to consider is how so-called "healthy aging" will be defined in the future. Is it simply a matter of maintaining functional abilities related to cognition, mobility, and daily tasks or rather does it encompass a sense of well-being and personal satisfaction? The answer should be obvious that longevity in itself is hardly a desired goal if it is accompanied by chronic suffering, limitations, and endless frustration. Then, of course, there is the actual cost of caring for the elderly, not only for the individual and family but for society. At what point is it still feasible to keep someone alive when the expense can exceed hundreds of thousands of dollars each year in medical expenses?

It is estimated that in the next few years as many as 20% of the population will be over 65 years of age. When this is combined with decreased physical exercise, increased obesity, escalating medical and prescription costs, and political inaction by government policies it is apparent that older caregivers are going to need considerable care themselves. After all, with current trends it is anticipated that two thirds of the national budget, after defense, will be consumed by Social Security and Medicare. This is one of the many reasons it is predicted that the future of healthy aging will likely take place in multigenerational living arrangements with mutual care taking place in the home (Super, 2021).

On a global scale nations are gearing up for the next stage in an aging world in which the number of elderly outnumber the children. This doesn't just mean that gerontology will replace pediatrics as the most in-demand medical specialty but that health care as we previously knew and understood it is likely to become transformed into a system that will be quite different in addressing the needs of a far more diverse population. Specifically it is predicted there will be more focus on age-inclusive institutions that empower older people to maintain their own safety and access to critical services.

It may very well be that the most remarkable collective achievement of our species isn't the invention of the wheel, tools, printing press, clock, or the internet, but our increased life span. There are, of course, inequities in this achievement, based on resources, finances, culture, gender, age, ethnicity, geography, medical care, environment, and context, but our

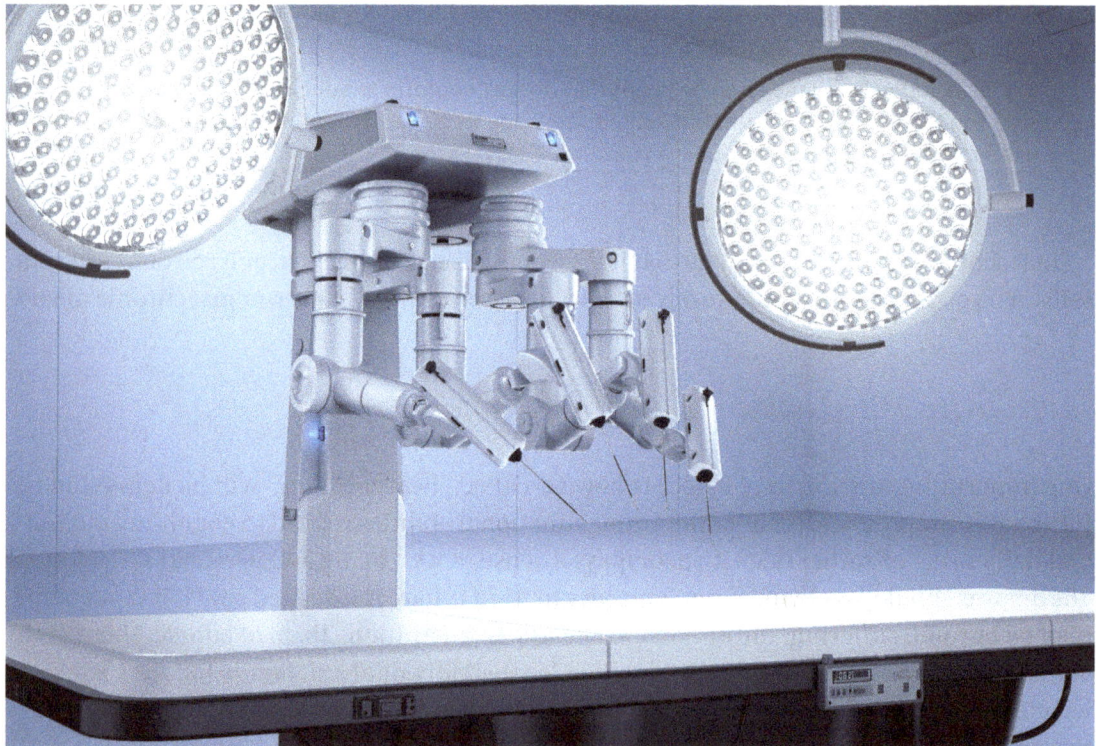

FIGURE 13.1   Is this the future? It is mind boggling to consider the innovations that will occur in health and medicine during the next few years that will continue to extend the human life span and lead to healthier aging. Soon it will be routine for surgeons to conduct robotic, long-distance operations anywhere in the world using remote, virtual technology to control the most precise and exacting procedures. This is not unlike the ways that that drones and self-driving vehicles will eventually become standard delivery services.

extraordinary longevity is still our defining feature. We've invented agriculture, vaccines, miracle drugs, robotic surgery, air conditioning and heating, and public health organizations, all of which have reduced child and maternal mortality, as well as extended life a few more decades. All of these improvements have also had a huge impact on "healthy aging," which has been described as maintaining functional abilities to the extent that it continues to contribute to a sense of well-being, joy, productivity, and satisfaction. This has now become a major priority of the World Health Organization that has developed a plan during the next decade focused on increasing healthy aging for the world's oldest citizens.

Much of the WHO plan proposes to invest greater resources in an integrated health infrastructure that makes health care more accessible, affordable, and targeted to the needs of the elderly. The goal is specifically focus on the most excluded, vulnerable groups who would otherwise not receive the support and care they require. In addition, we can expect quite a number of technological advances in the practice of medicine that will continue to cure diseases, treat illnesses, and provide even more precise and effective procedures that will continue to add quality years to human life expectancy. Some of the anticipated breakthroughs will likely include the following:

- DNA monitoring to predict future problems
- Early detection of the first cancer cells, long before they spread
- Breath analyzer to assess symptoms of immune disease
- Big data: Collection of imagery scans online that can be shared all over the world
- Wearable devices to monitor biological functions (earbuds, rings, implants, watches, contact lenses)
- Robotic surgical procedures that can be conducted long-distance to remote areas
- Telemedicine will become standard for office visits and even routine exams
- Regenerative medicine will restore functioning of cells and organs
- Medications will become personalized for each individual based on their condition, DNA, and unique composition
- Bionic implants will be installed in various parts of the body to compensate for loss of mobility or functioning
- Mobile devices will routinely self-diagnose various conditions and send data directly to health professionals
- Drones will deliver medications and health supplies
- Artificial intelligence will be better harnessed for greater diagnostic accuracy

In addition to these medical breakthroughs virtual reality will offer limitless ways that rehabilitation or mental health treatments can be offered remotely, just as this became standard during the COVID-19 pandemic. Throughout history it has often been disease outbreaks, world wars, or catastrophes that led to scientific breakthroughs that extended life span and improved health. Although World War I was partially responsible for the spread of the flu pandemic, as well as the first mass killing of the 20th century, it also led to a number of health and medical advancements that saved far more lives in the future. A few of these innovations included the

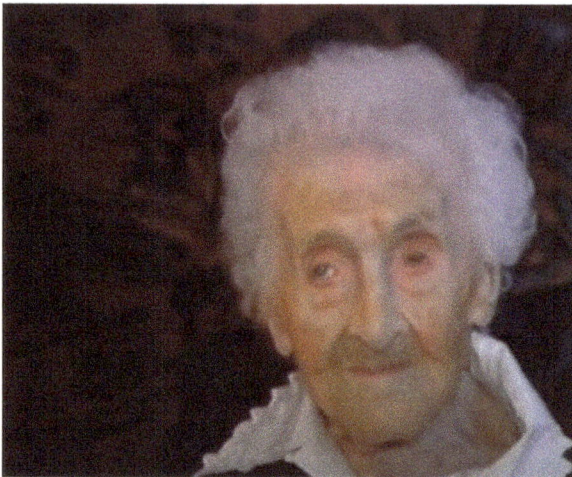

FIGURE 13.2   Jeanne Calment is considered the oldest person who ever lived at 122 (and ½!) years old. Interestingly, she didn't follow any of the guidelines, recommendations, or findings from health research since she was a lifelong smoker, claimed she didn't exercise regularly, never took medication (except aspirin for a headache), and reportedly didn't pay much attention to her diet. She didn't recall ever being vaccinated as a child, but if not, she seemed to have a natural immunity to measles and chickenpox. Her favorite thing to eat was dessert. Yet looking closer, she appeared to do everything in moderation—smoking only two cigarettes a day, drinking smoothies, even still riding her bike at age 100!

first hospital ship, ambulance services for transporting the wounded or sick, the use of antiseptics, and anesthesia, and the first diagnosis and treatment of "shell shock" (PTSD), treatments for venereal disease, use of splints for leg fractures (instead of amputation!), use of prosthetic limbs, plastic surgery, and blood transfusions (Bell, 2018). We can fully expect after surviving years of another pandemic that another revolutionary round of innovations will soon come on the scene in much the same way that "Zoom sessions" changed so much about education, human collaboration, and the nature of work.

There are other trends in the future that we can expect will change the nature of family composition and functioning, as well as the role of grandparents and great-grandparents (Silverstein, 2019). As mentioned, the proliferation of inexpensive, easily accessible forms of digital communication enhance and strengthen communication between family members, changing the nature of long-distance relationships. Just compare the options today versus decades ago when the only possibility was a long-distance, expensive phone call, or further back in time when it took days, or even weeks, to receive a posted letter.

Perhaps the technological advancements in communication will help compensate for those elders who are "left behind," so to speak. Increasingly, families are not only forced to relocate because of career opportunities but also due to displacement as refugees (internally or internationally), immigration, wars and violent conflicts, and health threats. Then there are grandparents who are left behind in the sense that they've been involuntarily cut off from the children—most often after divorce and/or remarriage.

We live in one of the few cultures that denigrates aging and sings the praises of youthful vigor. There are endless messages in popular culture, entertainment, and social media that describe the burden of old people as a drain on our resources, economy, and the medical system. It is young people who are heralded as our most precious resource for the future, and for good reason, but not necessarily as direct competitors of the aged. And yet, almost all of our advancements, development, and cultural evolution have resulted from the intergenerational transmission of knowledge. It is precisely the "invention" of old age that has made every other invention possible.

QUESTIONS FOR REFLECTION OR DISCUSSION

1. What would you predict will become trends in the future related to health practices?
2. What are some of the habits and behavior you currently engage in that will likely impact your life own life expectancy? Consider diet, exercise, drug and alcohol use, stress levels, risk taking, exposure to trauma, and neglect of self-care.
3. What were some of the most interesting ideas and new insights that you gained from reading this book?
4. In addition, what were some of the ideas discussed in the book that you strongly disagree with? Provide evidence to support your alternative position or opinion.

Figure Credits

Fig. 13.1: Copyright © 2018 Depositphotos/phonlamai.

Fig. 13.2: Source: https://www.youtube.com/watch?app=desktop&v=aUnWJk81-ho.

References and Sources

Adesman, A. (2017, May 6–9). *Grandparents who practice outdated health myths may pose safety threat on grandchildren* [Paper presentation]. Pediatric Academic Societies Meeting, Philadelphia, PA, United States.

Allen, K. R., Henderson, A. C., & Murray, M. M. (2019). Theoretical approaches to grandparenting. In B. Hayslip & C. A. Fruhauf (Eds.), *Grandparenting: Influences on the dynamics of family relationships* (pp. 3–16). Springer.

American Psychological Association. (2017). *Older adults' health and age-related changes: Reality versus myths.*

Anderson, L. R., Sheppard, P., & Monden, C. W. S. (2018). Grandparent effects on educational outcomes: A systematic review. *Sociological Science, 5*(6), 114–142. https://doi.org/10.15195/v5.a6

Arnett, J. J., Robinson, O., & Lachman, M. E. (2020). Rethinking adult development: Introduction to the special issue. *American Psychologist, 75*(4), 425–430. https://doi.org/10.1037/amp0000633

Attar-Schwartz, S., & Buchanan, A. (2020). Grandparenting and adolescent well-being: Evidence from the UK and Israel. In A. Buchanan & A. Rotkirch (Eds.), *The role of grandparents in the 21st century* (pp. 89–101). Routledge.

Barker, G., Garg, A., Heilman, B., van der Gaag, N., & Mehaffey, R. (2021). *State of the world's fathers.* Promundo.

Barnett, A. E., & Connidis, I. A. (2019). Grandparents in changing times: Negotiating gender across generations. In B. Hayslip & C. A. Fruhauf (Eds.), *Grandparenting: Influences on the dynamics of family relationships* (pp. 181–200). Springer.

Bates, J. S. (2009). Generative grandfathering: A conceptual framework for nurturing grandchildren. *Marriage and Family Review, 45*(4), 331–352. https://doi.org/10.1080/01494920802537548

Beer, J. (2019). *Why marking to seniors is so terrible.* Fast Company. https://www.fastcompany.com/90341477/why-marketing-to-seniors-is-so-terrible

Bell, L. (2018). *Medical developments in World War I.* British Library. https://www.bl.uk/world-war-one/articles/medical-developments-in-world-war-one

Berger, L. (2020, June 26). Why parents are the ultimate essential workers. *The Correspondent.* https://thecorrespondent.com/555/why-grandparents-are-the-ultimate-essential-workers/73423375905-488adac6

Bernhold, Q. S., & Giles, H. (2017). Paternal grandmothers benefit the most from expressing affection to grandchildren: An extension of evolutionary and sociological research. *Journal of Social and Personal Relationships, 36*(2), 514–534. https://doi.org/10.1177/0265407517734657

Bialik, K., & Fry, R. (2019). *Millennial life: How young adulthood today compares with prior generations.* Pew Research Center. https://www.pewresearch.org/social-trends/2019/02/14/millennial-life-how-young-adulthood-today-compares-with-prior-generations-2/

Biesele, M, & Howell, N. (1981). "The old people give you life:" Aging among !Kung hunter-gatherers. In P. T. Amoss & S. Harrell (Eds.), *Other ways of growing pld: Anthropological perspectives* (pp. 77–98). Stanford University Press.

Bone, V. (2018). Grandparenting: Created by evolution, revised by history, still in use today. *European Journal of Mental Health, 13*(1), 82–105. https://doi.org/10.5708/EJMH.13.2018.1.7

Boon, S. D., & Shaw, M. J. (2007). Grandchildren's perceptions of grandparents' health: Worries and impact on their own lives. *Journal of Intergenerational Relations, 5*(1), 57–78. https://doi.org/10.1300/J194v05n01_05

Boszormeny-Nagy, I., & Spark, G. M. (2013). *Invisible loyalties.* Routledge.

Bradley, J. (2020, March 23). Four in five grandparents "usually" provide childcare. *The Scotsman.* https://www.scotsman.com/news/people/four-five-grandparents-usually-provide-childcare-2506005

Brunissen, L., Rapoport, E., Fruitman, K., Adesman, A. (2020). Parenting challenges of grandparents raising grandchildren: Discipline, child education, technology use, and outdated health beliefs. *GrandFamilies: The Contemporary Journal of Research, Practice and Policy, 6*(1), 16–33. https://scholarworks.wmich.edu/grandfamilies/vol6/iss1/6/

Bryson, B. (2019). *The body.* Doubleday.

Buchanan, A. (2019). Grandfathers: Are their roles changing and is this having an impact on grandchildren? In B. Hayslip & C. A. Fruhauf (Eds.), *Grandparenting: Influences on the dynamics of family relationships* (pp. 133–146). Springer.

Buchanan, A., & Rotkirch, A. (2018). Twenty-first century grandparents: Global perspectives on changing roles and consequences. *Contemporary Social Science, 13*(2), 131–144. https://doi.org/10.1080/21582041.2018.1467034

Buchanan, A. & Rotkirch, A. (Eds.). (2020). *The role of grandparents in the 21st century: Global perspectives on changing roles and consequences.* Routledge.

Buss, I. O. (1990). *Elephant life: Fifteen years of population density.* Iowa State University Press.

Callaway, E. (2010). Grandmother hypothesis' takes a hit. *Nature.* https://doi.org/10.1038/news.2010.430

Cant, M. A., & Johnstone, R. A. (2008). Reproductive conflict and the separation of reproductive generations in humans. *PNAS, 105*(14), 5332–5336. https://doi.org/10.1073/pnas.0711911105

Caro, T. M., & Hauser, M. D. (1992). Is there teaching in nonhuman animals? *Quarterly Review of Biology, 67*(2), 151–174. https://doi.org/10.1086/417553

Caspari, R. (2012, November 1). The evolution of grandparents. *Scientific American.* https://www.scientificamerican.com/article/the-evolution-of-grandparents-2012-12-07/

Castel, A. D. (2019). *The psychology of successful aging.* Oxford University Press.

Celdran, M., Villar, F., & Triado, C. (2014). Thinking about my grandparent: How dementia influences adolescent grandchildren's perceptions of their grandparents. *Journal of Aging Studies, 29,* 1–8. https://doi.org/10.1016/j.jaging.2013.12.004

Chan, T. W., & Boliver, V. (2013). The grandparents effect in social mobility: Evidence from British birth cohort studies. *American Sociological Review, 78*(4), 662–678. https://doi.org/10.1177/0003122413489130

Chapman, S. N., Lahdenperä, M., Pettay, J. E., & Lummaa, V. (2017). Changes in length of grandparenthood in Finland 1790–1959. *Finnish Yearbook of Population Research, 52,* 3–13. https://doi.org/10.23979/fypr.65346

Chapman, S. N., Pettay, J. E., Lummaa, V., & Lahdenpera, M. (2019). Limits to fitness benefits of prolonged post-reproductive lifespan in women. *Current Biology, 29*(4), 645–650. https://doi.org/10.1016/j.cub.2018.12.052

Cherlin, A., & Furstenberg, F. F., Jr. (1985). Styles and strategies of grandparenting. In V. L. Bengtson & J.F. Robertson (Eds.). *Grandparenthood* (pp. 97–116). SAGE.

Condon, J., Luszcz, M., & McKee, I. (2018). The transition to grandparenthood: A prospective study of mental health implications. *Aging & Mental Health, 22*(3), 336–343. https://doi.org/10.1080/13607863.2016.1248897

Coughlan, J. F. (2017). *The longevity economy: Unlocking the world's fastest-growing, most misunderstood market.* Public Affairs.

Cox, C. (2018). Cultural diversity among grandparent caregivers: Implications for interventions and policy. *Educational Gerontology, 44*(8), 484–491. https://doi.org/10.1080/03601277.2018.1521612

Coxworth, J. E., Kim, P. S., McQueen, J. S., & Hawkes, K. (2015). Grandmothering life histories and human pair bonding. *Proceedings of the National Academy of Sciences, 112*(38), 11806–11811. https://doi.org/10.1073/pnas.1599993112

Crimmins, E. M., Shim, H., Zhang, Y., & Kim, J. (2019). Differences between men and women in mortality and the health dimensions of the morbidity process. *Clinical Chemistry, 65*(1), 135–145. https://doi.org/10.1373/clinchem.2018.288332

Croft, D. P., Brent, L. J., Franks, D. W., & Cant, M. A. (2015). The evolution of prolonged life after reproduction. *Trends in Ecology and Evolution, 30*(7), 407–416. https://doi.org/10.1016/j.tree.2015.04.011

Croft, D. P., Johnstone, R. A., Ellis, S., Nattrass, S., Franks, D. W., Brent, L. J. N., Mazzi, S., Balcomb, K. C., Ford, J. K. B., & Cant, M. A. (2017). Reproductive conflict and the evolution of menopause in killer whales. *Current Biology, 27*(2), 298–304. https://doi.org/10.1016/j.cub.2016.12.015

Crow, S., & Coleman, K. (2020, April 20). *60 things grandparents should never do.* BestLife. https://bestlifeonline.com/things-grandparents-should-never-do/

Dagg, A. I. (2009). *The social behavior of older animals.* Johns Hopkins University Press.

Danielsbacka, M., Křenková, L. & Tanskanen, A.O. (2022). Grandparenting, health, and well-being: A systematic literature review. *European Journal of Ageing, 19,* 341–368. https://doi.org/10.1007/s10433-021-00674-y

David, P. (2017). *Happiness grows with age.* AARP.

David, P., & Nelson-Kakulla, B. (2019, April). *Grandparents embrace changing attitudes and technology.* AARP Research. https://doi.org/10.26419/res.00289.001

de Becker, E. (2020). The abusive grandparent: Theoretical-clinical issues and networking practice. *Dialogue, 230*(4), 141–157.

Dolbin-MacNab, M., & Few-Demo, A. (2020). Grandfamilies in the United States: An intersectional analysis. In V. Timonen (Ed.), *Grandparenting practices around the world* (pp. 189–208). Policy Press.

Dolbin-Macnab, M. L., Stucki, B. D., & Natwick, J. E. (2019). Grandparenthood: Clinical issues and interventions. In B. Hayslip & C. A. Fruhauf (Eds.), *Grandparenting: Influences on the dynamics of family relationships* (pp. 217–232). Springer.

Dong, X., Milholland, B., & Vijg, J. (2016). Evidence for a limit to human lifespan. *Nature, 538*(7624), 257–259. https://doi.org/10.1038/nature19793

Dossey, L. (2018). The helper's high. *Explore*, *14*(6), 393–399. https://doi.org/10.1016/j.explore.2018.10.003

Driscoll, C. (2009). Grandmothers, hunters, and human life history. *Biology and Philosophy*, *24*(5), 665–686.

Duhigg, C. (2012). *The power of habit*. Random House.

Dvorsky, G. (2015, July 13). *9 different versions of what families will look like 50 years from now*. Gizmodo. https://gizmodo.com/9-different-visions-of-what-families-will-look-like-50-1717480917

Eisenberg, D., Rej, P. H., Duazo, P., Carba, D., Hayes, M. G., & Kuzawa, C. W. (2020). Testing for paternal influences on offspring telomere length in a human cohort in the Philippines. *American Journal of Biological Anthropology*, *171*(3), 520–528. https://doi.org/10.1002/ajpa.23983

Elias, N., Nimrod, G., & Lemish, D. (2019). The ultimate treat? Young Israeli children's media use under their grandparents' care. *Journal of Children and Media*, *13*(4), 472–483. https://doi.org/10.1080/17482798.2019.1627228

Ellis, S., Franks, D. W., Nattrass, S., Currie, T. E., Cant, M. A., Giles, D., Balcomb, K. C., & Croft, D. P. (2018). Analysis of ovarian activity reveal repeated evolution of post-reproductive life in toothed whales. *Scientific Reports*, *8*, Article 12833.

Endendjik, J. J., Groeneveld, M. G., Bakermans-Kranenburg, M. J., & Mesman, J. (2016). Gender-differentiated parenting revisited: Meta-analysis reveals very few differences in parental control of boys and girls. *PLoS One*, *11*(7), 1–33. https://doi.org/10.1371/journal.pone.0159193

Engelhardt, S. C., Bergeron, P., Gagnon, A., Dillon, L., & Pelletier, F. (2019). Using geographic distance as a potential proxy for help in the assessment of the grandmother hypothesis. *Current Biology*, *29*(4), 651–656. https://doi.org/10.1016/j.cub.2019.01.027

Erikson, E., & Erikson, J. (1998). *The life cycle completed*. Norton.

Evan-Zohar, A. (2019). Great-grandparenting in Israel. In B. Hayslip & C. A. Fruhauf (Eds.), *Grandparenting: Influences on the dynamics of family relationships* (pp. 96–109). Springer.

Evan-Zohar, A., & Garby, A. (2016). Great-grandparents' role perception and its contribution to their quality of life. *Journal of Intergenerational Relations*, *14*(3), 197–219. https://doi.org/10.1080/15350770.2016.1195246

Feldman, R. (2019). *Development across the life span* (9th ed.). Pearson.

Finch, C. B. (2010). Evolution of human lifespan and diseases of aging: Infection, inflammation, and nutrition. *PNAS*, *107*(1), 1718–1724. https://doi.org/10.1073/pnas.0909606106

Finlay B. L. (2019). Human exceptionalism, our ordinary cortex and our research futures. *Developmental Psychobiology*, *61*(3), 317–322. https://doi.org/10.1002/dev.21838

Fishel, A. (2015). *Home for dinner: Mixing food, fun, and conversation for a happier family and healthier kids*. Harper Collins.

Fishel, A. (2022). Family Dinner Project, Harvard Graduate School of Education. Retrieved from https://www.gse.harvard.edu/news/20/04/harvard-edcast-benefit-family-mealtime

Fisher, R. A. 1930. *The genetical theory of natural selection*. Clarendon Press.

Fossey, D. (1983). *Gorillas in the mist*. Houghton Mifflin.

Frankl, V. E. (1959). *Man's search for meaning*. Beacon Press.

Fraser, G. E., Cosgrove, C. M., Mashchak, A. D., Orlich, M. J., & Altekruse, S. F. (2020). Lower rates of cancer and all-cause mortality in an Adventist cohort compared with a U.S. census population. *Cancer, 126*(5), 1102–1111. https://doi.org/10.1002/cncr.32571

Freedman, V. A., Cornman, J. C., & Kasper, J. D. (2021). *National health and aging trends study chart book: Key trends, measures, and detailed tables.* Michigan Center on the Demography of Aging. https://micda.isr.umich.edu/wp-content/uploads/2022/03/NHATS-Companion-Chartbook-to-Trends-Dashboards-2020.pdf

Freeman, J., Elton, J., & South, A. (2019). "A second chance being a parent:" Grandparent caregivers' reported communication and parenting practices with co-residential children. *Journal of Family Communication, 19*(3), 261–276. https://doi.org/10.1080/15267431.2019.1632864

Freud, S. (1912). *On psychotherapy.* The Journal of Nervous and Mental Disease Publication Company.

Furstenberg, F. F. (2019). Family change in global perspective: How and why family systems change. *Family Relations, 68*(3), 326–341. https://doi.org/10.1111/fare.12361

Ganong, L., Sanner, C., & Coleman, M. (2019). Divorce and step-grandparenthood. In B. Hayslip & C. A. Fruhauf (Eds.), *Grandparenting: Influences on the dynamics of family relationships* (pp. 111–129). Springer.

Gazso, A., & McDaniel, S. A. (2015). Families by choice and the management of low income through social supports. *Journal of Family Issues, 36*(3), 371–395. https://doi.org/10.1177/0192513X13506002

Ge, W., & Adesman, A. (2017). Grandparents raising grandchildren: A primer for pediatricians. *Current Opinion in Pediatrics, 29*(3), 379–384. https://doi.org/10.1097/MOP.0000000000000501

Gendron, T. (2022). *Ageism unmasked: Exploring age bias and how to end it.* Steerforth.

Gershoff, E. T. (2010). More harm than good: A summary of scientific research on the intended and unintended effects of corporal punishment on children. *Law and Contemporary Problems, 73*(2), 31–56.

Gessa, G., Bordone, V., & Arpino, B. (2020). Becoming a grandparent and its effect on well-being: The role of order of transitions, time, and gender. *Journal of Gerontology: Social Sciences, 75*(10), 2250–2262. https://doi.org/10.1093/geronb/gbz135

Goodall, J. (1988). *My life with the chimpanzees.* Byron Press.

Gray, A. (2006). The time economy of parenting. *Sociological Review Online, 11*(3). https://doi.org/10.5153/sro.1393

Gurven, M., & Kaplan, H. (2008). Beyond the grandmother hypothesis: Evolutionary models of human longevity. In J. Sokolovsky, *The cultural context of aging: Worldwide perspectives* (pp. 53–66). Praeger Publishers.

Haber, C. (1985). *Beyond sixty-five: The dilemma of old age in America's past.* Cambridge University Press.

Hank, K., Cavrini, G., Di Gessa, G., & Tomassini, C. (2018). What do we know about grandparents? Insights from current quantitative data and identification of future data needs. *European Journal of Ageing, 15*(3), 225–235. https://doi.org/10.1007/s10433-018-0468-1

Härkänen, T., Kuulasmaa, K., Sares-Jäske, A., Joushilati, P., Peltonen, M., Borodulin, K., Knekt, P., Koskinen, S. (2020). Heavy stress and lifestyle can predict how long we life. *Science Daily, 10*(3). https://doi.org/10.1136/bmjopen-2019-033741

Havighurst, R. J. (1952). *Human development and education.* McKay.

Hawkes, K. (2004). The grandmother effect. *Nature, 428*, 128–129.

Hawkes, K. (2016). Ethnoarchaeology and Plio-Pleistocene sites: Some lessons from the Hadza. *Journal of Anthropology and Archaeology, 44*, 158–165. https://doi.org/10.1016/j.jaa.2016.07.005

Hawkes, K. (2020a). Cognitive consequences of our grandmothering life history: Cultural learning begins in infancy. *Philosophical Transactions of the Royal Society B Biological Sciences, 375*(1803). http://doi.org/10.1098/rstb.2019.0501

Hawkes, K. (2020b). The centrality of ancestral grandmothering in human evolution. *Integrative and Comparative Biology, 60*(3), 765–781. https://doi.org/10.1093/icb.icaa029

Hawkes, K., O'Connell, J., & Blurton Jones, N. (2018). Hunter-gatherer studies and human evolution: A very selective review. *American Journal of Physical Anthropology, 165*(4), 777–800. https://doi.org/10.1002/ajpa.23403

Hawkes, K., O'Connnell, J. F., Jones, N. G., Alvarez, H., & Charnov, E. L. (1998). Grandmothering, menopause, and the evolution of human life histories. *Proceedings of the National Academy of Sciences, 95*(3), 1336–1339. https://doi.org/10.1073/pnas.95.3.1336

Hayslip, B., Fruhauf, C., & Fish, J. (2021). Should I do this? Factors influencing the decision to raise grandchildren among custodial grandparents. *The Gerontologist, 61*(5), 735–745. https://doi.org/10.1093/geront/gnaa202

Hayslip, B., Toledo, R., Henderson, C., Rodriguez, R., & Vela, D. (2019). Cross-cultural differences in the experience of grandparent-grandchild relationships and related outcomes. *International Journal of Aging and Human Development, 89*(2), 151–171. https://doi.org/10.1177/0091415018769468

Hilbrand, S., Coall, D. A., Gerstorf, D., & Hertwig, R. (2017). Caregiving within and beyond the family is associated with lower mortality for the caregiver: A prospective study. *Evolution of Human Behavior, 38*(3), 397–403. https://doi.org/10.1016/j.evolhumbehav.2016.11.010

Homans, G. (1958). Social behavior as exchange. *American Journal of Sociology, 63*(6), 597–606.

Hoorens, V., & Buunk, A.P. (1992). Self-serving biases in social comparison: Illusory superiority and unrealistic optimism. *Psychologica Belgica, 32*(2), 169–194. https://doi.org/10.5334/PB.831

Horsfall, B., & Dempsey, D. (2015). Grandparents doing gender: Experiences of grandmothers and grandfathers caring for grandchildren in Australia. *Journal of Sociology, 51*(4), 1070–1084. https://doi.org/10.1177/1440783313498945

Hrdy, S. B. (1999). *Mother nature: A history of mothers, infants, and natural selection.* Pantheon.

Hrdy, S. B. (2005). Cooperative breeders with an ace in the hole. In E. Voland, A. Chasiotis, & W. Schiefenhovel (Eds.), *Grandmotherhood: The evolutionary significance of the second half of female life* (pp. 295–317). Rutgers University Press.

Hrdy, S. B. (2009). *Mothers and others: The evolutionary origins of mutual understanding.* Harvard University Press.

Hrdy, S. B. (2017). Comes the child before man: How cooperative breeding and prolonged postweaning dependence shaped human potential. In B. S. Hewlett & M. E. Lamb (Eds.), *Hunter-gatherer childhoods: Evolutionary, developmental, and cultural perspectives* (pp. 65–91). Routledge.

Hudomiet, P., Hurd, M. D., & Rohwedder, S. (2020). *The age profile of life-satisfaction after age 65.* U.S. National Bureau of Economic Research. https://doi.org/10.3386/w28037

Institute of Medicine. (2010). *Providing healthy and safe foods as we age: Workshop summary.* The National Academies Press. https://doi.org/10.17226/12967

Jackson, K. F., Mitchell, F. M., Snyder, C. R., & Samuels, G. E. (2020). Salience of ethnic minority grand-parents in the ethnic-racial socialization and identity development of multiracial grandchildren. *Identity*, *20*(2), 73–91. https://doi.org/10.1080/15283488.2020.1728535

Jamieson, L., Ribe, E., & Warner, P. (2018). Outdated assumptions about maternal grandmothers? Gender and lineage in grandparent-grandchild relationships. *Journal of the Academy of Social Sciences*, *13*(2), 261–274. https://doi.org/10.1080/21582041.2018.1433869

Jensen, B. K., Quaal, G., & Manoogian, M. M. (2018). Understanding the grandfather role in families. *PURE Insights*, *7*, Article 4.

Johansson, M., Benderix, Y., & Svensson, I. (2020). Mothers' and fathers' lived experiences of postpartum depression and parental stress after childbirth: A qualitative study. *International Journal of Qualitative Studies on Health and Well-being*, *15*(1), Article 1722564. https://doi.org/10.1080/17482631.2020.1722564

Johnson, S. (2021). *Extra life: A short history of living longer.* Riverhead.

Jongenelis, M. I., Morley, B. Worrall, C., & Talati, Z. (2021). Grandparents' perceptions of the barriers and strategies to providing their grandchildren with a healthy diet. *Appetite*, *159*, Article 105061. https://doi.org/10.1016/j.appet.2020.105061

Kahana, E., Kahana, B., Goler, T., & Kahana, J. (2019). Grandparent-grandchild relationships: A proposed mutuality model with a focus on young children and adolescents. In B. Hayslip & C. A. Fruhauf (Eds.), *Grandparenting: Influences on the dynamics of family relationships* (pp. 61–80). Springer.

Kaplan, H., Gurven, M., & Winking, J. (2009). An evolutionary theory of human life span: Embodied capital and the human adaptive complex. In V. L. Bengston, D. Gans, N. M. Pulney, & M. Silverstein (Eds.), *Handbook of theories of aging* (pp. 39–60). Springer.

Kaplan, L. (2022). This Women's History Month, here's a radical idea: Let women lead. *Fortune*. https://fortune.com/2022/03/01/it-is-past-time-for-women-to-lead/

Kelley, S. J., Whitley, D., Escarra, S. R., Zheng, R., Horne, E. M., & Warren, G. L. (2021). The mental health well-being of grandparents raising grandchildren: A systematic review and meta-analysis. *Marriage and Family Review*, *57*(4), 329–345. https://doi.org/10/1080/01494929.2020.1861163

Kim, H., Kan, H., & Johnson-Motoyama, M. (2017). The psychological well-being of grandparents who provide supplementary grandchild care: A systematic review. *Journal of Family Studies*, *23*(1), 118–141. https://doi.org/10.1080/13229400.2016.1194306

Kim, S. K., & Park, M. (2017). Effectiveness of person-centered care on people with dementia: A systematic review and meta-analysis. *Clinical Interventions in Aging*, *12*, 381–297. https://doi.org/10.2147/CIA.S117637

Kornhaber, A., & Woodward, K. L. (1985). *Grandparents/grandchildren: The vital connection.* Transaction Books.

Kottler, J. A. (2000). *Doing good: Passion and commitment for helping others.* Routledge.

Kottler, J. A. (2014). *Change: What leads to personal transformation.* Oxford University Press.

Kottler, J. A. (2015). *Stories we've heard, stories we've told: Life-changing narratives in therapy and everyday life.* Oxford University Press.

Kottler, J. A. (2018). *What you don't know about leadership but probably should: Applications to daily life.* Oxford University Press.

Kottler, J. A. (2022a). *Critical and provocative issues in human development.* Cognella.

Kottler, J. A. (2022b). *On being a therapist* (6th ed.). Oxford University Press.

Kottler, J. A. (2023). *Unexplained mysteries of everyday human behavior.* Cognella.

Kottler, J. A., & Balkin, R. (2017). *Relationships in counseling and the counselor's life.* American Counseling Association.

Kottler, J. A., & Balkin, R. (2020). *Myths, misconceptions, and invalid assumptions of counseling and psychotherapy.* Oxford University Press.

Kottler, J. A., Banu, S., & Jani, S. (Eds.). (2019). *Handbook of refugee experience: Trauma, resilience, and recovery.* Cognella.

Kottler, J. A., & Carlson, J. (2006). *The client who changed me: Stories of therapist personal transformation.* Routledge.

Kottler, J. A., & Carlson, J. (2016). *Therapy over 50: Aging issues in psychotherapy and the therapist's life.* Oxford University Press.

Kottler, J. A., Carlson, J., & Keeney, B. (2004). *An American shaman: An odyssey of ancient healing traditions.* Routledge.

Kottler, J. A., & Marriner, M. (2009). *Changing people's lives while transforming your own: Paths to social justice and global human rights.* Wiley.

Kottler, J. A., & Safari, S. (2019). *Making a difference: A journey of adventure, disaster, and redemption inspired by the plight of at-risk girls.* Cognella.

Kutubaeva, R. (2019). Analysis of life satisfaction of the elderly population on the example of Sweden, Austria, and Germany. *Population and Economics, 3*(3), 102–116. https://doi.org/10.3897/popecon.3.e47192

Lahdenpera, M., Mar, K. U., & Lummaa, V. (2016). Nearby grandmother enhances calf survival and reproduction in Asian elephants. *Scientific Reports, 6*(1), Article 27213. https://doi.org/10.1038/srep27213

Langhammer, B., Bergland, A., & Rydwik, E. (2018). The importance of physical activity exercise among older people [Special issue]. *BioMed Research International, 2018*, Article 7856823. https://doi.org/10.1155/2018/7856823

Langley, L. (2016, May 7). Schooled: Animals that teach their young. *National Geographic.* https://www.nationalgeographic.com/adventure/article/160507-animals-teaching-parents-science-meerkats

Lee, P. C., Fishlock, V., Webber, C. E., & Moss, C. J. (2016). Reproductive advantages of a long life: Longevity and senescence in wild female African elephants. *Behavioral Ecological Sociobiology, 70*, 337–345. https://doi.org/10.1007/s00265-015-2051-5

Lehti, H., Erola, J., & Tanskanen, A. (2019). Tying the extended family knot: Grandparents' influence on educational achievement. *European Sociological Review, 35*(1), 29–48. https://doi.org/10.1093.esr/jcy044

Lesperance, D. (2010). Legacy, influence, and keeping the distance: Two grandfathers, three stories. *Journal of Men's Studies, 18*(3), 199–217. https://doi.org/10.3149/jms.1803.199

Levitin, D. J. (2020). *Successful aging: A neuroscientist explores the power and potential of our lives.* Dutton.

Li, Y., Cui, N., Kok, H., Deatrick, J., & Liu, J. (2019). The relationship between parenting styles practiced by grandparents and children's emotional and behavioral problems. *Journal of Child and Family Studies*, *28*, 1899–1913. https://doi.org/10.1007/s10826-019-01415-7

Lieberman, D. E. (2013). *The story of the human body: Evolution, health, and disease*. Vintage.

Lieberman, D. E., Kistner, T. M., Richard, D., Lee, I., & Baggish, A. L. (2021). The active grandparent hypothesis: Physical activity and the evolution of extended human healthspans and lifespans. *Proceedings of the National Academy of Sciences*, *118*(50), e2107621118. https://doi.org/10.1073/pnas.2107621118

Livingston, G. (2015). *Americans are aging, but not as fast as people in Germany, Italy, and Japan*. Pew Research Center. https://www.pewresearch.org/fact-tank/2015/05/21/americans-are-aging-but-not-as-fast-as-people-in-germany-italy-and-japan/

MacLeod, S., Musich, S., Hawkins, K., Alsgaard, K., & Wicker, E. R. (2016). The impact of resilience among older adults. *Geriatric Nursing*, *37*, 266–272. https://doi.org/10.1016/j.geninurse.2016.02.014

Malonebeach, E., Hakoyama, M., & Arnold, S. (2018). The good grandparent: Perspectives of young adults. *Marriage & Family Review*, *54*(6), 582–597. https://doi.org/10.1080/01494929.2017.1414724

Mann, R. (2007). Out of the shadows? Grandfatherhood, age, and masculinities. *Journal of Aging Studies*, *21*(4), 281–291. https://doi.org/10.1016/j.jaging.2007.05.008

Mann, R., Kahn, H., & Leeson, G. W. (2013). Variation in grandchildren's perceptions of their grandfathers and grandmothers: Dynamic of age and gender. *Journal of Intergenerational Relationships*, *11*(4), 380–395. https://doi.org/10.1080/15350770.2013.839326

Mann, R., Tarrant, A., & Leeson, G. W. (2016). Grandfatherhood: Shifting masculinities in later life. *Sociology*, *50*(3), 594–610. https://doi.org/10.1177/0038038515572586

Margolis, R. (2016). The changing demography of grandparenthood. Journal of *Marriage and the Family*, *78*(3), 610–622. https://doi.org/10.1111/jomg.12286

Margolis, R., & Arpino, B. (2020). The demography of grandparenthood in 16 European countries and two North American countries. In V. Timonen (Ed.), *Grandparenting practices around the world* (pp. 23–41). Policy Press.

Margolis, R., & Iciaszczyk, N. (2015). The changing health of Canadian grandparents. *Canadian Studies in Population*, *42*(3–4), 63–76. https://doi.org/10.25336/P6J88R

Marlowe, F. (2000). The patriarch hypothesis: An alternative explanation of menopause. *Human Nature*, *11*(1), 27–42. https://doi.org/10.1007/s12110-000-1001-7

Matos, A. D., & Neves, R. B. (2012). Understanding adolescent grandchildren's influence on their grandparents. In S. Arber & V. Timonen (Eds.), *Contemporary grandparenting* (pp. 203–224). University of Chicago Press.

McComb, K., Shannon, G., Durant, S., Sayialel, K., Slotow, R., Poole, J. H., & Moss, C. J. (2011). Leadership in elephants: The adaptive value of age. *Proceedings of the Royal Society B: Biological Sciences*, *278*(1722), 3270–3276. https://doi.org/10.1098/rspb.2011.0168

McLain, D. K., Setters, D., Moulton, M. P., & Pratt, A. (2000). Ascription of resemblance of newborns by parents and nonrelatives. *Evolution and Human Behavior*, *21*(1), 11–23. https://doi.org/10.1016/S1090-5138(99)00029-X

Mead, M. (1972). *Blackberry winter: My earlier years*. William Morrow.

Medina, L., Sabo, S., & Vespa, J. (2020). *Living longer: Historical and projected life expectancy in the United States, 1960–2060.* U.S. Department of Commerce.

Mendoza, A. N., Fruhauf, C. A., & MacPhee, D. (2020). Grandparent caregivers' resilience: Stress, support, and coping predict life satisfaction. *International Journal of Aging and Human Development*, *9*(1), 3–20. https://doi.org/10.1177/0091415019843459

Miller, H. (1977). *Sextet: Six essays.* Capra Press.

Miller, T. (2011). *Making sense of fatherhood: Gender, caring, and work.* Cambridge University Press.

Miller, W. R., & de Baca, J. C. (2001). *Quantum change: When epiphanies and sudden insights transform ordinary lives.* Guilford.

Mitchell, B. (2019, September 11). British woman becomes oldest person to sail solo around the world. *The Scotsman.* https://www.scotsman.com/news/people/british-woman-becomes-oldest-person-sail-solo-around-world-1407996

Mollegaard, S., & Jaeger, M. M. (2015). The effects of grandparents' economic, cultural, and social capital on grandchildren's educational success. *Research in Social Stratification and Mobility*, *82*(42), 11–19. https://doi.org/10.1016/j.rssm.2015.06.004

Montoro-Rodriguez, J., & Ramsey, J. (2020). Grandparents and race/ethnicity. In V. Timonen (Ed.), *Grandparenting practices around the world* (pp. 313–330). Policy Press.

Moore, S., & Rosenthal, D. (2017). *Grandparenting: Contemporary perspectives.* Routledge.

Moorman, S. M., & Stokes, G. E. (2016). Solidarity in the grandparent-adult grandchild relationship and trajectories of depressive symptoms. *The Gerontologist*, *56*(3), 408–420. https://doi.org/10.1093/geront/gnu056

Morales, S., Tang, A., Bowers, M. E., Miller, N. V., Buzzell, G. A., Smith, E., Seddio, K., Henderson, H. A., & Fox, N. A. (2021). Infant temperament prospectively predicts general psychopathology in childhood. *Development and Psychopathology*, *34*(3), 774–783. https://doi.org/10.1017/S0954579420001996

Musil, C. M., Zauszniewski, J. A., Givens, S. E., Henrich, C., Wallace, M., Jeanblanc, A., & Burant, C. J. (2019). Resilience, resourcefulness, and grandparenting. In B. Hayslip & C. A. Fruhauf (Eds.), *Grandparenting: Influences on the dynamics of family relationships* (pp. 233–250). Springer.

National Center on Elder Abuse. (2021). *Research, statistics, and data.* https://ncea.acl.gov/What-We-Do/Research/Statistics-and-Data.aspx

National Institute on Aging. (2022). *10 myths about aging.* U.S. Department of Health and Human Services. https://www.nia.nih.gov/health/10-myths-about-aging

Neugarten, B. L., & Weinstein, K. K. (1964). The changing American grandparent. *Journal of Marriage and the Family*, *26*(2), 199–204. https://doi.org/10.2307/349727

Niechcial, M. A., Vaportzis, E., & Gow, A. J. (2022). Genes versus lifestyles: Exploring beliefs about the determinents of cognitive aging. *Frontiers in Psychology*, March. https://www.frontiersin.org/articles/10.3389/fpsyg.2022.838323/full

Nimrod, G., Lemish, D., & Elias, N. (2019). Grandparenting with media: Patterns of mediating grandchildren's media use. *Journal of Family Studies*, *28*(1), 70–88. https://doi.org/10.1080/13229400.2019.1679660

Olshansky, S. J., & Carnes, B. A. (2019). Inconvenient truths about human longevity. *Journal of Gerontology: Medical Sciences*, *74*(S1), S7–S12. https://doi.org/10.1093/gerona/glz098

Pavard, S., Metcalf, C., & Heyer, E. (2008). Senescence of reproduction may explain adaptive menopause in humans: A test of the "mother" hypothesis. *American Journal of Physical Anthropology, 136*(2), 194–203. https://doi.org/10.1002/ajpa.20794

Payne, K. (1998). *Silent thunder in the presence of elephants.* Simon & Schuster.

Pearce, M., & Raftery, A. E. (2021). Probabilistic forecasting of maximum human lifespan by 2100 using Bayesian population projections. *Demographic Research, 44*(52), 1271–1294. https://doi.org/10,4054/demres.2021.44.52

Peccei, J. S. (2001). A critique of the grandmother hypotheses: Old and new. *American Journal of Human Biology, 13*(4), 434–452. https://doi.org/10.1002/ajhb.1076

Pintado, A. P. (2022, April 21). Want to live independently in old age? An aging America needs to make some changes, experts say. *USA Today.* https://www.usatoday.com/story/news/nation/2022/04/21/aging-america-maintain-independent-living/7320888001/?gnt-cfr=1

Pontzer, H., Raichlen, D. A., Wood, B. M., Thompson, M. E., Racette, S. B., Mabulla, A. Z. P., & Marlowe, F. W. (2015). Energy expenditure and activity among the Hadza hunter-gatherers. *American Journal of Human Biology, 27,* 628–637. https://doi.org/10.1002/ajhb.22711

Post, S. G. (Ed.). (2007). *Altruism and health: Perspectives from empirical research.* Oxford University Press.

Post, S. G. (2011). *The hidden gifts of helping: How the power of giving, compassion, and hope can get us through hard times.* Jossey-Bass.

Price, D., Ribe, E., Di Gessa, G., & Glaser, K. (2020). Grandparental childcare: A reconceptualization of family policy regimes. In V. Timonen (Ed.), *Grandparenting practices around the world* (pp. 43–62). Policy Press.

Rapoport, E., Muthiah, N., Keim, S. A., & Adesman, A. (2020). Family well-being in grandparent-versus parent-headed households. *Pediatrics, 146*(3), Article e20200115. https://doi.org/10.1542/peds.2020-0115

Rice, M. A., Restrepo, L. F., & Ophir, A. G. (2018). When to cheat: Modeling dynamics of paternity and promiscuity in socially monogamous prairie voles. *Frontiers in Ecology and Evolution, 6,* 141. https://doi.org/10.3389/fevo.2018.00141

Rilling, J. K., Gonzales, A., & Lee, M. (2021). The neural correlates of grandmaternal caregiving. *Proceedings of the Royal Society, 288*(1963). https://doi.org/10.1098/rspb.2021.1997

Rizvi, S. I. (2021). The Zugswang hypothesis: Why human lifespan cannot be increased. *Gerontology, 67,* 705–707. https://doi.org/10.1159/000514861

Rose, F. (2021). *The sea we swim in: How stories work in a data-driven world.* Norton.

Ross, M. C. (2001). *Dangerous beauty.* Hyperion.

Rowe, J. W., & Kahn, R. (1987). *Successful aging.* Pantheon.

Russell, B. (1956). *Portraits from memory: And other essays.* Readers Union.

Sadruddin, A., Ponguta, L. A., Zonderman, A. L., Wiley, K. S., Grimshaw, A., & Panter-Brick, C. (2019). How do grandparents influence child health and development? A systematic review. *Social Science and Medicine, 239,* Article 112476. https://doi.org/10.1016/j.socscimed.2019.112476

Schniter, E., Wilcox, N. T., Beheim, B. A., Kaplan, H. S., & Gurven, M. (2018). Information transmission and the oral tradition: Evidence of a late-life service niche for Tsimane Amerindians. *Evolution and Human Behavior, 39*(1), 94–105. https://doi.org/10.1016/j.evolhumbehav.2017.10.006

Schulenberg, S. E. (Ed.). (2021). *Positive psychological approaches to disaster.* Springer.

Schuler, E., & Dias, C. (2021). Legacies from great-grandparents to their descendants. *Journal of Intergenerational Relationships.* Advance online publication. https://doi.org/10.1080/15350770.2021.1913275

Schwalb, D. W., & Hossain, S. (Eds.). (2018). *Grandparents in cultural context.* Routledge.

Seegert, L. (2018). *The health benefits of grandparenting.* Center for Excellence in Health Care Journalism.

Seligman, M. (2012). *Flourish: A visionary new understanding of happiness and well-being.* Atria Books.

Sheppard, P., & Monden, C. (2018). The additive advantage of having educated grandfathers for children's education: Evidence from a cross-national sample in Europe. *European Sociological Review, 34*(4), 365–380. https://doi.org/10.1093/esr/jcy026

Shlomo, S. B., & Taubman-Ben-Ari, O. (2017). What factors may assist social workers to promote life satisfaction and personal growth among first-time grandfathers? *Child and Family Social Work, 22*(1), 482–491. https://doi.org/10.1111/cfs.12267

Silverstein, M. (2019). Growing old and growing up: Grandparents and their adult grandchildren in the context of multigenerational families. In B. Hayslip & C. A. Fruhauf (Eds.), *Grandparenting: Influences on the dynamics of family relationships* (pp. 81–94). Springer.

Sinclair, D., & LaPlante, M. D. (2019). *Lifespan: Why we age—and why we don't have to.* Atria.

Sokolovsky, J. (Ed.) (2020). *The cultural context of aging* (4th ed.). Praeger.

Song, S., & Geyer, H. (2018). Predictive neuromechanical simulations indicate why walking performance declines with aging. *The Journal of Physiology, 596*(7), 1199–1210. https://doi.org/10.1113/JP275166

Sorensen, P., & Cooper, N. J. (2010). Reshaping the family man: A grounded theory study of the meaning of grandparenthood. *Journal of Men's Studies, 18*(2), 117–136. https://doi.org/10.3149/jms.1802.117

Stephan, Y., Sutin, A. R., Luchetti, M., & Terracciano, A. (2019). Facets of conscientiousness and longevity: Findings from the Health and Retirement study. *Journal of Psychosomatic Research, 116*, 1–5. https://doi.org/10.1016/j.jpsychores.2018. 11.002

Sterelny, K. (2012). *The evolved apprentice: How evolution made humans unique.* The MIT Press.

Strassman, B. I., & Garrard, W. M. (2011). Alternatives to the grandmother hypothesis: A meta-analysis of the association between grandparental and grandchild survival in patrilineal populations. *Human Nature, 22*(1–2), 202–222. https://doi.org/10.1007/s12110-011-9114-8

Strauss, C. A. (1943). Grandma made Johnny delinquent. *American Journal of Orthopsychiatry, 13*(2), 343–346. https://doi.org/10.1111/j.1939-0025.1943.tb06003.x

Strom, R. D., & Strom, P. S. (2017). Grandparent learning and cultural differences. *Educational Gerontology, 43*(8), 417–427. https://doi.org/10.1080/03601277.2017.1314642

Super, N. (2021). Three trends shaping the politics of aging in America: An update. *Journal of Gerontology and Geriatric Medicine.* Advance online publication. https://doi.org/10.24966/GGM-8662/100107

Tedeschi, R. G., & Moore, B. A. (2020). *Transformed by trauma: Stories of posttraumatic growth.* Boulder Crest.

Thiele, D. M., & Whelan, T. A. (2006). The nature and dimensions of the grandparent role. *Marriage and Family Review, 40*(1), 93–108. https://doi.org/10.1300/J002v40n01_06

Thomson, E. S. (1942). *Wild animals I have known.* Scribners.

Thouzeau, V., & Raymond, M. (2017). Emergence and maintenance of menopause in humans: A game theory model. *Journal of Theoretical Biology, 430*, 229–236. https://doi.org/10.1016/j.jtbi.2017.07.019

Timonen, V. (Ed.). (2020). *Grandparenting practices around the world.* Policy Press.

Touron, D. R. (2015). Memory avoidance by older adults: When "old dogs" won't perform their new tricks. *Current Directions in Psychological Science, 24*(3), 170–176. https://doi.org/10.1177/0963721414563730

Tropp, L. (2019). *Grandparents in a digital age.* Lexington Books.

Ungvari, Z., & Adany, R. (2021). The future of healthy aging: Translation of geroscience to public health practice. *European Journal of Public Health, 31*(3), 455–456. https://doi.org/10.1093/eurpub/ckaa212

Urtamo, A., Jyvakorpi, S. K., & Strandberg, T. E. (2019). Definitions of successful ageing: A brief review of a multidimensional concept. *Acta Biomed, 90*(2), 359–363. https://doi.org/10.23750/abm.v90i2.8376

U.S. Census Bureau. (2019). *Older people projected to outnumber children for first time in U.S. history.* U.S. Department of Commerce. https://www.census.gov/newsroom/press-releases/2018/cb18-41-population-projections.html

Vogel, J. M. (2017). *Family resilience and traumatic stress: A guide for mental health providers.* National Center for Child Traumatic Stress.

Watkins, A. (2021). Reevaluating the grandmother hypothesis. *History and Philosophy of the Life Sciences, 43*(3), 1–29. https://doi.org/10.1007/s40656-021-00455-x

Weinberg, B. A., & Galenson, D. W. (2019). Creative careers: The life cycles of Nobel Laureates in economics. *Economist, 167*, 221–239. https://doi.org/10.3386/w11799

Westreich, S. (2018, July 27). Why do we even have grandparents? *Medium.* https://medium.com/a-microbiome-scientist-at-large/why-do-we-even-have-grandparents-d3e483bf6a21

Wille, B., Wiernik, B., Vergauwe, J., Vrijdags, A., & Trbovic, N. (2018). Personality characteristics of male and female executives: Distinct pathways to success? *Journal of Vocational Behaivor, 106*, 220–235. https://doi.org/10.1016/j.jvb.2018.02.005

Williams, G. C. (1957). Pleiotropy, natural selection, and the evolution of senescence. *Evolution, 11*(4), 398–411. https://doi.org/10.2307/2406060

Williams, P. T., & Thompson, P.D. (2013). The relationship of walking intensity to total and cause-specific mortality. Results from national walkers' study. *Plos One, 8*(11). https://doi.org/10.1371/journal.pone.0081098

Williams, S. (2016). Genetic mutations you want. *PNAS, 113*(10), 2554–2557. https://doi.org/10.1073/pnas.1601663113

Willingham, E. (2021a, May 25). Humans could live up to 150 years, new research suggests. *Scientific American.* https://www.scientificamerican.com/article/humans-could-live-up-to-150-years-new-research-suggests/

Willingham, E. (2021b, November 24). Physical activity could be an evolutionary adaptation for grandparenting. *Scientific American.* https://www.scientificamerican.com/article/physical-activity-could-be-an-evolutionary-adaptation-for-grandparenting/

Wilson, C., Walker, D., & Saklofske, D. (2021). Developing a model of resilience in older adulthood: A qualitative meta-synthesis. *Ageing and Society, 41*(8), 1920–1942. https://doi.org/10.1017/S0144686X20000112

Wooster, E. M., & Maniate, J. M. (2019). Reimagining medical education: Part II—practicing in an age of uncertainty and change. *Archives of Medicine and Health Sciences, 7*(1), 92–95.

World Health Organization. (2021a). *Decade of healthy aging 2021-2030.* https://www.euro.who.int/en/health-topics/Life-stages/healthy-ageing/news/news/2021/01/decade-of-healthy-ageing-2021-2030

World Health Organization. (2021b). *Obesity and overweight.* https://www.who.int/news-room/fact-sheets/detail/obesity-and-overweight

Yaeger, D. S., & Dweck, C. (2020). What can be learned from the growth mindset controversies? *American Psychologist, 75*(9), 1269–1284. https://doi.org/10.1037/amp0000794

Yahirun, J. J., Park, S. S., & Seltzer, J. A. (2018). Step-grandparenthood in the United States. *Journal of Gerontology, 73*(6), 1055–1065. https://doi.org/10.1093/geronb/gbx164

Yorgason, J. B., & Hill, M. S. (2019). Grandparents and health. In B. Hayslip & C. A. Fruhauf (Eds.), *Grandparenting: Influences on the dynamics of family relationships* (pp. 201–216). Springer.

Zannas, A. S., & West, A. E. (2014). Epigenetics and the regulation of stress vulnerability and resilience. *Neuroscience, 264,* 157–170. https://doi.org/10.1016/j.neuroscience.2013.12.003

Ziglio, E., Currie, C., & Rasmussen, V. B. (2004). The WHO cross-national study of health behaviors in school-aged children from 35 countries: Findings from 2001–2002. *Journal of School Health, 74,* 204–206. https://doi.org/10.1111/j.1746-1561.2004.tb07933.x

Index

About the Author

Jeffrey A. Kottler is one of the most prominent authors and presenters in the fields of counseling, psychotherapy, health, education, and advocacy. He has written over 100 books about a wide range of subjects, including many with Oxford University Press such as: *On Being a Therapist (6th ed); Stories We've Heard, Stories We've Told: Life-Changing Narratives in Therapy and Everyday Life; Myths, Misconceptions, and Invalid Assumptions of Counseling and Psychotherapy; What You Don't Know About Leadership but Probably Should: Applications to Daily Life; Therapy Over 50: Aging Issues in Psychotherapy and the Therapist's Life;* and *Change: What Leads to Personal Transformation.*

Jeffrey has been a counselor, therapist, supervisor, researcher, and educator for 45 years, having worked within preschool, middle school, mental health center, crisis center, hospital, medical school, refugee resettlement agency, nongovernmental organization (NGO), university, community college, private practice, and disaster relief settings. He is the founder of Empower Nepali Girls, a charitable organization that supports and mentors at-risk children. He has served as a Fulbright scholar and senior lecturer in Peru and Iceland, as well as worked as a visiting professor in New Zealand, Australia, Hong Kong, Singapore, and Nepal. Jeffrey is Professor Emeritus of Counseling at California State University, Fullerton. He currently lives in Houston, where he works on projects related to refugee trauma with the Alliance for Multicultural Services.